Investigating BUSINESS

COLIN PARSONS

Inspector for Economics and
Business Education
Surrey County Council

JOHN CAIN

Deputy Headteacher
Warlingham School

Longman

Acknowledgements

We are grateful to the following for permission to reproduce photographs and cartoons:
Basingstoke Gazette, page 40; The Bowater Organisation, page 179; British Waterways, page 80; Camera Press, pages 51 *above* (photo: ILN), 113 *above right* (photo: Poly-Press), 113 *centre right* (photo: Les Wilson), 113 *centre left* (photo: G/S), taken from the book *Castaway*, by Lucy Irvine, Victor Gollancz, page 24 *above*; J Allan Cash, page 23 *below*, page 39, page 78, page 97, page 185; Bruce Coleman, page 157 *above left*, 157 *centre left* (photo: John Newby), 186 *above*; James Davis Travel Photography, page 28; Mark Edwards/Still Pictures, pages 186 *below left*, 186 *below right*; By courtesy of Ford Motor Co. Ltd., pages 56, 67, 113 *below right*; R.G. Fox, page 81; L. Gibbard, pages 127, 143; John Hillelson, page 41 *above* (photo: Andanson/Sygma); Hulton Deutsch Collection, page 50; Robert Hunt, page 147; Phil Kerkhoff, Merryfall Graphics, page 91; Bryan McAlister, page 142; Network, pages 25 *above* (photo: Mike Abraham), 25 *below* (photo: Steve Benbow), 27 (photo: John Sturrock), 113 *above left* (photo: Laurie Sparham); Oxfam, page 23 *above* (photo: J. Hartley), 157 *above right* (photo: Ben Fawcett), 157 *centre right* (photo: D. Jacques), 157 *below* (photo: Chris Fagg), 173 (photo: J. Hartley), 189 *above* (photo: J. Hartley), 189 *below* (photo: J. Hartley); Ingram Pinn/*Sunday Times*, page 41 *below*; Popperfoto, page 51 *below*; *Private Eye*, page 165; *Punch*, page 164; Cartoon by Ken Pyne, *Employing People* – The ACAS Handbook for Small Firms, page 110; Spectrum Colour Library, page 29; TR Trustees Corporation, page 85, 94; The Telegraph Colour Library, page 113 *below left*; *Western Mail & Echo Ltd*, page 167.

We are unable to trace the copyright holders of the following and would be grateful for any information that will enable us to do so:
pages 24 *below*, 112, 187.

We are grateful to the following for permission to reproduce copyright material:
page 14, Crown copyright, reproduced with the permission of the controller of Her Majesty's stationery office. page 29, 'Crown Corporations in Canada', J.R.S. Prichard; page 34, Social Trends 18, 1988, HMSO; page 35, *The Guardian*, 30.9.1987; page 36, *Britain 1988: An Official Handbook*, HMSO; page 38, *Basingstoke & North Hampshire Gazette*; page 40, *Farmers Weekly*, Ministry of Agriculture Fisheries & Food, © Crown Copyright 1988; page 42 *above*, Economic Progress Report, 1986, HMSO; page 42 *below*, Royal Bank of Scotland; page 44, Royal Bank of Scotland; page 46, *The Economist*, 9.5.1987; page 47 *above*, *The Economist*, 21.2.1987; page 47 *below*, Social Trends 18, 1988, HMSO; page 48 *above*, *The Economist*, 27.6.1987; page 48 *below*, Halifax Building Society, Press Association Graphic; page 49 *left*, *The Economist*, 9.5.1987; page 51, *Britain 1988: An Official Handbook*, HMSO; page 52 *above*, *The Economist*, 10.10.1987; page 52 *above centre*, OECD; page 52 *below*, *The Financial Times*, 18.3.1988; page 52 *below centre*, Employment Gazette, July 1984, HMSO; page 53, *Employment Gazette*, November 1987, HMSO; page 55 *above*, Economic Progress Report, 1987, HMSO; page 55 *below*, Department of Employment, *After Industrial Society*, J.I. Gershunny; page 56, *The Economist*, 5.10.1985; page 57, *The Economist*; page 64, Association of British Insurers; page 68, Bank of Scotland; page 69 *below*, Barclays Bank plc; page 79, Report of the Director General of Fair Trading, 1986, HMSO; page 82, British Rail Network SouthEast; page 96 *left*, *The Guardian*, 17.4.1988; page 96 *right*, *Britain 1988: An Official Handbook*, HMSO; page 98, *Britain 1988; An Official Handbook*, HMSO; page 101, Storey, D.M., 'The Performance of Small Firms', *Economic Review*, September 1987; page 104, *Financial Weekly*, No. 466, 24.3.1988; page 108, *The Guardian*, 30.3.1988; page 124, Datastream: Dewe Rogerson: Company reports; page 131 *centre left*, Employment Gazette, November 1987; page 131 *below left*, Lloyds Bank Economic Bulletin, May 1987; page 131 *right*, *Britain 1988; An Official Handbook*, HMSO; page 132, Southampton City Council; page 133 *above*, G. Cook, 'Economics Update 1988'; page 133 *below*, *The Economist*, Autumn Statement 1987; page 134 *above*, Key Data 1987, HMSO; page 134 *below*, Public Expenditure White Paper 1988, HMSO; page 135, Economic Progress Report, 1987, HMSO; page 138 *above*, *The Independent*, 16.4.1988; page 138 *centre*, *The Guardian*, 16.4.1988; page 138 *below*, H.M. Treasury; page 140 *above*, *The Independent*, 16.4.1988; page 140 *below*, Economic Progress Report, HMSO; page 142 *below*, *The Economist*, 11.7.1987; page 148, *Britain 1988: An Official Handbook*, HMSO; page 150, *Britain 1988: An Official Handbook*, HMSO; page 152, British Airports Authority; page 176 *above*, Al Coe, European Water Supply & Plumbing Practices.

Contents

Introduction

What is business?
How are we going to 'investigate' it?

These are interesting questions which we hope this book will help you to answer. You may already feel that you have a fairly good idea of what business is about. Firms undertake some kind of activity and, in the process, they employ people. They may produce something or supply a service which they sell. People who buy are their customers and the price they pay allows firms to cover their costs and make a profit.

If you investigate 'business' you will need to look at all these issues – employment, production, profits, costs, revenue, sales and a whole lot more. You will look at trade and the way in which trade is supported by banking, insurance and many other commercial services.

This is not all there is to our study, however. We need to investigate how business fits into the whole pattern of the national economy: how businesses compete with one another, how they sometimes cooperate and sometimes come into conflict. We will investigate the role of the government in controlling business and explore some of the arguments behind decisions which the government may take. We shall also try to understand how people fit into this pattern as producers and consumers.

Investigating business today involves even more than this. It is clear that we live in a world which is becoming smaller; not only because we are using scarce resources but because modern communications are so quick that we can pass information to and fro in an instant. This change in business information technology is very much part of our investigation. It is quite normal for business people to communicate with the latest technology and we hope that you, the student, will want to use modern technology as an important tool in your investigation. It is for this reason that many exercises are included in this book which encourage the use of information technology (IT).

Finding your way about the book

The book is divided into 39 units. Each is a complete study unit in itself but is also part of a group of related topics. These groups are:

The information technology background
The economics background
The commercial background
The organisational background
The government background
The international background
The financial background

Within each study unit you will find important information and a list of points to remember. There are also tasks for you to complete and questions to answer. Some of these tasks are designed to be done in groups, others by you alone. Those tasks which involve the use of information technology are highlighted with one of the symbols below:

IT WORDPRO — a microcomputer word processor

IT GRAPHICS — a software package which will produce graphs and charts

IT DESKTOP — a desktop publishing package

IT SPREADSHEET — a suitable simple computer spreadsheet

IT DATABASE — a simple educational database

Investigating the
INFORMATION TECHNOLOGY
Background

Business Communications

People at work find the need to communicate with others all the time. Sometimes they need to speak, sometimes to use signs, sometimes they use machines or the written word. By all these methods they pass information. In addition to this, people communicate things about themselves by the way they dress, speak or react when they are spoken to.

Look at your own behaviour

Many people do not realise that it is often their own behaviour which determines how somebody else will react. Consider a simple example. You walk into a room for an interview and the person you see knows you are there but is busy doing something else. You immediately feel unimportant and the interviewer may feel he has shown his authority. If, instead, there had been an immediate smile and 'hello' you would feel differently about the situation. This may seem obvious but just keep a note of how many times in a day you fail to be cheerful and friendly towards other people.

Ways of communicating

Businesses often require different things from their different methods of communication. Sometimes speed will be all important, but at other times, secrecy or low cost communication may be more so. Possibly, for reasons of safety, clarity or because a record is required, we may need to use written rather than spoken communication. For communication with their employees many firms issue a company handbook which includes matters like:

what to do if you are away ill.
who is in charge of what.
rules which must be obeyed.
what to do if you have a complaint.
the social facilities the firm has.

They will also use notice boards for matters of general interest and may even include information in your pay packet.

Letters and telephones

Letters and telephones are probably the main methods of communications used by most businesses. Many countries can now be dialled direct and the call is routed through one of the many satellites orbiting the earth.

In Britain, British Telecom is often criticised for its failure to provide a reliable service. The directory enquiry system is considered very poor and lines are often engaged. The postal system, although very

Group Task: Naming a chocolate bar

Four people, A, B, C, and D have been gathered together to decide the name of a new chocolate bar. A, B, and C should each decide on a name which they want to propose, but they should not tell the others. D will make the final decision. You will need to think of a different name for each situation.

There are three situations which you have to play through. You are allowed to talk to another person only if the communication arrow allows you to do so. The conversation must not be overheard by anybody with whom you are not allowed to communicate.

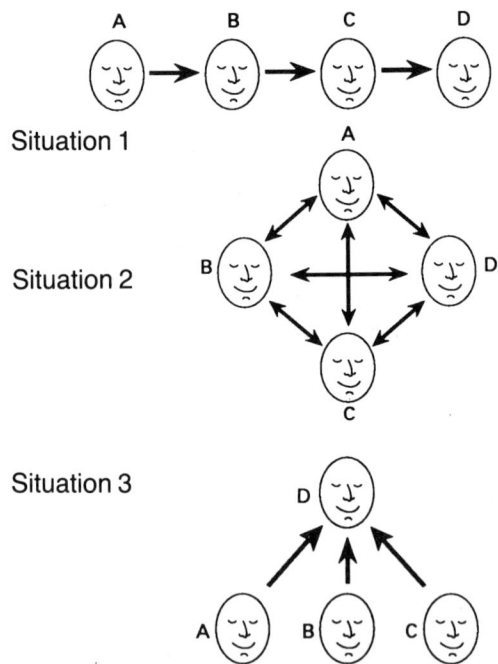

Situation 1

Situation 2

Situation 3

Questions

1 What name was decided on in each case?

2 In which situation did you feel you had the best chance of getting your name adopted?

3 In which situation did you feel you had least chance of getting your name adopted?

4 Can you suggest real life applications for each of the above situations?

efficient in comparison with those in many other countries, gets much criticism for its failure to provide a reliable first class letter service. Such failings hamper the efficiency of businesses.

Radio telephones

Within a business, memoranda (brief written messages) and telephone calls are cheap and efficient. Radio phones are now common and allow a user to walk up to 100m away from the base of the phone to check documents or move to another office. The main disadvantage of this system is that it is not strictly private so your call could be overheard.

Portable telephones, which can be used in cars or outdoors, are now in use. One of these systems is called Cellnet, which does not yet cover the whole of the country so the mobile phones can be used only in certain areas.

Paging systems

Bleeper systems, like 'Radiopager', are becoming more and more common. These tell the wearer to contact their base. Usually they would go to a phone to do so. Their main advantage is that they are relatively cheap and key personnel can always be contacted in an emergency. Over shorter distances, for example within a factory or town, short-wave radios may be used.

Confravision

Air travel is increasing rapidly but it can present the problems of jet lag. This occurs when you leave Britain at midday and travel for eight hours only to find you arrive in another country at 2pm local time. Your body thinks it is 8pm. Three hours later your body is ready to sleep but it is still only 5pm! A possible alternative is to use Confravision where you can go to linked studios and talk to people abroad and see them on a television screen.

Video phones

Within offices, many telephone systems will already allow several people to talk together. The Japanese are experimenting with video phones but one of the main problems will be finding an internationally standard way of transmitting the pictures. The problem is rather like the struggle between VHS and Betamax for a standard video system. There is no doubt the video phone will come, but we will have to rethink the way we communicate on the phone if people can see us as well as hear us!

Telex

For many years now use has been made of the telex system. In this case two teleprinters (which look very much like ordinary typewriters) are linked together. The system's main advantage is that it provides a permanent record of the message which is printed out. These can operate unattended so time differences around the world do not matter, the message is ready and waiting when business starts in another country.

Pie charts

Pie charts are a very common method of communication in business. You will see them in annual reports and sales brochures. You will find them a very useful way of displaying data you have collected. You can construct them by hand, doing all the calculations yourself, or you can use a computer graphics package which will do all the work for you. If you have to do them yourself, the method is given below.

Exercise

The results of a survey asking for peoples' favourite TV programme were:

Eastenders	25
The Match	20
Neighbours	15
Total	60

Method

1 Total the number who replied = 60.
2 360 degrees divided by 60 = 6 degrees.

This means every 1 reply takes up 6 degrees of the circle.

Degrees for Eastenders	$= 25 \times 6 = 150$
Degrees for The Big Match	$= 20 \times 6 = 120$
Degrees for Neighbours	$= 15 \times 6 = 90$
Check this adds up to 360 degrees	$-\,360$

The final pie chart would then look like this

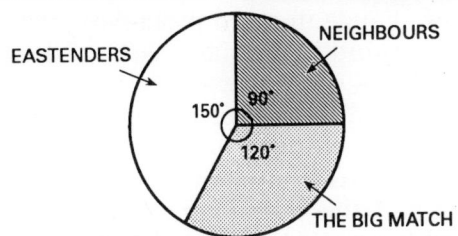

Questions

Draw pie charts to show the following information.

1 Passengers (in millions) at three airports in 1986:
   Heathrow 31   Manchester 8   Belfast 2

2 Readership of newspapers in 1987 in millions:
   Sun 4   *Times* 0.4   *Express* 1.6
   Star 1.2   *Mirror* 3   *Guardian* 0.5

IT ▶ **GRAPHICS**

You can also complete these questions using a graphics package.

Electronic mail

This system links a computer to the telephone lines through a modem. Messages can be sent to another computer and displayed on the screen or printed. This system can be used by a company for either internal or external communications. It is also possible to get the computer to answer for you. It can for example reply that you are out for a few days.

Fax

Many firms also have Fax (this is the abbreviation for 'facsimile' which means an exact copy) which allows them to transmit pictures or documents down telephone lines. The receiving machine reproduces the picture or document. There are also portable versions of Fax which can send documents from a car via the Cellnet mobile telephone system to other machines in cars or offices.

Teletext

Much information is now available on text systems on suitably adapted TVs. The BBC offers Ceefax which carries a wide range of regularly updated information on business, sport, weather and travel news. The Prestel system allows subscribers to display information about their company which other people can use. For example holidays which are available can be seen on the system and travel agents can book them using a special code. This saves a great deal of time for both the travel agent and the customer. Some supermarkets display all the items they have for sale and people who are subscribers to Prestel can order their groceries. Banks also use the system to allow people to see their own bank statement and undertake transactions.

Word processors

The pace of change in word processing is becoming increasingly rapid. Although you will still find manual and electric typewriters in many smaller offices, the word processor is becoming standard equipment for dealing with the written word. It allows instant correction, movement and redesign of paragraphs and the production of standard letters. Those word processing systems which are part of an integrated package can also accept information from databases and spreadsheets for editing into a report.

Desk-top publishing

The power of microcomputers made high quality desk-top publishing possible for many firms. This enables them to present reports and advertisements in high quality at a low cost. Firms can use different sizes of letters and type styles to make their reports more eye-catching and graphics to display charts and diagrams.

POINTS TO REMEMBER

★ Good communications between people helps to make a business successful.

★ Advances in technology are improving the speed and quality of communications.

Super smart cards

These advanced credit cards can:

store bank balances.
convert currencies.
tell the time.
act as an electronic diary.
go on line to a computer to get information like share prices.

Smart Card Shopping

All the major banks are currently involved in experiments using IC cards for shopping and other credit services. The

Credit with chips, the new VISA card

common feature of these is that they all use cards which can store money transferred to the card's memory from the customer's bank accounts or which set a predetermined credit limit. These experiments are not only looking for ways to develop new customer services. One major motivation is to find more efficient ways to circulate money electronically between shoppers, stores and banks.

Questions

1 Suggest three items of personal information which it might be useful to hold on this sort of card.

2 What are the dangers of storing personal information on a card like this?

TASK 1

1 Can you find out why satellites have been so important in improving telecommunications?

2 Explain what is meant by each of the following:
 a a fax system.
 b Prestel.
 c electronic mail.
 d word processor.
 e confravision.
 f bleeper system.
 g telex.
 h Ceefax.
 i desk-top publishing.
 j Cellnet.
 k short-wave radio.

TASK 2

BUSINESS LETTER

Layout of a letter that is fully blocked with open punctuation:

IT ▶ DESKTOP

1 Design a suitable letter heading for use by
 M.I.E. Communications
 Fairmeade Industrial Estate
 Longport Road
 Liverpool
 L23 5JU   Tel. 051 923 8999

IT ▶ WORDPRO

2 Compose a letter from the above company's sales manager, Ms S Robson, to Dataformic Ltd of 56 Merton Way, Wandsworth, London, pointing out the possible benefits of buying a fax machine and offering to come and demonstrate it.

REF
(blank line)
TODAY'S DATE
— Do not use punctuation in this section of the letter

(blank line)

NAME
ADDRESS
ADDRESS
ADDRESS
POSTCODE
(blank line)
Dear Sir (Miss Smith)
— This section contains the name and address of the person to whom you are sending the letter. Do not use punctuation in this section

(blank line)
Text
Text
Text
(leave one blank line to show a new paragraph)
Text
Text
Text
(blank line)

Yours faithfully (sincerely)
(blank line)
(blank line)
(blank line)
(blank line)
(blank line)
Name of person sending the letter
(blank line)
Enc
— Do not use punctuation in this section

Databases

Fields, records and files

Nowadays a great deal of information is stored on computers. Computer programs are written which allow you to store the information in different formats. One of the ways of storing information is in a database. A telephone directory is a database which contains three 'fields', these are:

name
address
telephone number

There are many thousands of 'records' such as:

Jones A   37 Lime Street   0823-7617

Each telephone book covering an area is a 'file'.

Finding information

Once the information has been put into a database you can then ask the computer to find a certain piece of information, e.g. the telephone number of A Jones who lives at 37 Lime Street. You can then select which fields you want printed out, in this case you might only want the phone number printed.

This last example points to one of the major problems people have when using databases. You need to be quite clear about the question you are going to ask the database and, having done that, you then need to tell it which fields you want printed out.

Abbreviating field names

When creating a database it is a good idea to abbreviate field names as this saves space in the computer's memory. For example,

Field Name

Add 1   37 Lime Street
Add 2   Newton
Add 3   Ayrshire

Splitting up the address like this means that you can search on each individual field – so you could find the names of people living in Newton or Ayrshire. Also you can use abbreviations when entering information, for example

Female   F
Male   M

Explaining abbreviations

The meanings of these abbreviations can be stored in the database. This might be called 'Explain Text' or something similar, depending on which database you are using.

The uses of databases

Once information has been collected on a database, it is a very valuable asset to the owner. Think about a mail order firm which has hundreds of agents and thousands of customers. Some will be up to date with their payments, others in arrears. It is very easy to select people who are up to date to send them a particular letter, perhaps one encouraging them to buy more, and to send all the others a letter encouraging them to pay their debts.

Retailing database

Questions

Create the following database and insert the abbreviations to the codes in the appropriate part of your database.

SHOP	SELLS
Woolworth	THCS
Littlewoods	CF
BHS	CF
Harrods	THCSEF

where T = Toys
      H = Household goods
      C = Clothes
      S = Sweets
      E = Sports equipment
      F = Food

1 Which sells toys?

2 Which sells toys and sweets?

3 What does Littlewoods sell?

4 Which sells food?

5 Print out the entire database and the explanations.

In the same way, products could be tested on people living in a certain part of the country by selecting them on the basis of the town in which they live.

Companies which hold information on databases will also sell this to others; once one has your name and address, many other companies can get it. This is how we receive so much unwanted mail, advertising all sorts of products.

Databases and the law

It is now a legal requirement that all computer users who hold personal information on people are registered with the Data Protection Registrar and they must state what information they hold and why they are holding it. The reason for this is the fear that information held may be incorrect and damaging to people.

Credit references

One of the most sensitive areas in the use of databases is in giving consumers credit. If you go into a shop and ask for credit, the shop will almost certainly check your name and address with credit reference agencies. These hold information about people who have been declared bankrupt or who have failed to meet previous credit repayments. If you are refused credit you have the right to know which agency was used and, on payment of a fee, you can have access to the information held on you. If you can show it to be incorrect you can insist that it is altered.

The need for controls on databases

Whilst factual information held in databases may present few problems, some databases may go beyond this and contain opinions or rumours about you. This is an area which needs careful monitoring as more and more organisations hold personal information on databases.

POINTS TO REMEMBER

★ A database can store a great deal of information about people, events or products.

★ Legal safeguards are needed to protect people from the misuse of databases.

Entering a database

A simple database is set out below. Enter it into the database on your computer.

Name	Sex	Age
Johnson	Male	27
Williams	Female	16
Blake	Female	19
Sheardon	Male	16

Questions

1 How many fields are there?

2 What are they called?

3 How many records are there?

4 Write down all the information in one record.

Find the answers to the following questions by using the database and then check from the table that you are correct.

5 Print all the information known about Johnson. (Name = Johnson; Print Name, Age and Sex)

6 Print an alphabetical list of all the names (Alphabetical sort on Name; Print Name)

7 Who is 19 years old? (Age = 19; Print Name)

8 List the names of the females (Sex = Female; Print Name)

9 List all the names and ages in numerical order of age. (Numerical Sort on Age; Print Names and Ages)

10 Who is 16 and female? (Age = 16 and Sex = Female; Print Name)

11 List all the information about anybody who is 27. (Age = 27; Print Name, Age and Sex).

12 List the age of everybody whose name contains the letter 'e'. (Name contains e; Print Age).

13 List the name and age of anybody older than 18. (Age greater than 18; Print Name and Age).

14 Print out the entire database. (Print all records and all fields).

15 Who is less than 17? (Age less than 17; Print Name).

16 Whose name starts with 'W' and how old is that person? (Name starts with 'W'; Print Name and Age)

TASK 1

Create the following database on the main export markets for the United Kingdom in 1986.

Country	value of exports £m	% share
Fed Rep Germany	8542	11.7
France	6210	8.5
Netherlands	5443	7.5
Eire	3558	4.9
United States	10380	14.2
Belgium	3833	5.3
Spain	1905	2.6
Italy	3472	4.8
Sweden	2308	3.2
Canada	1698	2.3

1 To which countries did the UK export over £5000m worth of goods?

2 What is the total value of exports to the countries included in the database?

3 List the countries in ascending order of percentage share of exports.

4 What is the average value of exports to a country?

TASK 2

SCHOOL CANTEEN

Create a database to include all the items sold in your school canteen. The fields should include:

Item   Price   Colour coding

You need to apply a colour coding system where:

Red is bad for you, i.e. sticky buns, crisps;

Yellow is alright, provided you do not eat too much of it;

Green is good for you, eat as much as you want.

Now answer the following questions:

1 Which items cost less than 15p?

2 List the items you should not eat.

3 List the items which are good for you.

4 Which items cost more than 20p?

5 I have only 12p to spend. What can I buy?

TASK 3

DRIVER & VEHICLE LICENSING CENTRE

All the records of cars and drivers are held on a computer at Swansea. This can be used to record convictions against drivers and to check on who owns a particular car. The information on this computer is not available to the general public.

Department of Transport   T 437608

Vehicle Registration Document

ALEXANDER BERT KENB
24 DAYS CLOSE
LINGHAM
CAMBRIDGE
CB5 7LE

V5
Rev. Jan/88

| Registration Mark | D305 VDA | 2 | Validation Character | X | 3 |

PLEASE QUOTE THE REGISTRATION MARK IN ALL CORRESPONDENCE

Taxation Class	PRIVATE/LIGHT GOODS (PLG)
Make	ZASTAVA
Model/Type	YUGO 55 L
	3 DOOR SALOON
Colour(s)	WHITE
Type of Fuel	PETROL
VIN/Chassis/Frame No.	VX1345A0D348427
Engine No.	300GL064924512
Cylinder Capacity	1116 CC
Seating Capacity	
Taxable Weight	726.0 KG UNLADEN
Date of Registration	21.04.87
Last Change of Keeper	22.08.88
No. of Former Keepers	1

1 Look at the vehicle registration document. What fields are there on this?

2 Make a list of the organisations which you think should be able to have access to the information stored on this computer.

TASK 4

RADIO CASSETTE PLAYERS

Name	Price £	General features	Radio features	Cassette features
DECCASOUND	70	ADF	NP	BDKNPR
AIWA	70	ADF	PQ	BDNPQ
AKAI	130	ABCEFGH	NPQR	BCDEL
FISHER	80	ADG	KPQ	DGLNPQR
TOSHIBA	90	ADFH	Q	BDNPQR
SONY	110	ADG		BELN
PANASONIC	80	ACD	KPQ	DGNPQR
GRUNDIG	110	ADFH	PQ	DKN

Construct a database with five fields and eight records on the topic of stereo radio cassette recorders.

1 Print out an alphabetical list of all recorders showing their target price, general features, radio features and cassette features.

2 Print out an alphabetical list of the names only of the cassette recorders.

3 Print out an explanation of the codes of the radio features. (The teacher should check this is correct on the screen if a printout cannot be obtained.)

4 Print out the names of recorders with a target price of £80.

5 Print out the names and general features of recorders with a target price of more than £80.

6 Print out the names of recorders with a tone control and a short wave radio.

7 Print out all the details of recorders which work off batteries, have a stereo/mono switch and have built-in microphones.

8 Owing to improvements in technology the AKAI machine is now to be sold at £110. Alter the database to show this and print out all the details of the AKAI machine.

Explanation of codes

General features

A – headphone sockets
B – sockets for external speakers
C – stereo widening switch
D – tone control
E – graphic equaliser
F – balance control
G – works off batteries
H – connects to other equipment
J – clock with radio alarm

Cassette features

B – sockets for microphones
C – autostop for fast wind
D – autostop from play
E – auto reverse
G – cue and review
K – tape counter
L – programme search
M – microphone mixing
N – built in microphones
P – two cassette decks for copying
Q – double speed copying
R – continuous play

Radio features

N – tuning selector
P – stereo indicator
Q – stereo/mono switch
R – socket for FM aerial
K – short wave

(Adapted from Which? Dec 1986)

Spreadsheets

This section is intended to give only a very brief outline of the way in which spreadsheets work. Although they all operate on the same principle, different computers have different spreadsheets and each has its own set of operating instructions. You will need to be familiar with the instructions for one system before you can complete the questions in this section.

What would happen if . . . ?

Spreadsheets are now very commonly used in business to display financial information and to show what the effects of changes in the information would be. For example, a firm might want to know how its profits would be affected if they were to increase the selling price of their product.

You could set up the spreadsheet to complete a particular calculation. For example:

Sales − Purchases = PROFIT
£200 − £50   = £150

This could be put into a spreadsheet just as it is, except that you would not put in the figure of £150. In that position you would put a simple formula telling the spreadsheet to take away the contents of purchases (£50) from the contents of sales (£200).

The spreadsheet can be displayed on the computer as a grid:

Each slot has its own reference number, three are shaded. In each slot (or cell) you can put a:

label   that is a word like 'sales'.
value   that is a number.
formula   this tells the spreadsheet to do something.

For example, you could tell it to add the contents of slot B3 to the contents of slot B4. This would be done by the formula B3+B4. You could put this formula

in slot B5. If you were to change the contents of B3 or B4 the spreadsheet would automatically put the new answer into slot B5!

Spreadsheets will accept:

Add   use +
Subtract   use −
Multiply   use *
Divide   use /

Also it is possible to use formulae which obey the rules you learnt in maths lessons. For example, (B5*B6) + (B7−B8) could be used.

When you try to prepare a spreadsheet it is usually a good idea to map out on a piece of paper what headings you will need and what spacing you will have to use.

POINT TO REMEMBER

★ Spreadsheets are widely used in business to quickly show the effects of making financial changes.

Calculations

Using a spreadsheet find the answers to the following.

1 200 + 234	**10** 12 900 × 980
2 34 × 12	**11** 1235
	+4678
3 12 / 2.5	+2917
4 £23.78 × 4	**12** 8622
	−1975
5 45 − 12	
	13 +VAT Total
6 23 + 12 − 3	86.40 +15% =
	19.78 +15% =
7 67.23 × 34	34.89 +15% =
8 £123.90 + £12.87	**14** 12.60
	+14.28
9 56 / 6	+19.58

The bakery problem

The Tasty Bakery has a varied range of products including

	Cost of production
Medium brown loaf	25p
Bun loaf	24p
French stick	19p
Eccles cake	7p
Fairy cake	14p
Doughnut	9p

It operates on five days per week. The selling price is found by adding fifty per cent to the cost of making the item, and rounding up any ½p.

Unit sales per day are always about 5 percent greater than the previous day from Monday to Friday. The sales on Monday of one week were

MBL	200
BL	50
FS	50
EC	20
FC	10
D	5

Questions

Devise a single spreadsheet to find all of the following:

1 the selling price of each item.

2 the revenue from sales on each day.

3 the total revenue for the week.

4 the unit sales for each day.

5 the unit sales for the week.

6 If prices were to be calculated by adding 60 per cent to the cost what would be the new daily and weekly revenue?

TASK 1

AIRWORLD TRAVEL

Airworld Travel wants to produce a guide to foreign currencies and the values in terms of pounds (£).

1 Devise a spreadsheet to show the value of £1, £2, £5, £10, £20, £50, £100, £500 and £1000 in terms of French francs, Japanese yen and American dollars if £1 = 9.85 francs = 234.24 yen = 1.61 dollars. Print out your answer.

The great benefit of using a spreadsheet for this purpose is that it is easy to update if exchange rates alter.

2 Alter the spreadsheet to cope with:

£1 = 9.90 francs = 241.10 yen = 1.60 dollars. Print out your answer.

3 Find out two reasons why the exchange rate for the pound varies from day to day.

TASK 2

MONEY

1 Construct a spreadsheet to show for a list of 10 of your friends:
   a the total pocket money received.
   b the total money received from part time jobs.
   c the total money received from both sources.

2 If part-time employers gave everybody a 6.5% pay rise how much extra would each student receive?

3 What would the average total money received by one person in the group now be?

TASK 3

DRY CLEANING SHOPS

The spreadsheet set out below shows the sales on the six days (Monday to Saturday) for three branches of shoe shops in Corby, Oldham and Bolton.

	A MON	B TUES	C WED	D THURS	E FRI	F SAT	G TOTAL	H BRANCH
1	MON	TUES	WED	THURS	FRI	SAT	TOTAL	BRANCH
2	247.01	256.78	432.89	379.89	128.56	356.90		CORBY
3	321.78	256.90	213.67	200.02	234.76	235.90		OLDHAM
4	563.00	235.87	199.00	674.90	216.09	235.90		BOLTON
5	------	------	------	------	------	------	------	
6								
7	======	======	======	======	======	======	======	
8								
9	Average	Sales	Per	Day	=			
10								

1 Put the above information into your spreadsheet.

2 Use a formula to complete G2, G3 and G4 to find the sales for the week for each branch.

3 Use a formula to complete A6, B6, C6, D6, E6 and F6 which is the total daily sales.

4 What are the three possible formulae that could be used to find G6?

5 Insert the formula to find the average sales per day.

6 Print out the completed spreadsheet.

7 You receive a phone call from the Oldham branch saying that the figures they submitted were incorrect. Wednesday should have been £564.98 and Saturday should have been £236.89. Make these alterations on the spreadsheet.

8 What is the new overall total for Oldham for the week?

9 What is the new overall total for the three branches for the week?

10 What is the new average sales per day?

TASK 4

PETROL PROBLEM

A 24 hour garage sells Gulf petrol. On each day of the week it serves:

MONDAY   20 cars per hour

TUESDAY   15 cars per hour

WEDNESDAY   7 cars per hour

THURSDAY   17 cars per hour

FRIDAY   20 cars per hour

SATURDAY   18 cars per hour

SUNDAY   25 cars per hour

Each car on average buys 25 litres of petrol. The price of petrol per litre is displayed on the sign. The garage can buy it for 26p per litre.
  Each day wages are £50, except for Saturday and Sunday when they are £60.
  Rent is £100 per day and rates are £90 per day.

1 Construct a spreadsheet to show
    a the number of litres of petrol sold per day.
    b the number of litres of petrol sold per week.
    c the daily sales revenue.
    d the weekly sales revenue.
    e the daily costs.
    f the weekly costs.
    g the profit made for each day.
    h the profit made for the week.

    Print out your answer.

2 How much extra profit would they make if the selling price was increased to 36p per litre and the weekend wages were reduced to £55?

    Print out your answer.

TASK 5

PLANNING FOR AN OVERDRAFT

One of the most common uses of spreadsheets is to see what would happen if certain changes were made. If you think about the process of setting up a business, you will see the need to be able to work out how much cash you will need to get through each month. This may lead to your realising that, at certain times during the first year, you might need an overdraft from the bank.

Consider the following situation.

A company starts business in January with a balance at the bank of £5000. Cash payments for sales are received in the month after the goods are sold. Expenses have to be paid in the month they occur.

	JAN	FEB	MARCH	APR	MAY	JUN
Predicted sales	£4000	£3500	£2000	£4500	£4700	£4890
Predicted expenses	£8000	£3000	£4500	£1000	£1000	£8000

1 Construct a spreadsheet which shows clearly the opening balance and the balance on the bank account each month. Remember that the balance at the end of each month should always be carried forward to the next month.

2 In which months would you need to arrange an overdraft?

3 BAD NEWS! You now suspect that the people who buy your goods will pay you in the second month after they receive them. By altering the amounts you expect to receive in each month, if you have the right formula, the spreadsheet will recalculate the bank balance in each month.

4 In which months do you now require overdrafts?

Investigating the ECONOMICS Background

THE TROUBLE WITH US, CLAUDE . . . . THE MORE WE HAVE, THE MORE WE WANT.

The Economic Problem

Satisfying basic economic wants

Imagine living on a desert island. Endless sun, sand and sea . . . but, before you can enjoy these pleasures, you have to make sure that you can stay alive. You will need to find food and shelter. You must keep warm at night and be able to prepare food.

Let us take the problem of food. You could be a gatherer – shellfish from the seashore, berries from bushes, fruit from trees. Or you can be a trapper – rabbits perhaps, or a hunter – catching fish or crabs, maybe a wild boar. You will probably try your hand at all three and balance your time according to your level of skill or your particular needs.

There is only one of you so you might fish late at night when shoals come inshore and you may gather berries early in the morning. Of course, if several of your friends had been shipwrecked on the island too, you would have divided your time. Perhaps one was the best hunter, another better at fishing and a third the best cook. Perhaps you were best at sitting down and organising them.

Economic society

Of course, very few of us live on desert islands. We live in crowded towns and cities, or small village communities. As members of a 'society' we learn to live with one another and we come to rely on one another. In Britain we are rather like one very large island community, although there are very few palm trees about. Some people produce foodstuffs from farms, others contribute to making goods and yet others provide services like shops or air travel.

The role of the government

It is the job of government to try to ensure that this system of working and living together works successfully. The government doesn't own or control everything but it creates rules to try to make living together easier. There are laws to control the way in which firms operate. The government collects taxes to spend on pensions for the old and care for the sick.

The economic system

We call all this the 'economic system'. How people, firms, institutions and government work together to solve the economic problem. Of course, although Britain is an island, it is part of a world economy and the government is also concerned about our relationship with other countries.

The economic problem

All countries have more or less the same economic

Group discussion In groups of 4 decide your answers to the following questions and compare your answers with other groups.

Questions

1 You have been shipwrecked on a desert island with five other people. Which five jobs would you like them to have done? The following list may help you, or you can select jobs of your own.

Doctor   Comedian   Chef   Lawyer
Police officer   Computer programmer
Nurse   Farmer   Sailor
Teacher   Car mechanic   Carpenter
Hairdresser   Judge
Newspaper reporter   Coal miner

2 A person's job may not be the best indication of their worth to you on a desert island. What qualities would your group want from the six people, in order to make the most of life there?

IT ▶ WORDPRO

Once you have decided on your group decision, use the word processor to present your conclusions as a group report.

List the five selected jobs you have chosen and, for each one, list the qualities you would want to find.

problem – deciding on:

a what to produce,

b how to produce it and

c how to distribute it fairly amongst the population.

Most countries solve the first two problems through production by privately owned firms. They use natural resources to manufacture products which they sell to those who wish to buy. A farmer may produce carrots which he sells, using the money to buy a car made by lots of people working in a city far away. It is money which allows the system to work.

Often the food and raw materials have to be bought from abroad, because we don't have enough of what we need. We pay for these by selling things, which we do have, to foreign countries – oil, tractors or even insurance.

Even if we solve part of our economic problem through production and trade in goods and services, we still have to make sure that the population benefits from the system. People who work are paid for their labour and this allows them to buy the goods and services they need. In a caring society we must also consider those who are not able to get work – unemployment is a big problem. There are also the young and old who must be cared for even though they are not actually 'earning a living'.

This, then, is the basic economic problem. How to make the 'system' work. Later units will explore the ideas further.

POINTS TO REMEMBER

★ The basic economic problem is:

what to produce
how to produce it
how to distribute it.

★ Everyone has basic economic wants like food, clothing and shelter.

★ We all have to allocate our time to satisfy our wants. Society too, must allocate time and resources.

★ Sometimes the system does not work very well and people are unemployed, homeless or hungry – sometimes all three.

★ We trade with one another but also with countries overseas. This is increasingly important.

Scarce resources: water

The picture shows an area of the world where water is very scarce.

Questions

1 Suggest how the way in which you pay for water might be different from how water is paid for in this African village.

2 State three ways in which you would use water differently if you had to fetch it in water jars several times a day.

Trade: a street market

The picture shows a street market in Hong Kong where local farmers can sell vegetables which they have grown.

Questions

1 Why do you think food prices in this market are cheaper than in nearby shops?

2 Why does the farmer prefer to sell some of his goods rather than feed them all to his family?

You might discuss your answers here with others in your group.

TASK 1

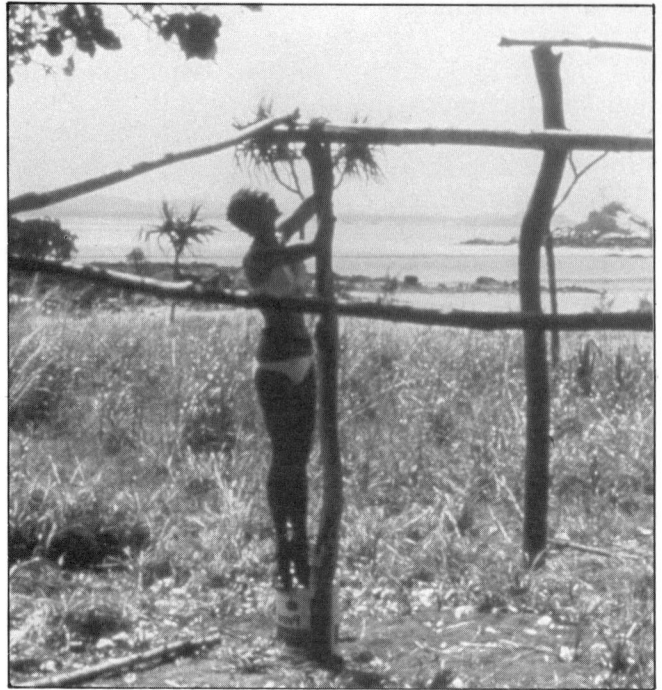

Castaway

CASTAWAY WITH SCARCE RESOURCES

I learned quickly where the most abundant catches of fruit were, and to get these entailed a trek through the interior. If I observed something potentially edible or useful, some mechanism inside would snap awake and a mental note would be made of how to find the spot again. . . . First I select the most deeply coloured, perfect specimens off the vine. . . . Where there are only two fruit, I eat one and keep the other, where there are eight, eat four keep four.

The passage above is taken from *Castaway*, the story of two people who lived alone together on a Pacific Island for a year. The story is told by one of them, Lucy Irvine. Gathering fruit is the easiest way of finding food. Lucy soon found that growing crops was more difficult but much more reliable.

Lucy and her companion could not gather food all the time. They had to spend time tilling the soil and planting seeds so that, later, food would be plentiful.

1 Suggest reasons why:
   a Lucy could not rely on living from gathered fruit on its own.
   b Lucy chose the best specimens of fruit first.
   c Where there are eight fruit, Lucy ate four and kept four.

2 Explain:
   a What is meant by the term 'capital investment'.
   b Give three different examples of capital investment schemes going on somewhere near you.
   c Imagine that you have to explain to a Pacific island community why it is better to build a canning factory than to extend the existing pineapple plantation.

▶ WORDPRO

Present your argument in the form of a letter to the Island Council. This should be 10–20 lines in length and should be addressed to the Secretary from your home address.

Bhakra Dam Project, India

An economic society makes the same kind of decision. It builds factories and roads as well as video recorders and cars. We call this capital investment whereas video recorders and cars are consumer goods.

TASK 2

POVERTY IN BRITAIN

These two boys and the man live in poor housing in an inner city. Imagine their thoughts about the future and their hopes for a better life ahead.

Think of a suitable phrase or caption, for each photograph, which sums up what you think they might want to say about their own situation.

TASK 3

POVERTY AND INEQUALITY

The gap between rich and poor is widening in Britain.

★ The rich are getting richer:

The top 10% of wage earners earned 118% more in 1986 than in 1979.
The bottom 10% of wage earners earned 80% more in 1986 than in 1979.
Prices rose by 80% between 1979 and 1986.

★ The poor are getting poorer:

In 1979 6 million people were below the official poverty line.
In 1986 10 million people were below the official poverty line.

Look at the figures above.

1 Are the lowest wage earners better or worse off in terms of what they could buy in 1986 compared with 1979?

2 The richest 10% are not only better off than in 1979 but they have improved more than the poorest 10%, Write down the figures which proves these two statements.

3 Think of three likely reasons why more people are living in poverty in Britain in 1986 than in 1979.

4 What questions do these figures raise in your mind about the way in which Britain is facing up to 'the economic problem'?

TASK 4

DIVISION OF LABOUR

Most economies divide up jobs so that they can be done more efficiently. For example some people specialise in being doctors, others farmers. This division of labour also occurs within jobs. If you visit a factory you will see many people contributing to making a product, each often performing just one small task.

1 What examples are there of the division of labour:
   a within your school?
   b in a fast food shop?

2 What advantages and disadvantages can you think of in operating a division of labour?

The Mixed Economy

Desert island economics

Robinson Crusoe is a desert island 'castaway' known to almost everyone. On his desert island he was in complete control of how he organised his time. He could use the natural resources of the island in any way he wished. He could use his own skills freely and he had to answer only to himself – although he was fairly limited in what he could do and the choices he could make.

A 'capitalist' economy

If Robinson Crusoe had returned to live in a modern western country – like the United States for instance – he would have found life very confusing. Shops would be full of an unbelievable range of goods to buy, made in factories all over the world. He would be able to ride in any number of different makes of car. Streets would be well lit, running water would be readily available. Very few services are provided by the government in the US – people pay privately for most things they receive. People contribute the capital to run industry and commerce so it is often known as a 'capitalist' economy.

A 'command' economy

In some Eastern European countries he would have found life different again. People would appear well-fed and warmly clothed but the shops would have fewer things to sell. The range of cars on the streets would be far fewer than in the US. People's choices would be restricted. On the other hand, everyone would be sure of somewhere to live, transport would be cheap and very few would be out of work. The state would own most of the factories and would control what was produced and would fix the prices which were to be charged for many things. This is often called a 'planned' or 'command' economy, like the Soviet Union or East Germany.

A 'mixed' economy

He would have found the modern British economy an interesting mixture. Like the United States, factories in Britain are mainly privately owned. In fact, they are owned usually by shareholders who use their savings to purchase shares in large companies. Often these firms are in competition with one another, which is healthy because it keeps their prices down when the consumer has to pay. Most people live in homes which they are buying for themselves. They own their own cars and are free to choose holidays and how they spend their leisure time.

On the other hand, he would soon become aware

Robinson Crusoe.

I might have raised ship-loadings of corn, but I had no use for it; so I let as little grow as I thought enough for my occasion. I had tortoise or turtles enough; but now and then one was as much as I could put to any use. I had timber enough to have built a fleet of ships. I had grapes enough to have made wine, or to have cured into raisins, to have loaded that fleet when they had been built.

But all I could make use of was all that was valuable. I had enough to eat and to supply my wants, and what was all the rest to me? If I killed more flesh than I could eat, the dog must eat it, or the vermin. If I sowed more corn than I could eat, it must be spoiled. The trees that I cut down were lying to rot on the ground; I could make no more use of them than for fuel, and that I had no occasion for but to dress my food.

Making choices: Robinson Crusoe

This passage is taken from the book *Robinson Crusoe* by Daniel Defoe. It tells the story of Crusoe, a shipwrecked mariner and his adventures on a desert island. He had lots of 'economic' choices to make.

Questions

1 The only things which he considered of 'value' to him were those which he could use. List them.

2 Think of six items which you have bought recently. Which would have been of 'value' to Robinson Crusoe? List those which
   a would have been of use to him
   b you think would not have been useful.

that many of the services in the British economy were actually provided for him by the government – often referred to as the 'state' – the postal service for example, and the railway system.

The state charges taxes on goods and demands tax payments from individuals and firms to raise the revenue they needed to provide pensions for the elderly, child allowances for the young, grants for industry, roads, policing and many other important services.

This kind of system is called a 'mixed' economy. That means that it is a mixture of things privately owned and things owned by the state. Britain is certainly not the only mixed economy. In fact it is much more like the US or Japan in its support of private ownership in recent years. You are probably aware that the government has been 'selling off' some of the industries it owned through the process of 'privatisation'. Perhaps France or Sweden are now better examples. Some controlled or 'command' economies are also becoming much more 'mixed' these days. Yugoslavia is a good example, and China seems to be moving that way.

'State', 'public' or 'government'?

We often use the terms 'state', 'government' and 'public' as if they mean the same thing. Usually, they can be.

Solving the basic economic problem

All these modern countries are trying to solve the same basic economic problem, but in slightly different ways. They want to help the population of their country to enjoy as high a standard of living as possible – to maximise their 'welfare'. Some are more concerned about freedom of choice, others more about equality.

POINTS TO REMEMBER

★ The 'mixed economy' combines some private ownership with some state control.

★ All countries are trying to solve the same economic problem, but often in different ways.

★ There are lots of versions of the mixed economy. Different political parties in Britain argue for a different balance. The same arguments go on in many other countries.

★ There is no 'right' or 'wrong' answer to the problem, just different viewpoints.

Fur coats before basic clothing?

Question

Write a paragraph to explain why an economy produces expensive fur coats for some people to buy whilst others may not be able to have basic clothing.

ADAM SMITH:
The Invisible Hand

The key to his system and his great gift to conservative economists is the 'Invisible Hand' – the assumption that a society of individuals making logical decisions in pursuit of economic self-interest will, as if guided by some unseen hand, produce an expanding, self-balancing economy.

All men sell their goods and labour as expensively as possible and buy as cheaply as possible. Goods are produced in response to demand. If supply is lacking it becomes profitable to expand production.

The price system is the self-regulator with the 'market price' the point at which supply equals demand. If governments interfere they will distort the self-correcting mechanism to disastrous effect.

The search for greater profits leads automatically to greater efficiency – increasing both the volume of goods produced and the income of workers. This increases demand and restarts the growth cycle again.

Adam Smith: The first 'economist'?

Many people think of Adam Smith (1723–1790) as the founder of modern economics. He believed that the state should leave the economy to the workings of market competition.

Question

Read the passage above carefully and try to identify what Adam Smith is saying.

TASK 1

China Notes that Marx is Dead

The Economist, 22 December 1984.

Parts of the economy, including heavy industry and energy, will remain firmly under the central planners' thumb. Most other firms will be able to vary the prices they charge within certain guidelines, and will have to learn to produce what their customers want; it will be harder to dump unsellable goods in state warehouses. Some small firms, and the growing number of businesses owned by individuals or small groups, will be able to offer their wares at whatever price the market will stand. There is even talk of a stock market.

This passage was written at a time when the Chinese government, under the leadership of Deng Xiaoping, was first moving away from a strictly regulated command economy, which had isolated the country from the rest of the world. The first reforms were in agriculture. It was not long before industry followed.

1 Which phrase in the passage means:
   a 'the government still retains firm control'?
   b 'there will still be some government control of prices'?
   c 'firms will have to produce what customers want to buy'?
   d 'small firms can fix their own prices as long as the goods will sell'?

2 After these reforms, what economic term would you use to describe the Chinese economy?

IT ➤ DESKTOP

3 The Chinese Trade Board in the United Kingdom wishes to design an appropriate logo for Chinese goods of all kinds. It must clearly reflect a suitable image of quality and reliability whilst, at the same time, reflect the country of origin.
   Use a sheet of A4 paper to design an appropriate logo.

TASK 2

"NO ROOM FOR ANY MORE RICE UNTIL WE MANUFACTURE SOME NEW GEARBOXES"

OVER PRODUCTION IN CHINA

1 Explain why planned economies will sometimes overproduce certain goods.

2 What would happen if a firm operating in a capitalist economy produced more goods than it could sell?

See if you can find examples of products which China now sells on the world market for the first time.

Two billion people discover the joys of the market

TASK 3

A PRODUCE MARKET IN MOSCOW

This photograph shows that private enterprise still has a place in a 'command' economy like the Soviet Union. Whereas most industry in the Soviet Union is state owned and controlled, the new political regime, under Mr Mikhail Gorbachev, is allowing more and more room for free enterprise and for industrial managers to make their own decisions.

Give two reasons why the Soviet Union is allowing more street markets to exist.

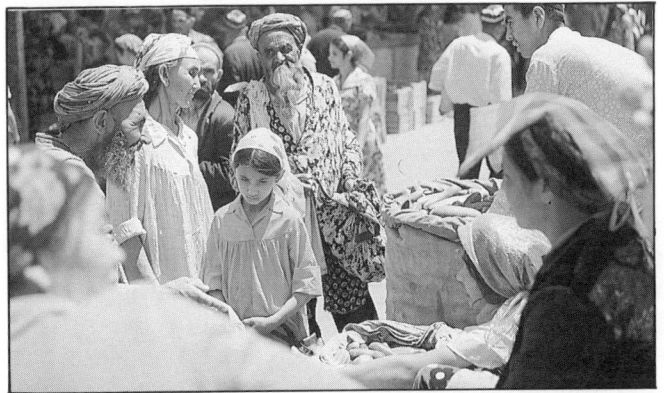

TASK 4

Frontiers of the state: the international extent of public enterprise

Private sector:
- ○ More than 75%

Public sector:
- ◔ 25%   ◑ 50%
- ◕ 75%
- ● More than 75%

	Posts	Telecommunications	Electricity	Gas	Oil production	Coal	Railways	Airlines	Motor industry	Steel	Shipbuilding	
Australia										na		Australia
Austria										na		Austria
Belgium					na							Belgium
Brazil												Brazil
Britain												Britain
Canada												Canada
France				na								France
West Germany												West Germany
Holland					na	na						Holland
India												India
Italy					na	na						Italy
Japan												Japan
Mexico												Mexico
South Korea				na								South Korea
Spain				na								Spain
Sweden				na	na							Sweden
Switzerland					na	na					na	Switzerland
United States												United States

*Including Conrail

THE EXTENT OF PUBLIC ENTERPRISE ('STATE' OWNERSHIP)

This table shows eighteen countries which have some government ownership of industry and commerce. In some of them, most industries on the list are 'state' owned (a black circle) and some have mostly 'private' ownership (a white circle).

1 What do you notice about the ownership of postal services and railways? Suggest two reasons why this happens.

2 The motor industry and shipbuilding are different in Britain from most other countries shown. In what way?

3 How does state ownership in the United States differ from Austria? How does Britain fit into this pattern?

TASK 5

A NEW SOVIET LAW

The new law, which is due to come into effect next January and will apply to all Soviet factories by 1991, aims to make companies responsible for their own profits and losses and to free them from day-by-day supervision by ministries and central planners. Instead of simply taking all their instructions from above, factories will now be able to buy some supplies directly from each other, by-passing the state distribution agency, Gossnab.

Companies that cannot pay their way will face reorganisation or closure. The old practice of allowing ministries to cream off the profits of better-run factories to bail out the rest is supposed to end. And to keep even the successful managers on their toes, all of them will have to submit themselves for election every five years. This is heady stuff, and worrying for managers of the old school who have survived by obeying orders rather than the guiding hand of Mr Gorbachev's "socialist market".

The Law on Socialist Enterprise was passed in June 1987.

1 What are company managers likely to find different under the new law?

2 What effects do you think this approach might have to prices of goods produced by Soviet factories?

Opportunity Cost

Choice

We all have to make economic choices. As individuals, we have to choose how we allocate our time, how we spend our money and how we satisfy our wants. Business managers must choose what goods and services they are going to produce, what resources they are to use and how they are to set about selling to customers. We know that governments have choices to make on behalf of us all – how much to raise in taxation, whether to spend money on defence, pensions, industrial support or road improvements.

Satisfying wants

These choices are really caused by the fact that we all have a large number of wants but limited resources to satisfy them. Most of us satisfy wants by using our 'labour' to earn us money which we spend on the goods and services we want – food and drink, new clothes, somewhere to live, leisure and entertainment. If we are lucky and are able to earn a lot of money, we can satisfy many of our wants.

For some people, very few of these wants can be satisfied. Some people live in countries with few natural resources or a poorly developed economic system. Even if they work very hard, it will be difficult to earn enough money to satisfy all but the basic wants. Even in quite rich economies, some people can find only poorly paid jobs, and some can't find a job at all. It is very difficult to choose between wants when your resources are very limited.

However, we must be careful not to mix up terms like 'happiness' and 'well-being' with satisfying lots of economic wants. In the West, we sometimes leap to wrong conclusions when we see people living in simple peasant communities. Everyone needs to be able to satisfy basic wants, but these are easy to misjudge. Happiness may have very little to do with a well-paid factory job and a new car.

Making choices: personal choices

Let us consider some of the choices we make nearly every day. Some of your friends may choose whether to walk to school or to spend money on bus fare. For others, the choice is between bus, train or a lift in the car. Do you spend money during a morning break? Do you buy crisps, chocolate or an apple? Perhaps you are hungry and buy all three. Do you have a packed lunch in the middle of the day, provided at home, or do you buy a lunch somewhere?

How do you make a decision? Is it related to how much money you have available, how much the item

THE TROUBLE WITH US, CLAUDE.... THE MORE WE HAVE, THE MORE WE WANT.

Questions

1 Make a list of your **essential** wants during a week.

2 How much money would you need to meet these wants?

3 What forces in society makes us feel we always need more goods and services?

Consumers' Expenditure in 1976 and 1986

	1976	1986	
	per cent	per cent	£ million
Food (household expenditure)	18.4	13.8	32,342
Alcoholic drink	7.5	7.0	16,474
Tobacco	4.1	3.2	7,471
Clothing and footwear	7.6	7.0	16,388
Housing	13.4	14.9	34,951
Fuel and power	4.7	4.8	11,148
Household goods and services	7.5	6.6	15,432
Transport and communications	14.9	16.5	38,557
Recreation, entertainment and education	9.2	9.4	21,927
Other goods and services	11.8	14.5	34,063
Other items	0.9	2.3	5,414
Total	100.0	100.0	234,167

costs, whether it suits you? Do your friends make the same kind of choices, based on the same kind of reasons?

Making choices: 'rational' choices

When we make a choice, we reject some alternatives. If we choose to spend money on a bus journey to school, we reject the alternatives of walking (and therefore saving our money), taking a train or scrounging a lift from home. When we buy snacks at breaktime, we cannot use the same money at lunchtime or to put towards a new record or pair of jeans. If we do a Saturday job we cannot meet our friends in town on Saturday morning.

We must make these choices sensibly. They are sometimes called 'rational' choices. We ought to think carefully about them. Usually we do, although some of our choices are made from habit.

Opportunity cost

Every choice we make involves us in something called an 'opportunity cost'. This is the next best alternative choice, which we reject, when we make a decision. Of course, one favoured choice means lots of others which we can't then choose. It is only the next best choice which we call the opportunity cost – the cost in terms of 'lost opportunity'.

POINTS TO REMEMBER

★ All of us have to make choices about how we use our time, spend our money, etc.

★ Business managers make choices also about production and sales and lots of other things.

★ Governments make choices about taxation, expenditure and all sorts of legislation.

★ All choices involve an opportunity cost – the next best alternative choice which is given up.

⬛ GRAPHICS

Use a suitable computer graphics program to draw two pie graphs (divided circles), one for 1976 and one for 1986, which show the percentage of consumers' expenditure in each of the categories listed.

Questions

1 Which category of consumer expenditure has increased most between 1976 and 1986?

2 Which category of consumer expenditure has decreased most between 1976 and 1986?

3 Give two reasons why expenditure on tobacco has fallen over the 10 year period.

4 Explain why the fall in the percentage of expenditure on food does not mean we are eating less.

5 What would be the 'opportunity cost' to you of spending more of your weekly income on clothing?

A LOCAL COUNCIL AND THE PROBLEM OF OPPORTUNITY COST

Southdown District Council have a problem and have called a full council meeting to discuss it. A sewer pipe has collapsed under the town high street and has to be replaced urgently. No money was allowed for this work in the annual budget. The cost is estimated to be £80 000 and the contractors need to start immediately.

In order to find the money to pay for the work one of three other schemes has to be postponed – at least for the present financial year. It is the job of the local councillors to decide which scheme must be dropped to make way for the urgent repair. Council officers have offered the following three alternatives:

1 The construction of twelve new bus shelters at a cost of £7000 each.

2 Providing two new football pitches and changing rooms in the park – a scheme twice postponed in the past and now considered urgent. Cost £78 000.

3 Saving labour costs by making redundant four school crossing patrol ladies and all the canteen workers in an old people's day centre, saving £86 000.

There are strong arguments against any of these cuts, but one of them must be made to find the money for the sewer repair. Decide which of the cuts you would argue for, and make a list to summarise your case.

Group activity

A speaker can be chosen to argue for each of the cuts – three in all. They will make the case for cutting one of the three choices and will, therefore, argue against cutting either of the other two.

The other members of the class or group may vote as members of the council. The activity may take the form of a debate, with views welcomed from the floor, before a vote is taken.

The photographs show the facilities currently available

TASK 2

You have saved £300 to go on a skiing holiday with a friend.

You have both looked closely at alternative ways of organising the trip and you have to decide on which way you prefer – and then try to persuade your friend why your choice is best.

The alternatives are:

a Package tour
   Cost: £260
   Includes: Everything, except spending money.
   (Ski and clothing hire, lessons, hotel with full board, charter flights, etc.)

b Independent fly and stay
   Flights: – choices at £80 or £100
   Hotel – choices at £80, £100, £120, £140
   Hire and tuition: £30
   Service charges: £20

c Drive and book
   Use of friend's red sports car – free
   Petrol: 1400 miles at 30 mpg × £2.00 per gallon
   Hotel as above – but you can move about.
   Hire, tuition and service also same.

Examine each choice carefully. Think of all the advantages and disadvantages of each, in particular you might consider:

   convenience
   cost
   quality
   satisfaction.

Decide on your choice

Now think of all the arguments which you feel support your final choice. There is no right or wrong answer – it is up to you.

Make a list of your final reasons.

Group activity: holiday choice

All those members of the group who have chosen each option should group themselves together – all the a's, b's and c's.

They have to make a presentation of their own decision and the arguments in favour of it to the other groups. If possible, an overhead projector should be used and the group should put their ideas together and use an OHP transparency to present their main points.

There is no right or wrong answer. Any choice is as good as any other but there are arguments for and against each. The group will benefit from the ideas of several members. They should make their case as strongly as possible and indicate their second preferred choice. This would represent the 'opportunity cost' of their decision.

Personal Budgeting

Consumers

You will often hear people referred to as 'consumers'. We often use the term 'consume' when we refer to eating food but 'consumer' in business means more than this. We are all 'consumers' of goods and services. We purchase goods like washing machines and motor bikes. These goods last for a time and we call them 'durable' consumer goods. Foodstuffs, newspapers and boxes of matches are also consumer goods.

We also 'consume' services. We buy holidays at home and abroad. We have cars repaired and we post letters. We use banks and insurance companies. As consumers we have the right to spend our money on more or less anything we like.

The weekly budget – a few years ago

In the past it was often essential for every family to live within its weekly means. Since most people were paid in cash each Friday, this was an important day for family budgeting. Sometimes money would be put away in a cocoa tin for the rent, fuel and groceries and the rest, whatever little there might be for an ordinary family, used to buy 'extras' like clothes and furniture. Some would be saved in case of some problem as yet unknown. There was very little borrowing in most households. This was partly because it was regarded as rather dangerous to live

Questions

1 What percentage of their incomes do
a pensioners on low incomes, and
b households on high incomes (with children) spend on fuel and light?

2 Does your answer to question 1 above, mean that pensioners have warmer homes than high income households with children?

IT ▶ GRAPHICS

3 Use a suitable computer graphics package to present the spending patterns of:
a a one parent household, and
b a high income household without children. You can select any appropriate form of presentation.

IT ▶ WORDPRO

4 Memorandum.
Think of any reasons for the differences found in your answer to question 3.
   Imagine that you are employed as a clerical assistant in the Department of Health and Social Security. You are asked to communicate your findings from the graph to the Section Head of your department in the form of a memo. Use the standard memo format.

MEMORANDUM   Ext
                              My ref
                              Your ref

To   From   Date

Can you think of any reasons for the differences found in your answer to question 3?

6.12 — Pattern of household expenditure: by household type and income level, 1985

United Kingdom

Percentages and £s per week

	Percentage of all households	Food	Housing	Fuel and light	Alcohol	Tobacco	Clothing and footwear	Durable household goods	Transport and vehicles	Other goods, services, miscellaneous	Average total expenditure £s per week (= 100%)
Pensioner households											
Low income	14	26.0	20.8	13.2	2.5	2.8	5.3	3.9	5.3	20.4	55.79
Other	12	20.6	21.6	7.9	3.4	2.1	5.4	6.1	12.0	20.8	122.66
One-parent households											
Low income	1	30.9	7.2	13.8	2.5	6.5	10.7	5.6	5.2	17.6	62.25
Other	2	23.8	14.6	8.2	2.1	3.3	10.8	5.0	11.1	21.2	111.42
Other households with children											
Low and middle income	22	23.7	14.8	6.6	4.2	3.4	8.1	7.1	13.9	18.2	164.84
High income	8	18.3	14.8	4.6	4.8	1.7	8.7	8.8	15.0	23.2	307.83
One person households											
Low income	3	23.5	18.4	11.2	4.8	5.1	5.5	3.3	11.2	17.0	57.24
Other	7	14.8	20.1	5.0	5.9	2.4	6.0	6.7	19.1	20.1	128.76
Other households without children											
Low income	1	23.7	17.0	9.7	5.0	5.0	5.2	4.3	15.8	14.2	100.71
Middle income	19	20.1	15.9	6.0	5.7	3.4	6.8	7.8	15.9	18.4	165.78
High income	11	16.9	14.0	4.1	6.2	2.1	7.7	7.3	19.5	22.2	294.40
All households	100	20.2	16.1	6.1	4.9	2.7	7.4	7.2	15.2	20.2	161.87
Low income	20	25.7	18.8	12.4	3.2	3.7	5.8	4.0	7.7	18.8	60.70
Middle income	60	21.3	16.7	6.5	4.7	3.1	7.2	7.1	14.6	18.8	150.62
High income	20	17.4	14.5	4.4	5.6	1.5	8.0	8.0	17.6	22.7	296.81

Percentage of reported expenditure

beyond your weekly means, and partly because there were few opportunities for working-class people to borrow.

The weekly budget – today

Circumstances have changed in the last ten or twenty years in many respects, and so have attitudes. Most employees are now paid through a bank account and the banks are one group only too anxious to lend money. Families tend to budget on a monthly or even longer term basis. That is not to say that everyone is better off.

We still have to careful about what we spend but it is easier to make longer term spending decisions to buy goods on credit. There are better opportunities for saving and less pressure on us to budget on a weekly basis.

Personal saving

It is a good idea to organise some of our income into savings, not only for that rainy day, but because we can earn interest on what we save. It is the money which we save that banks and other financial institutions use to lend at a profit. It is the source of borrowing for companies and government, essential for a healthy and expanding economy.

Consumer spending – credit

We spend from our income in the form of cash and cheques. Some of our spending these days is of money we have borrowed from banks in the form of loans and overdrafts. A lot of it is also transacted through credit cards – often referred to in the media as 'plastic money'. This gives us access to very easy credit at a high rate of interest – 2½% per month or 30% per year. Since we can usually borrow from a bank at 10–15%, you can see that we pay a high price for easy credit card borrowing. Of course, it is possible to pay off a credit card account each month and not incur any interest charges at all. Credit card companies are happy for us not to do this because they make their money by charging interest on their accounts.

The consumer society

It is often said that we live in a consumer society. There is a lot of pressure on us to spend money. A great deal of money each year is spent on advertising by virtually all firms. We are pressured into buying the latest in cars, clothes, holidays and cosmetics. A successful advertising campaign can be worth millions to a company. It is hardly surprising that many of us overspend and learn to live on credit. For others, the lesson comes too late and easy spending leads to financial ruin.

Value for money

If we are to resist the pressures of advertising by big business, we must learn to identify what is good value for our money.

Everything we wish to buy has some value to us. It

Buy, buy Baby

How much money do young people get? Do they save it? And what do they spend it on? The Carrick James spending survey tells all, as Tim Madge reports

IT'S GOOD news for the sugar industry and very bad news for your teeth. The annual Carrick James survey into how young people get and spend their money shows, once again, that a lot is spent on sweets and soft fizzy drinks, whatever you beg' borrow or earn.

Among 11-17-year-olds, between a half and three-quarters of those asked admitted to frequent spending on chewing or bubble gum, chocolate or other sweets, soft or fizzy drinks.

The survey also found that three-fifths of 11-12-year-olds get from £1 to £3 a week in pocket money, part-time jobs and gifts (and 84 per cent between 70p and £7).

At 13-14, 70 per cent get from £1 to £7 a week. From 15-17 weekly income rises to between £2 and £70 a week for 77 per cent, although 40 per cent in this age group received between £11 and £30.

At this age not all income is pocket money. While around 80 per cent of 11-14-year-olds get pocket money, only 49 of 15-17-year-olds do.

Within the 15-17 year group 50 per cent have a full or part-time job, while as many as 26 per cent of 13-14-year-olds say that they have some kind of regular job. But young people also have supplementary income from running errands, doing odd jobs, or by getting money for specific purposes from parents or relatives.

Taking just pocket money, among 11-12-year-olds 60 per cent get between 75p-£2; 54 per cent of 13-14-year-olds get between £1-£3; and a third of 15-17-year-olds get between £2.50-£5.

At the same time quite a lot of saving outside the home is taking place. As many as 35 per cent of 11-12-year-olds say they save between £2.50-£5 a month; 43 per cent of 13-14-year-olds between £2.50-£10 a month. Among 15-17-year-olds, 42 per cent say they save from £2.50-£20. Ten per cent in this older age group say they save £30 and up a month.

Young people spend appreciably on many items other than sweets and soft drinks. Snacks and fast food, comics and magazines, pens and paper, fares, clothes, jewellery and make-up, computer games, records and tapes all figured in the survey results.

It is now though that the annual disposable income among 7-17-year-olds exceeds £4 billion a year. Of this, another Carrick James (1984) survey found £414 million was spent on sweets, snacks and ice-cream, while £320 million went on clothes and £110 million on soft drinks.

But young people also buy or won a mass of consumer goods ranging from television sets to bikes and computers. Around two-fifths to a half of 11-17-year-olds have personal stereos; a third to a half have cameras; two thirds to a half bikes; a quarter to a third own a musical instrument.

About a quarter of 11-14-year-olds own a home computer and around a quarter own a colour television.

The Carrick James Annual Income and Media Spending (AMIS) Survey was a representative quota sample of 1,628 7-24-year-old young people interviewed in the home in June, 1987, throughout Great Britain.

Food, right (picture by Garry Weaser), tapes and records, clothes, jewellery and books (pictures by Justin Leighton) are where it goes

Question

IT ▶ WORDPRO

The above article is to be used again in a local newspaper. It is considered too complex for the style of presentation required.

You have to rewrite the feature in about 30 lines, picking out the main points. The editor has sent you the following memo.

MEMORANDUM

To   Editorial assistant
From The editor

Please bear in mind the following points in your re-write.

Copy is to be presented in a standard format:
1 A4 paper
2 Left margin 30mm
3 Columns to be 75mm wide with 10mm between columns
4 Please include a suitable illustration or cartoon to accompany your article.

UK consumer goods 1975–1985

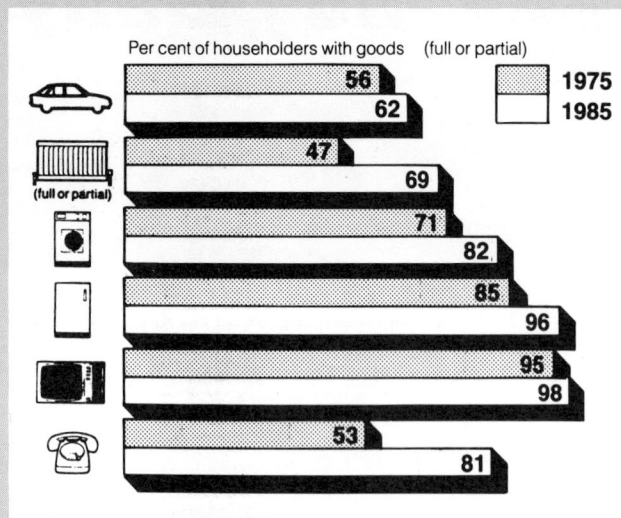

Per cent of householders with goods   (full or partial)

1975
1985

56
62

47
69

71
82

85
96

95
98

53
81

(full or partial)

These goods are sometimes referred to as 'consumer durable' goods, because they are things we buy and keep for some time. They are often used as a measure of how well off we are. Societies where people have a lot of 'consumer durables' are often thought to have a high standard of living.

Questions

1 Which goods seem to have grown most in UK homes?

2 Can you suggest reasons for this change?

3 Do you agree with the statement that "societies where people have a lot of 'consumer durable' goods have a high standard of living?"

IT ▶ WORDPRO

Discuss the issue of living standards in question 3 with other members of your group. Summarise your views in a ten line paragraph produced on a word processor.

Question

Use the word processor to compose a brief report of your findings and display your results for the rest of the class to see.

is very difficult to measure that value. How do we compare the 'worth' of a pound of sausages with a weekly magazine. If both cost £1 and we have just £1 to spend, which do we buy? Perhaps the answer depends on whether or not we are hungry? But we don't eat only when we are hungry and we don't buy a magazine only when we feel the urge to read. What else conditions our desire to spend wisely? Is it habit? Perhaps we always buy the same magazine. Perhaps we always buy sausages on Saturday mornings.

Becoming a 'rational' consumer

If we could learn to make sensible or 'rational' spending decisions, we would organise our lives much more effectively – but that might be rather boring. The best we can do is to think about why we spend money on sausages one day and a magazine another. These spending decisions are very important to firms when they come to decide what to produce. They will try very hard to persuade us that what they produce is what we really want to buy.

It is certainly true that the more we have of something, the less we want more of it, and this means that we are prepared to pay less for it as our stock grows. We may pay 30 pence for the first orange when we have decided that we want an orange, but we will pay only 20 pence for a second orange and only 5 pence or so when we have eaten two oranges.

Producers know that they will have to drop the price of a good if they want to sell a lot of it. It is often said that a firm can decide:

a what price to charge (and 'sales' will take care of itself), or

b how much to sell (and price will settle at a particular level), but

c it cannot do both things – decide on price *and* the quantity to be sold.

Saving and borrowing

You are asked to compare saving and borrowing charges at two institutions in your local area, e.g. a bank, post office or building society. Choose two likely establishments.

Borrowing: imagine that you need £800 towards the cost of a house improvement. Find out what interest rates would be charged in each of your two chosen places.

Saving: imagine now that you have £800 to save. Compare the interest rates paid by the two institutions, assuming that you wish to get your money out at seven days notice.

Question

Write a brief report of your findings and display your results for the rest of the class to see.

POINTS TO REMEMBER

★ Many people operate a 'budget' so that they plan income, expenditure, borrowing and saving.

★ Some consumers plan to borrow money or buy on credit if they wish to spend more money than they have currently available.

★ Borrowing almost always involves repayment of interest.

★ It is important to make 'rational' spending decisions to ensure that we make the best use of our scarce resources.

★ Producers try to influence consumers through advertising but consumers themselves make final choices based on price.

TASK 1

CALCULATE A WEEKLY PERSONAL BUDGET

Below is a weekly budget form designed for someone just starting work.

1 Design a form appropriate for yourself on which you can record any income you receive (pocket money, Saturday job, etc.) and your weekly outgoings.

2 Discuss your budget with a group of friends and compare your ideas. Do you wish to change your plan after talking to them?

THE PERSONAL BUDGET

YOUR PERSONAL WEEKLY BUDGET	
INCOME	£..........
Reserves/Paying the bills FARES (Season ticket to college or work)	£..........
Spend now BOARD (Living at home)	£..........
MIDDAY MEALS	£..........
INSTALMENT PAYMENTS (HP on stereo/motorbike etc)	£..........
ENTERTAINMENT	£..........
Saving CLOTHES	£..........
CHRISTMAS EXPENSES/ BIRTHDAY PRESENTS	£..........
HOLIDAY	£..........
Other items	£..........
TOTAL	£..........
BALANCE LEFT FROM INCOME	£........

TASK 2

FAMILY BUDGET ACCOUNT

Most high street banks will offer their customers a budget account. It is designed to help people with a regular, fixed income (monthly or weekly) to cope with household bills. The cost of these is spread over the whole year.

1 Visit your local bank to pick up a budget account leaflet.

2 Talk to your parents or a family known to you and try to complete the form.

3 You will notice, at the bottom of the form, that a regular amount is transferred from the customer's current account each month.

   Complete this figure.

4 What charge does the bank make for operating this account? How is it calculated? (You will need to do some research to find this answer).

BUDGET ACCOUNT FORM _____ BANK

Schedule of Estimated Annual Commitments

Nature of Payment	Estimated Maximum Annual Expenditure £	p	Month(s) when payment(s) become due
General Rates			
Water Rates			
Telephone			
Electricity			
Gas			
Fuel (including Oil and Coal)			
Life Assurance			
House and Contents Insurance			
Car Insurance			
Car Licence			
Season Ticket			
Television Licence			
Holidays			
Annual Subscriptions			
Clothing			
Christmas Expenses			
Total Estimated Annual Expenditure			
Amount, hereby authorised, of monthly transfer from Current Account, being 1/12th of the total			

Signature(s) _____

Date _____

The Price System

Consumers, firms and prices

You know that we refer to people who buy things as 'consumers'. We will now refer to 'firms' – business managers who supply the goods and services which consumers wish to buy. They may make the goods themselves (manufacturers), they may simply sell them (retailers) or they may offer the sale of services.

Goods and services are offered for sale at a 'price'. This will have to be high enough to allow the firm to cover all its costs but low enough to attract the consumer to buy. You will know, of course, that it is often competition which makes firms keep their prices down, where several firms produce the same kind of goods and the consumer can buy the cheapest.

Satisfying wants

As a consumer you have a limited amount of money to spend. We have seen in an earlier unit that you have many 'wants' – things you would like to buy – but you can satisfy only some of them. Let us assume that you want a new pair of jeans.

You will spend money to satisfy your want according to:

a how strong the want is – do you **really** want another pair of jeans?

b how much money you have to spend – £30 for petrol and clothes this week.

c how much the good costs – £20 for the jeans you like most.

Let us assume that there are five shops selling jeans. In each case, the shopkeeper has bought jeans, like the ones you want, for £12. Each charges about £20 for them to cover the operating costs and to make a profit. The shops are all close together and, as far as you can tell, all the jeans at this price are more or less the same.

Consumer demand

If there was only one shop selling jeans, the price might be £24. Competition has kept the prices to more or less the same level. Just one of the shops has your jeans for sale at £19.50. If you are absolutely sure that these are what you want, you would decide between three alternatives:

a to buy them now at this price,

b to do without new jeans and save your money,

c to wait and shop around for a few weeks.

The consumer's decision

As the consumer, you are influenced by the strength of your want and the price. (At the moment we can ignore other factors like differences in the quality of

Satisfying your demand for jeans

The advertisement is offering jeans for £9.99.

We will assume that you want a pair of jeans and that these are more or less what you would wear. They seem very cheap at £9.99. Are they good enough quality? Are they really fashionable? You know that you can buy **just** what you want at £20. This now becomes a 'demand' decision.

Before you finally make a decision, you will consider lots of issues, if you are a sensible consumer. Not all of these considerations will be about the jeans themselves, because you have to allocate some of your scarce budget to them. If you buy these and not the £20 pair you will have some money left over. Perhaps you will buy two pairs like this?

Questions

1 List as many factors as you can which will influence this spending decision. You may be surprised at how many things, some of which may not often occur to you, actually influence an important spending decision.

2 Discuss your list with others. How do they compare?

3 Explain whether you are a 'rational' consumer of jeans?

the jeans, how they are advertised, what kind of bag they are sold in). You compare the price of the jeans with just how much you want them. Only you can really make this decision.

If jeans were on offer at £10, would you buy two pairs? Perhaps you would buy three. Perhaps you want only one. We call this your 'demand' for jeans. We measure your demand at any given price – at £20 you buy one pair, at £10, you buy three pairs. It depends on all the factors mentioned – price, your want, how you feel, how much money you have.

Supply by firms

The firm would like to charge as much as possible for jeans. There are two constraints:

a what the consumer will pay (you may not buy jeans at all).

b what competitors charge for the same goods.

We assume that firms will try to sell lots more jeans if the price is high since this allows a lot more profit to be made.

The price system

The system which brings consumers and firms together is called the 'price system'. Consumers exert a 'demand' for goods and services and firms offer a 'supply'. How much is bought and sold is determined by the price. Although firms seem to set the price they charge, consumers have just as much say because they determine how much, if any, will be sold at that price.

A market

Where goods and services are bought and sold is called a 'market'. This need not be a particular place. The market for second-hand cars in your locality probably covers a wide area and includes lots of newspaper advertisements as well as car dealers like Arthur Daley.

Some markets are very local and very short term – fresh fruit and vegetables for example. Others are worldwide – dealers buy oil and wheat every day by telephone from every corner of the globe. In all these cases, consumers and firms are brought together in one way or another and a price is agreed.

POINTS TO REMEMBER

★ 'Consumers' and 'firms' buy and sell goods and services in the market place. The prices of goods and services are determined in this market by competition.

★ The consumer makes the final decision over whether or not to buy, but firms try to persuade consumers by advertising.

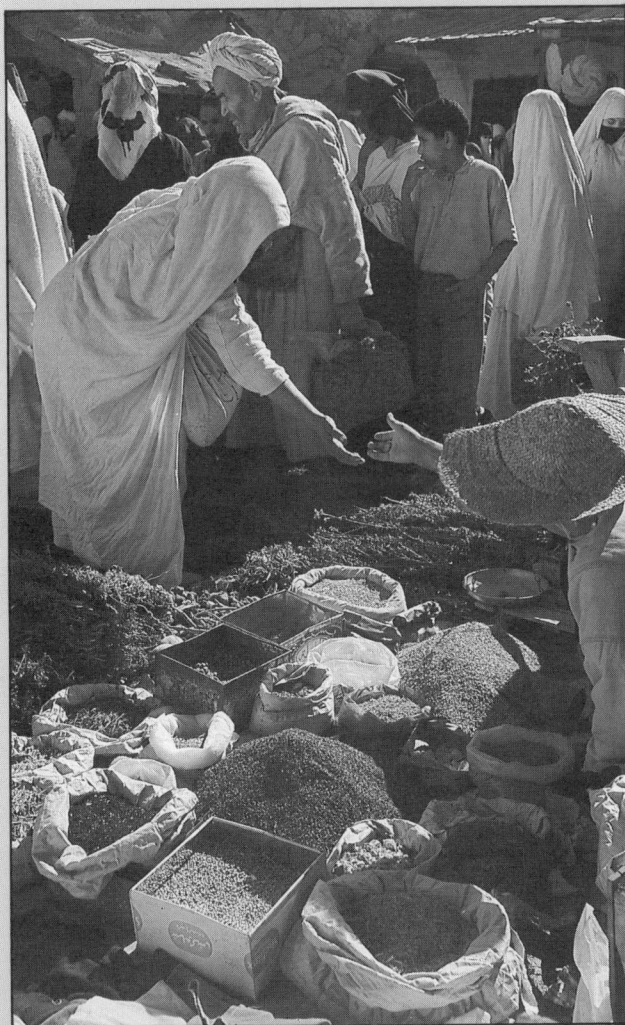

African street market

This is a photograph of a crowded street market in a busy African town. People are crowded together buying and selling. Many of the goods are sold by 'barter' – the price is not fixed by the seller but is negotiated between the seller and the customer.

This kind of market probably keeps prices down because it is very competitive. On the other hand, you have to be able to bargain effectively or you may pay too much.

Questions

1 What do you think are the main advantages and disadvantages of this method of market trading?

2 How do you think your local market trader would react if you started to bargain with her when buying fruit?

TASK 1

HOLD AN AUCTION SALE

You can set up your own auction sale – possibly for a charity of your choice. You will need an auctioneer and a range of goods to sell. This will need careful planning and you will need to advertise well to ensure success. Display the goods carefully and you may wish to produce a catalogue. Hold the item up for everyone to see as the bidding begins.

Start the bidding at a suitable price and go up in small stages. This is considered to be a very fair system for fixing prices because everyone knows what good is being offered and at what price.

Another way is to have a 'written' auction. Place the goods for sale out on a large table, each with a piece of paper beside it. The buyers write the amount they will pay and their name beside the item, so each bid gets higher until no-one else wishes to buy. The bottom name on the list will then be the highest bidder and will pay for the article at the end of the auction.

TASK 2

MARKET DAY – THE WEEKLY FATSTOCK AUCTION SALE

The photograph is of an animal auction in a typical market town. Farmers come from miles around to buy and sell livestock and all the local butchers will be represented if the animals are ready for slaughter.

1 Can you find out how an auctioneer makes money?

2 What is a 'reserve price' in an auction? What would happen if an auction item did not reach its reserve price?

TASK 3

DAIRY CATTLE

Week ended Tue, Feb 23

	COWS 1st qual £	Trend	2nd qual £	Trend	No sold
Banbury (W)	650	−3	526	−12	37
Beeston Castle (F)	645	+3	548	−27	23
Carlisle (F)	—	—	—	—	—
Carmarthen (W)	636	−34	475	−24	53
Chippenham (F)	646	+20	473	−27	15
Gisburn (Th)	653	+18	565	−13	31
Gloucester (Th)	686	+6	531	−12	11
Hereford* (F)	659	−24	526	+1	9
Holsworthy* (Th)	720	+20	551	−30	14

FARM PRICES: DAIRY CATTLE

These prices show what a farmer could obtain for selling first or second quality Friesan cows in milk on February 23 1988.

1 Which market has the lowest price? How many cows were sold there during the week?

2 Which market showed the highest increase in prices during this particular week?

3 Suggest two reasons why prices might vary between markets at any one time.

TASK 4

Pepsi-Cola became popular in the Soviet Union in the early 1970s and bottling plants were opened. In 1980 the Soviets licensed Coca-Cola as the official drink of the Moscow Olympic Games! China was the last major cola frontier, with a quarter of the world's population as a new market. It was sold openly to the Chinese people for the first time in 1980.

▶ DESKTOP

1 Design an advertisement for either Coke or Pepsi which you feel would appeal to the 900m population of China, mainly on very low incomes, which will persuade them that the product is worth drinking.

> ● In the beginning was the Real Thing. Then came the imitators . . . hundreds of them, hoping to cash in on Coca-Cola's astonishing success. Most were easily chased out of business under trademark laws but one slipped through the net: Pepsi-Cola. As the two companies battled to dominate the market they made friends in US politics, even in the White House. Coke was a Democratic drink; Pepsi became Republican. Finally, in the search for ever-increasing sales across the globe, they assumed an unprecedented role in world affairs. Such was their importance that when China emerged from years of isolation, it made a treaty first with Coca-Cola, and then with the US government.

Frontier of fizz:
Coke reaches the
Great Wall of China.

TASK 5

THE 'COLA' WARS

Can you tell 'Coke' from 'Pepsi'?

Try a blind test on your friends. Test them with six different colas and see if they can pick out the two brand leaders. We may prefer one brand because we are conditioned to believe that this is what 'cola' should taste like.

Coca-Cola was invented by mistake in 1885 when an American drugstore owner mixed a tonic syrup (made from coca leaves and kola nuts) with soda water. It soon became a successful drink.

Coca-Cola was born. Even the famous bottle was a mistake. The designers copied the shape of the cacao bean instead of the coca bean but the end result was splendid. There were many attempts to copy the product, including something called Koca Nola! Only one competitor survived – Pepsi-Cola.

Pepsi was also invented as an 'elixir' to relieve dyspepsia (wind!) – hence its name. It was modelled on Coca-Cola and took a long time to become successful. The firm went bankrupt in 1932. Pepsi-Cola re-started when it was bottled in cheap beer bottles which gave twice as much drink for the same price. By 1938 the two drinks were in competition and the first lawsuit was filed. The rivalry has been bitter ever since and the competition very intense.

Coke and Pepsi are the most advertised products in history, sold in 140 countries and rivalling coffee as the world's most popular drink.

Advertising now tends to concentrate on two themes. Pepsi is the young person's cola – 'lipsmackin' 'thirstquenchin'. . . The idea is that Coke is for tired fuddy duddies. Coke on the other hand is simply 'the real thing'.

1 Collect advertisements for the two products. Make two competitive displays. Perhaps two groups could be formed to support one product against the other.

2 Try to identify the image which the firms are trying to create.

3 How do you as consumers, react to this pressure?

4 Do you buy the cheaper product?

5 Is there really any difference?

The Cost of Living

Living with rising prices

You may have heard older people tell you of the days when you could go to the cinema on the bus, have a bag of chips on the way home and still have change from sixpence. What can you buy with 2½p nowadays? What they don't always remember to point out is that an average wage in those days may have been as little as £1.50 per week. The evening out was perhaps one sixtieth of the weekly wage. One sixtieth of a modern wage is about £3.30. I imagine that you could still have the same evening out for £3.30.

On the whole, we manage to live with rising prices. It is a feature of all modern societies that prices tend to rise month by month, year by year. Sometimes prices rise rapidly – in Britain during the 1970s for example, prices rose by over 25% in one year. In recent years, the annual rate of price rises has slowed down to less than 5%.

The problem of inflation

We call this tendency of prices to rise 'inflation', at least, that is the term we use when prices are rising steadily for a long time. Inflation became a problem in Britain during the 1970–1980 period. The cost of living was rising rapidly each year and the government were unable to get it under control. Since that time, inflation has fallen and is not now considered to be an economic problem, although we still tend to complain when rail fares and gas prices go up.

The causes of inflation

Imagine there are ten camels in a large tent in the middle of the Sahara desert. Five Arab chieftains want to buy these camels and they have two dollars each to spend. If we assume that they use all their money, they will pay one dollar for each camel and buy two each. If we give each chieftain five dollars, they can still buy only two camels each, but camels will cost $2.50. By increasing the amount of money in the tent without making more camels available, we have increased the price of camels and caused inflation.

Arguments over the causes of inflation

Some economists argue that this increase in the 'supply' of money is the main cause of inflation. Others would disagree and argue that much more complex forces are at work in the economy. For example, if workers are paid higher wages, costs of production will rise and firms will charge more for goods. Yet other economists would argue that rises in prices cause workers to seek higher wages, which in turn are passed on as price increases.

Government policy to control inflation

In the early 1980s, government policy was directed to controlling the constant rise in prices by controlling the amount of money we had to spend. One way of doing this was to print less money at the Royal Mint. More realistically, it was lending by banks and other financial institutions which was more closely controlled. In fact, many economists now believe that the supply of money in the economy (the dollars in the tent) was not reduced by much at all. However, for whatever real reason, the annual rate of price rises has fallen since the early 1980s.

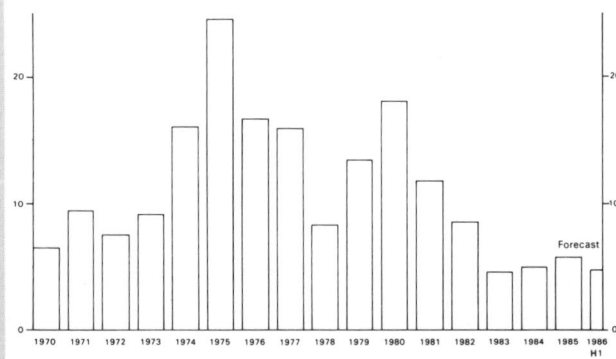

Chart 1 Inflation
Annual percentage increase in retail prices index

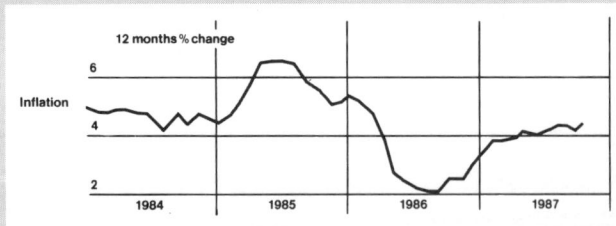

UK inflation

Look at the two tables.

Questions

1 Identify the year in which the rate of inflation was:
 a highest
 b lowest.

2 Looking at the table, when do you think government policy started to become successful in controlling inflation?

3 What is happening to the level of inflation after 1986?

Is controlling inflation a 'good' thing?

We must always answer a question like this by asking 'good for whom?' If you are an ordinary consumer with a steady job you will probably not worry much about inflation. Your wages will probably rise each year to keep up with the rise in prices.

Who suffers from inflation?

Those who suffer badly are those who do not receive sufficient annual income rises. These are often employees in the 'state' sector of the economy – where the government is the employer and won't allow large pay increases. Anyone who receives most of their income in one form of benefit or another will almost certainly suffer – pensioners and the unemployed rarely receive income increases large enough to cover annual price rises.

Savers are the other group which may suffer. Savings get larger as they gain interest but, if interest rates are lower than inflation rates, your savings are worth less each year.

Who benefits from inflation?

People who owe money benefit from inflation. If you borrowed £100 ten years ago it would have been worth much more then than now when you have to pay it back. Families with large mortgage loans do better when prices and incomes are rising steadily.

Inflation or unemployment

The government set about controlling inflation with a wide range of policies. Amongst these was the control of the money 'supply' which we referred to above. Another solution was to control annual wage rises. Taken together, all these policies have caused some problems for firms. Many have closed because they were not competitive, others have had to make some of their workforce redundant. This has resulted in a lot of unemployment, although the government would argue strongly that the economy needed to be 'slimmed down' in this way anyway.

Is high inflation preferable to high unemployment? Does one necessarily cancel the other?

These are questions on which economists and politicians rarely agree. This is why economic policies are so important at election time. Not only do we not agree with one another on how different policies fit together, we don't agree on whether or not one set of consequences of our policies is better or worse than another. It is very important that you begin to understand that there are no simple solutions to economic problems. It is even more important that you learn to listen to arguments, to think about them and form your own opinion.

POINTS TO REMEMBER

★ Inflation occurs when prices are rising steadily over a long period of time.

★ Government policies may try to cure one problem but create another.

★ There are few simple solutions.

'UK INFLATION SOARS – WHAT ARE THE CAUSES? ECONOMISTS DISAGREE.'

The alarming rise in prices which began in Britain in 1974 has sparked off a major debate amongst economists. They don't agree about the causes, the consequences or the policy solutions which the government should adopt. How much more disagreement can you have amongst so-called 'experts'?

The causes put forward are mostly linked to three things:

★ the crisis in the Middle East which led to fast rising oil prices. Oil has become the basis of so much of what we produce today and, with rising petrol costs, this has certainly forced up the level of the cost of living for everyone.

★ the granting of high wage increases to workers in industry which have put up the costs of production.

★ the ease with which people and institutions have been able to borrow money which has allowed them to 'bid up' prices of goods and services, especially property and housing.

All these different possible causes lead to different policy solutions.

★ For many years economists would have argued for a policy agreed with Trade Unions to restrict wage increases.

★ In the 1970s many would have liked to see controls on the amount of money the government allowed in the economy and strict controls on government spending and, if necessary, on levels of employment.

★ There are now economists who argue for a different approach altogether – one where the government takes very little part in controlling the economy at all – with resultant low direct taxation, low government spending and lots of competition to keep prices down. It is this policy which appeals most to the Conservative Government of the 1980s.

This article is a journalist's view of the debate about inflation in the early 1980s.

Question

1 How does the most recent government view differ from the viewpoint of the earlier economists?

2 What would you say in answer to the question: 'What caused high rates of inflation in Britain in the mid-1970s?'

TASK 1

EC INFLATION RATES

Average EC Inflation Rates				
1982	**1983**	**1984**	**1985**	**1986**
10.2%	8.2%	6.6%	5.1%	3.5%

EC Inflation Rates			
	1986	**1985**	**Change**
Greece	22.5%	17.1%	(+5.4%)
Portugal	12.0%	–	–
Spain	8.0%	–	–
Italy	5.6%	8.1%	(−2.5%)
UK	3.3%	5.9%	(−2.0%)
Ireland	2.9%	5.5%	(−2.6%)
France	2.4%	5.7%	(−3.3%)
Denmark	2.4%	3.9%	(−1.5%)
Belgium	1.2%	4.7%	(−3.5%)
West Germany	0.0%	2.1%	(−2.1%)
Netherlands	0.0%	2.3%	(−2.3%)
Luxembourg	−0.8%	4.2%	(−5.0%)

IT GRAPHICS

Use your graphics package to plot the changes in the rates of inflation in all 12 countries 1985/6.

Choose your own style of presentation which should include plus and minus figures.

1 How does the rate of inflation in the UK compare with:
   a the average rate in the EC (European Community)?
   b other member states?

2 Can you think of reasons why Greece and Portugal have such high inflation rates?

3 What do you notice about changes in inflation (1985/86) in almost all the EC countries?

TASK 3

MEASURING CHANGES IN PRICES: A RETAIL PRICES INDEX

We usually use the 'retail prices index' as our measure of price changes. This takes an average 'basket' of the goods we buy and compares the prices of the same contents at different times. We have to include petrol, rent, electricity charges and the like in our 'basket', as well as the more obvious baked beans and coffee! In national figures, goods are 'weighted' according to their importance in our weekly spending.

1 Make a list of items which you consider are typical of your own spending pattern in a normal week. Multiply each item by the number of times you might buy it. This becomes your own 'basket of goods'. Make sure that you include less obvious expenditure like bus fares.

2 Check the price of your 'basket' from time to time, say once a month, and try to remember to keep a record throughout the term or school year.

3 Keep a graph which plots your result. This will allow you to keep a check on your own personal 'inflation' rate. You may prefer to do this as a group exercise. How do your results compare?

The RPI in a nutshell

The RPI measures the overall change in the prices of things people buy, including services like travel and entertainment as well as goods from shops. Only savings and income tax are left out. Some things are more important than others in terms of the amount of money spent on them and this is allowed for in the index. For example, a given percentage increase in the price of bread has about four times the effect of a similar increase in the price of butter. The change in the index is therefore an average of the individual price changes for practically all goods and services, with more weight being given to those items on which people spend most.

TASK 2

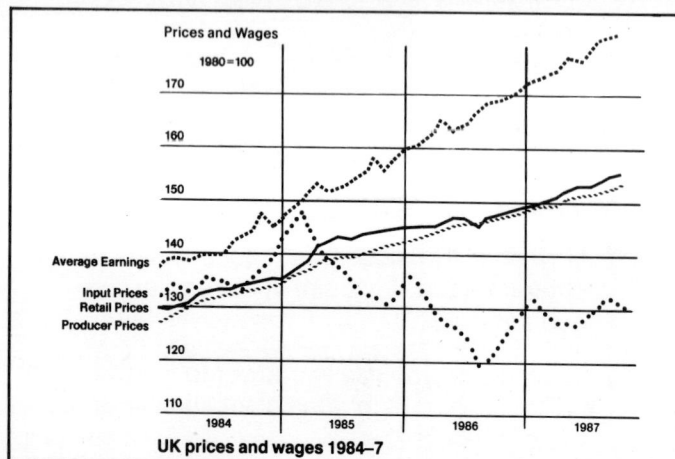

Prices and Wages
1980 = 100

Average Earnings
Input Prices
Retail Prices
Producer Prices

UK prices and wages 1984–7

PRICES AND WAGES

1 How have changes in retail prices compared with average earnings in the UK 1984–87?

2 Does this mean that average families have been better or worse off?

TASK 4

Structure of the Retail Prices Index in 1987

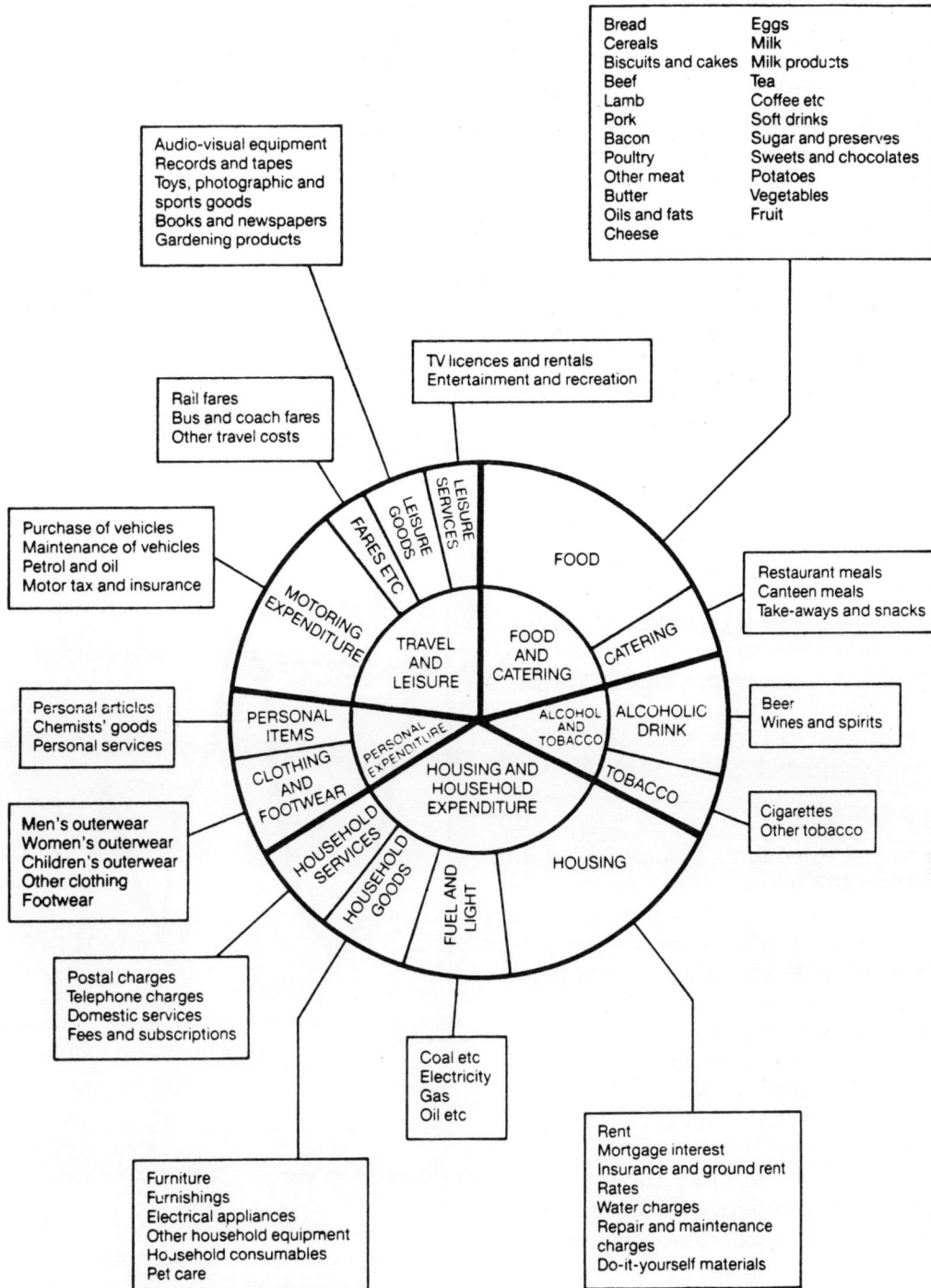

Bread	Eggs
Cereals	Milk
Biscuits and cakes	Milk products
Beef	Tea
Lamb	Coffee etc
Pork	Soft drinks
Bacon	Sugar and preserves
Poultry	Sweets and chocolates
Other meat	Potatoes
Butter	Vegetables
Oils and fats	Fruit
Cheese	

Audio-visual equipment
Records and tapes
Toys, photographic and sports goods
Books and newspapers
Gardening products

TV licences and rentals
Entertainment and recreation

Rail fares
Bus and coach fares
Other travel costs

Purchase of vehicles
Maintenance of vehicles
Petrol and oil
Motor tax and insurance

Restaurant meals
Canteen meals
Take-aways and snacks

Personal articles
Chemists' goods
Personal services

Beer
Wines and spirits

Men's outerwear
Women's outerwear
Children's outerwear
Other clothing
Footwear

Cigarettes
Other tobacco

Postal charges
Telephone charges
Domestic services
Fees and subscriptions

Coal etc
Electricity
Gas
Oil etc

Furniture
Furnishings
Electrical appliances
Other household equipment
Household consumables
Pet care

Rent
Mortgage interest
Insurance and ground rent
Rates
Water charges
Repair and maintenance charges
Do-it-yourself materials

Wheel diagram segments:
LEISURE SERVICES, LEISURE GOODS, FARES ETC, FOOD, CATERING, MOTORING EXPENDITURE, TRAVEL AND LEISURE, FOOD AND CATERING, ALCOHOL AND TOBACCO, ALCOHOLIC DRINK, PERSONAL ITEMS, PERSONAL EXPENDITURE, TOBACCO, CLOTHING AND FOOTWEAR, HOUSING AND HOUSEHOLD EXPENDITURE, HOUSEHOLD SERVICES, HOUSEHOLD GOODS, FUEL AND LIGHT, HOUSING

RETAIL PRICES INDEX (RPI)

1 Which is the largest category group in the 1987 RPI 'basket of goods'?

2 Where does spending on 'food' rank in the overall 'basket'?

3 Why do you think that some pensioners claim that this basket of goods should not be used to calculate their yearly rise in pensions?

The Standard of Living

The problem of measurement

When we talk about the standard of living, we are usually referring to how well off people are. The term is often used without careful thought. Do we mean all people – the rich, the poor, an average family? What do we mean by 'how well off'?

Most people would use the term 'standard of living' as if it referred to family income and wealth. A basic living standard in Britain would mean having enough money to buy or rent somewhere to live, enough to eat and drink, heating and clothing to an adequate standard.

Standards in different countries

However, what might be considered adequate in one country might be quite poor in another. Different societies apply different standards. In the United States, most families have a car and a telephone. In China, few people have either. We might conclude that general living standards are higher in the US than in China. There are, however, lots of people in the US who are homeless and nearly destitute. There are very few indeed in China who are in this position.

The 'quality of life'

The 'standard of living' must have something to do with things other than the wealth of the majority or of the average family. What do we mean by the term 'quality of life'? This is much more difficult to define. It has something to do with 'happiness', 'freedom' and health. It is perfectly possible to enjoy a life of the highest quality living in a small village in a poor part of Brazil – with few of the facilities which money can buy – and equally to be very unhappy with very obvious wealth in a modern Western society.

Part of what we want to achieve includes the provision of basic living standards for everyone – including not only material goods but also freedom to worship, work, think and travel.

Economic growth

Economic growth refers to the amount of goods and services we can produce in an economy in a year. It is achieved by the output of everyone at work in the economy – factory workers, miners, insurance sales representatives and teachers. Everyone at work contributes to the level of national output in one way or another. (We refer to this output in different ways – 'national income', 'gross national product', 'gross domestic product'; all these are different ways of measuring more or less the same thing.) We want to produce more goods and services each year and this is what we call economic growth.

Distributing wealth

Economic growth should ensure that we are better off. It will only do this if it is distributed fairly. If everything goes to a few people, we can't really say that living standards are improving. On the whole, rising economic growth in Britain does mean that people become better off. This might not be true at

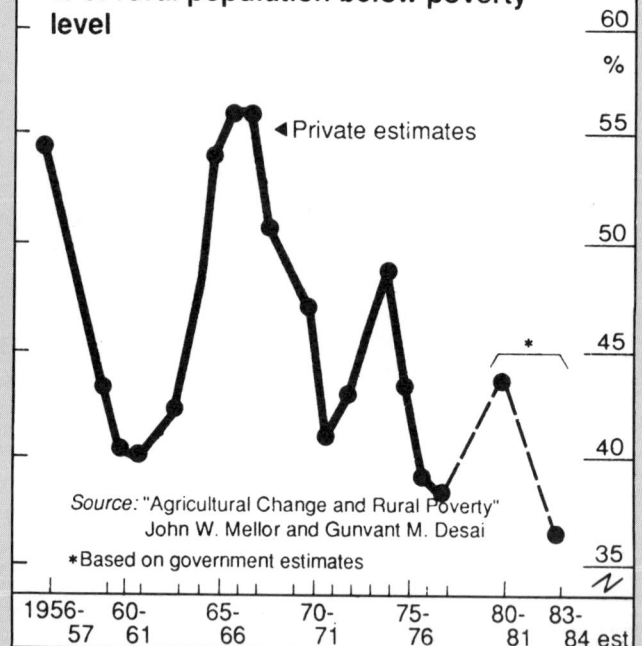

The poverty cycle

% of rural population below poverty level

◄ Private estimates

Source: "Agricultural Change and Rural Poverty"
John W. Mellor and Gunvant M. Desai

*Based on government estimates

1956-57   60-61   65-66   70-71   75-76   80-81   83-84 est

Poverty in India

This graph shows the percentage of Indian people who live outside towns and cities who are below the 'poverty line'.

Questions

1 What do you think is meant by the term 'poverty line'?

2 Why does the line fluctuate up and down as it does? (remember that it refers to agricultural communities.)

3 Why is the overall picture quite encouraging?

all in a country like Brazil, where so many people live in shanty towns or in remote communities outside the 'economic system' that rising general living standards don't help a lot of people at all.

Measurement of living standards

The usual measure we use is 'national income per head'. This simply calculates the total amount we produce in a year and divides it by the size of the population. If wealth is evenly and fairly distributed, it is the best measure we have. If wealth is poorly or unfairly distributed, it is a poor measure indeed.

Other measures we might use would refer to different aspects of the quality of life: the number of people per doctor; the number per telephone or car; the percentage who can read or write. Life expectancy refers to the average age at which people die. If you think about it, this is quite a good measure.

POINTS TO REMEMBER

★ It is not always clear how we should set about measuring the standard of living of people who live in a country.

★ 'Standard of living' may not have much to do with wealth or even with the quality of life.

★ Average figures are very misleading. They may disguise the fact that some people within a country are very poor and others very rich – whatever that means.

★ Economic growth examines how economic output in one year compares with the next. Because we use percentage figures, a modest change in a poor country can look very good indeed.

Britain in profile

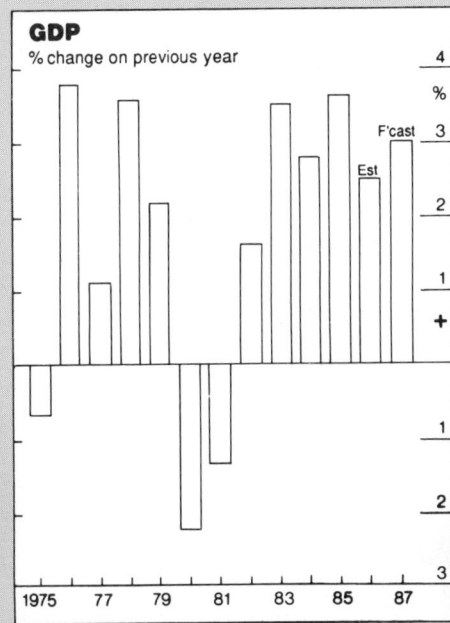

GDP
% change on previous year

Economic growth in Britain

The graph shows the annual level of economic growth in the UK 1975–1987.

Questions

1 What has been the best level of growth achieved?

2 What does it mean when these figures are negative?

3 Can you think of some reasons why growth rates were so poor in 1980 and 1981?

Households with selected consumer goods

One way in which we might measure the standard of living in developed western countries would be to look at the consumption of 'luxury' goods. For example, if 80% of households in Britain have a telephone and 92% have a 'phone in the US, is it reasonable to conclude that families in the US are generally better off?

Question

IT ▶ WORDPRO

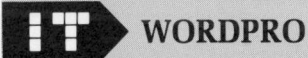

1 Newspaper report – you have been asked to contribute a newspaper article for the *Daily Globe* on changes in the standard of living in Britain between 1972 and 1984/5. The article must not exceed 10 lines in length with columns 75mm wide.

Use your word processor to complete this article and produce a suitable headline.

Households with selected durable goods

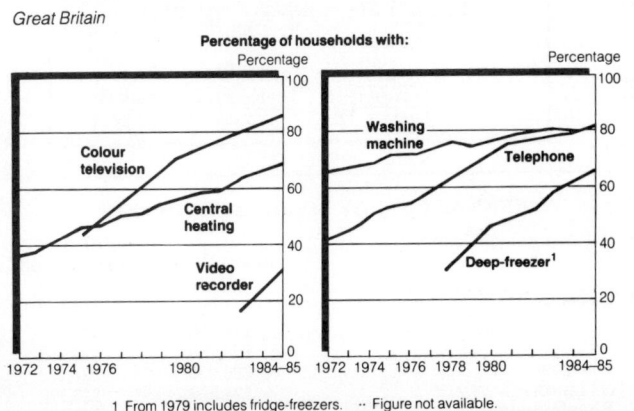

Great Britain

Percentage of households with:

1 From 1979 includes fridge-freezers. ·· Figure not available.

TASK 1

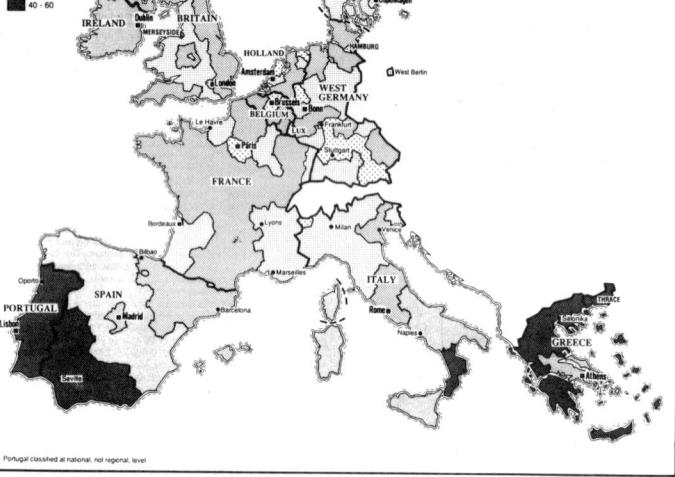

For richer, for poorer

GDP per person, 1985
Current purchasing-power parities
EEC average=100

	Over 120
	100 - 120
	80 - 100
	60 - 80
	40 - 60

Portugal classified at national, not regional, level

GDP PER PERSON IN THE EC 1985

This map shows which regions of Europe are above and below the average level of GDP per head.

1 Which countries are mainly below average and which are mainly above?

2 Can you suggest any reasons for these differences?

TASK 2

1985

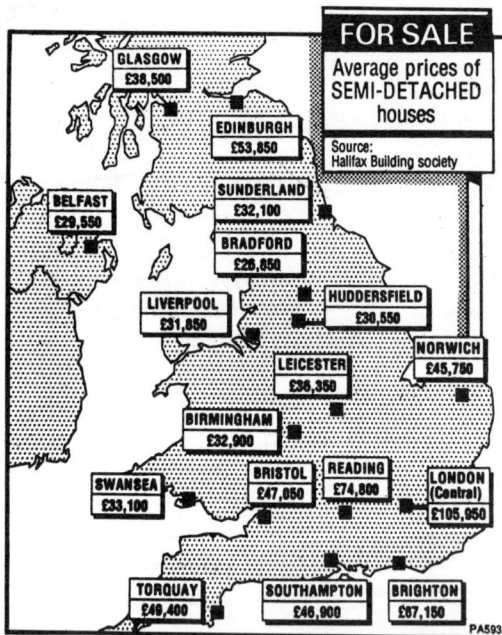

FOR SALE

Average prices of
SEMI-DETACHED
houses

Source:
Halifax Building society

GLASGOW £38,500
EDINBURGH £53,650
BELFAST £29,550
SUNDERLAND £32,100
BRADFORD £26,650
LIVERPOOL £31,850
HUDDERSFIELD £30,550
NORWICH £45,760
LEICESTER £36,350
BIRMINGHAM £32,900
SWANSEA £33,100
BRISTOL £47,050
READING £74,800
LONDON (Central) £105,950
TORQUAY £40,400
SOUTHAMPTON £46,900
BRIGHTON £57,150

PA593

1987

ANNUAL COST OF LIVING BY LOCATION

Location	House Price	Total Annual Living Cost
London	£133,000	£33,527
Reading	£81,550	£26,717
Bristol	£76,150	£26,318
Edinburgh	£70,750	£26,250
Glasgow	£66,850	£26,170
Swindon	£74,200	£25,775
Birmingham	£69,950	£25,484
Aberdeen	£65,900	£25,408
Milton Keynes	£69,850	£25,312
Newcastle	£58,750	£25,048
Manchester	£57,900	£24,289
Norwich	£57,350	£24,158
Leeds	£53,850	£23,723
Liverpool	£52,600	£23,355

The Liverpool FC striker John Wark, late of the substitute's bench and keen for a move to another club, had agreed satisfactory terms for a transfer to Watford FC, on the outskirts of the capital.

The move was aborted when Wark, in consultation with his wife, came to the conclusion that the difference in property prices would prove too costly to warrant the move.

The situation is unlikely to change.

COST OF LIVING: REGIONAL DIFFERENCES IN HOUSE PRICES

The tables above are for two years, 1985 and 1987.

1 Of those towns which are in both tables, in which town has the increase in house prices been most?

2 How has this apparently influenced the transfer decision of John Wark?

3 Look at the 'league table' of cost of living for the town in table 2. Why are these differences not similar to those for house prices?

This last question is quite an important one and it would be a good idea to spend some time discussing it with other members of your group.

TASK 3

GDP AND ECONOMIC GROWTH: MEASURING A NATION'S OUTPUT

GDP, or gross domestic product, is the term we usually use to measure the size of a country's output. If we divide it by the size of the population (GDP per head) we have an idea of the economic living standard. If we compare one year with another, we have a measure of economic growth. If a country is very poor, then a small increase in GDP can produce quite large percentage growth rates.

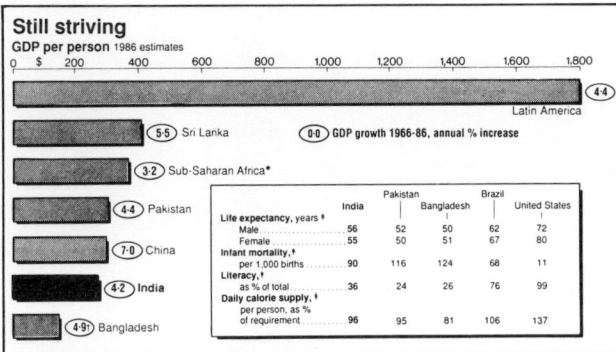

Still striving
GDP per person 1986 estimates

	India	Pakistan	Bangladesh	Brazil	United States
Life expectancy, years †					
Male	56	52	50	62	72
Female	55	50	51	67	80
Infant mortality,† per 1,000 births	90	116	124	68	11
Literacy,† as % of total	36	24	26	76	99
Daily calorie supply,† per person, as % of requirement	96	95	81	106	137

COMPARISON OF LIVING STANDARDS IN THE DEVELOPING WORLD

Look at these figures for developing countries. They show how Latin American countries, which used to be thought of as underdeveloped, are now much more prosperous than those in Africa and the Indian sub-continent. They also show one year's economic growth and use some other figures which might measure the standard of living.

1 Why is GDP per person not always a good measure of how well off people are?

2 Which country has the highest rate of economic growth and why is its GDP per person still relatively low?

3 Of the other measures of well-being, which would you choose as a reliable guide to living standards and why.

TASK 4

Length of time necessary to work to pay for selected commodities and services

Great Britain

	Married couple with husband only working	
	Hrs mins	Hrs mins
	1971	1986
1 large loaf (white sliced)	9	7
1lb of rump steak	54	45
500gr of butter (home produced)	20	16
1 pint of fresh milk	5	4
1 dozen eggs (medium size)	22	14
100gr of coffee (instant)	22	22
125gr of tea (medium priced)	9	6
1 pint of beer	13	12
1 bottle of whisky	4 17	2 04
20 cigarettes	22	22
Weekly gas bill	55	1 15
Weekly electricity bill	1 04	1 03
1 gallon of petrol (4 star)	33	26
1 cwt of coal	1 19	1 26
Weekly telephone bill	50	37
Motor car licence	39 59	25 38
Colour television licence	19 40	14 52
Cinema admission	29	..
Long-playing record (full price)	3 16	..

STANDARD OF LIVING: COMPARING OVER TIME

It is sometimes very difficult to compare how well off we are at one time with another. Price comparisons are no good on their own because earnings change too – a television may cost twice as much as five years ago, but we earn a lot more now.

The table looks at the cost of things in terms of how long we have to work to obtain them. For example, it took 9 minutes to earn enough to buy a loaf of bread in 1971 but only 7 minutes in 1986.

If these calculations are accurate, nearly everything was cheaper in 'real' terms in 1986 than in 1971.

1 Which two items were 'dearer' in real terms in 1986?

2 Which item has fallen in price most in 'real' terms?

3 How would you feel about these figures if you were a pensioner or one of the unemployed in 1986? Give your reasons.

Unemployment

Measuring unemployment

We almost always use the term 'unemployed' to refer to the number of people who are willing and able to work who can't find a job. In the UK, for example, the total population is now 56.5 million of whom 27.6 million are counted as the 'workforce'. This includes all men aged 16–65 and all women 16–60 who are available for work.

The figure varies because, for example, not all women consider themselves as 'looking for work'. The figure rose by 1 million between 1983 and 1985 because more women entered the labour market. The number unemployed in 1986 was 3.3 million. That is, of the 27.6m workforce, 3.3m could not find a job. This represents 11.9% of the working population.

The problem of unemployment

In 1975 unemployment was below 1 million (845,000). It reached 2 million in 1981 and 3 million in 1985. By the end of 1988 it had fallen to 2.2 million.

High unemployment in an economy is a bad thing. People are a resource which should be used to create economic wealth. However, they also need to have money to spend as consumers, and to be able to take pride in the work they do. If you want a job and can't find one, not only is there economic hardship, but also social hardship and loss of self confidence and, sometimes, of self respect.

Unemployment in the 1930s and the 1980s

The last period of very high unemployment in Britain was during the 1930s when over 3 million were out of work. Times were very bad then because the level of unemployment pay ('dole') was low and families were often hungry and cold. It was the demand for labour during the Second World War which brought an end to this mass unemployment.

After the war, it was thought that a lesson had been learned and that such high unemployment would not occur again. Although high unemployment has occurred again, we have learned to provide a better living standard for those out of work, through the welfare state, but money is still very tight and problems are often severe.

The causes of unemployment: changing the nature of jobs

Any economy which is to grow and develop is likely to require changes in the jobs it needs. Progress means that new machines and new technology, replace labour. We would not have progressed if this were not so – for example, fewer people work in

The Thirties – Wigan

Unemployment in the 1930s

This is a family photograph taken in Wigan in 1939. It shows the sadness and hopelessness of long-term unemployment through the eyes of the children and the stance of the unemployed man. In a town of 85,000 people, 9,500 were out of work – 11% of the workforce.

Question

Can you think of an appropriate caption for this photograph?

factories operating machines. However, in a successful economy, new types of job are created and people are taught to perform them. In Britain, old types of employment have declined but not enough of the new jobs have been created.

The causes of unemployment: imports

Much of what we buy is now made abroad. It is sometimes hard to find any make of some products which are made entirely in Britain – motorbikes are a good example, but this is now true of electrical goods and even cars. Unless we find alternative job opportunities for people, we will always have to face the problem of unemployment.

Solutions to the unemployment problem

Until we agree what causes high unemployment, it is difficult to agree on solutions to the problem. Politicians often disagree strongly. Some would argue that high wages have been a major cause of job losses, others would call for limits on the amount of goods we import. Just as many would call for an increase in government spending to help UK industry, others argue for further spending cuts to make the economy healthy.

Solutions to the unemployment problem: government policy

Government policy in the 1980s has argued that a strong and competitive economy is the first ingredient for success. Some firms have to close, they say, to remove out-of-date techniques so that new and successful businesses can prosper. They have used the term 'real jobs' – implying that keeping out of date practices going is only artificially keeping people in jobs. On the other hand, it is argued that the government is uncaring in its attitude to people who want to work and is sacrificing their jobs in order to change the face of the economy. It is important to remember that there are often lots of sides to these questions and no simple answers.

POINTS TO REMEMBER

★ The number unemployed is a figure which we measure in Britain by including all those actively seeking employment but who are unable to get a job.

★ This figure (3.3 million in 1986) is expressed as a percentage of the working population (27.7 million in 1986).

★ There are lots of different ideas as to which are the main causes of high unemployment and, therefore, lots of different preferred solutions.

★ Perhaps the solution over which there is most agreement requires that, as we run down jobs in older and declining industries, we must generate new employment opportunities in the economy, and encourage workers to retrain in readiness for them.

Manpower in Britain

Table 38: Manpower in Britain 1976–1986

thousands

Year (June)	Employees in employ-ment[a]	Self-employed	Unem-ployed[b]	Armed forces	Working population[c]
1976	22,557	1,952	1,179	336	
1977	22,631	1,907	1,251	327	
1978	22,789	1,907	1,226	318	
1979	23,173	1,906	1,141	314	
1980	22,991	2,013	1,452	323	
1981	21,891	2,119	2,270	334	
1982	21,414	2,170	2,626	324	
1983	21,067	2,221	2,867	322	
1984	21,238	2,496	2,999	326	
1985	21,509	2,610	3,114	326	
1986	21,594	2,627	3,180	322	

[a] Part time workers are counted as full units.
[b] Figures are adjusted for discontinuities and seasonal factors, and exclude school-leavers.
[c] Not seasonally adjusted and including school-leavers.

Questions

IT ▶ SPREADSHEET

The information in the table above may be set up as a spreadsheet. This would require rows for each of the years 1976 to 1986 and columns for the five categories of manpower.

1 Complete the column for totals of working population.

2 Calculate the percentage rate of unemployment in each year (of total working population).
   The result of these calculations could be plotted as a bar graph using your graphics package or integrated package, if you have one.

3 Write a brief passage to comment on the trends you observe about these figures.

The Jarrow Crusade – march to London 1936

'March for Jobs' – 1986

Question

Can you explain why unemployment has always been higher in some parts of the country than others?

TASK 1

UNEMPLOYMENT RATES

% unemployment: percentage of total working population unemployed.

% long term: those out of work for a period of 12 months or more.

youth rate: unemployment percentage rate amongst 16–20 year olds.

Working populations:
USA 105m.
Japan 55m.
Canada 11m.

Look at the tables which appear on this page.

1 You know that 11.8% unemployment in the UK represents about 3.3m unemployed. Can you find out what the level of unemployment would be in the US and Japan, using the percentage figures in the table.

2 Why is 'long-term' unemployment such a serious element in the unemployment statistics presented here?

3 Which age groups appear to suffer most from the problems of unemployment? Can you suggest reasons why this may be so?

4 What measures have the UK government taken to decrease the problems of unemployment amongst young people?

5 In which regions of the UK is unemployment the greatest problem? What do these regions appear to have in common?

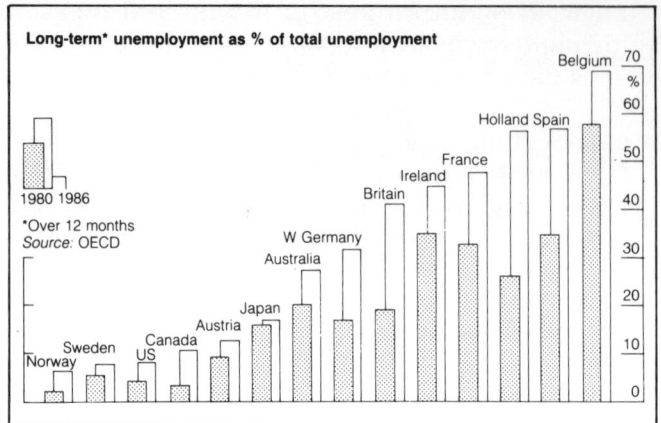

Long-term* unemployment as % of total unemployment

1980 1986

*Over 12 months
Source: OECD

Footnotes applicable to all tables. All figures seasonally adjusted except * not seas. adj.
† Average of latest 3 months compared with avg. of previous 3 mos. at annual rate.
na not available.

Unemployment rates

	Total** %			% long term†	youth* rate
	1985	1986	1987	1985	1985
America	7.2	7	6.8	9.5	13.0
Japan	2.6	2.8	3	15.2‡	4.8
W Germany	8.3	8	7.3	31.0	9.5
France	10.2	10.3	10.3	46.8	25.6
Britain	11.9	12	11.8	41.0	21.7
Italy	10.6	11	11.5	47.9‡	33.7
Canada	10.5	9.5	9.5	10.3	16.5
Total	**7.5**	**7.5**	**7.3**	**—**	**15.3**

*15–24 year-olds; **national definitions
adjusted by OECD; †12 months and over; ‡1984.

Unemployment and age, July 1984

Age	Unemployment rate (male and female, UK)
<18	19.4
18–19	25.1
20–24	20.9
25–34	13.0
35–44	9.1
45–54	8.8
55–59	12.5

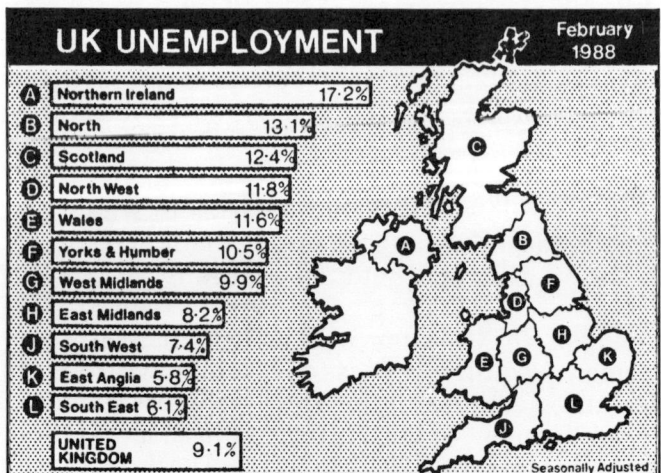

UK UNEMPLOYMENT   February 1988

A	Northern Ireland	17.2%
B	North	13.1%
C	Scotland	12.4%
D	North West	11.8%
E	Wales	11.6%
F	Yorks & Humber	10.5%
G	West Midlands	9.9%
H	East Midlands	8.2%
J	South West	7.4%
K	East Anglia	5.8%
L	South East	6.1%
	UNITED KINGDOM	9.1%

Seasonally Adjusted

TASK 2

UNEMPLOYMENT

In October 1987 (according to official statistics) the seasonally adjusted unemployment rate fell to below 10% for the first time in 5 years. Sixteen consecutive monthly falls produced a total reduction of nearly 500,000 since the peak of June 1986. There are a number of reasons why unemployment has fallen.

☆ Rapid economic growth has meant the creation of genuine new jobs, though many of these are part-time and only account for about 50% of the improvement.

☆ The Youth Training Scheme (YTS) has been expanded by 113,000 places.

☆ The Community Programme and Job Training Scheme (for adults) were expanded slightly to 280,000 places.

☆ Many of the long-term unemployed people interviewed under the "Restart" programme have stopped claiming benefit, either because they have failed the new (tougher) availability for work test or because they were "moonlighting" and feared prosecution.

☆ People who give up work voluntarily face a longer disqualification period for unemployment benefit. In October 1986 the disqualification was raised from 6 to 12 weeks, and in November 1987 it was extended further to 6 months.

UNEMPLOYMENT AND VACANCIES: United Kingdom

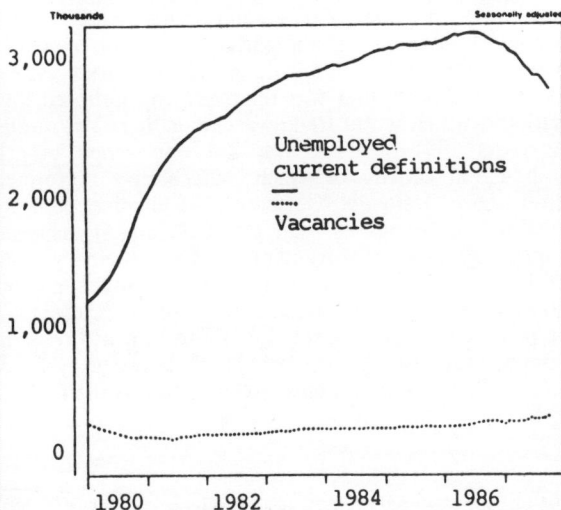

Thousands   Seasonally adjusted

Unemployed
current definitions
═══
Vacancies

3,000

2,000

1,000

0

1980   1982   1984   1986

The government has made a large number of changes to the way unemployment is calculated. These have reduced "official" unemployment by 424,000. In addition, "special measures" such as YTS have taken many people off the register of unemployment. Without these measures, unemployment would have reached 4 millions by 1986.

1 What is happening to the trend in unemployment figures shown in the article above?

2 Look at the reasons put forward to explain this trend.

Why does the article conclude: 'without these measures, unemployment would have reached 4 million by 1986'?

TASK 3

How we can all benefit from unemployment – the case for job sharing schemes

Most people in Britain work at their jobs for an average of 38 hours each week. Some work longer hours and earn overtime and some are only part-time employees – but the average working week has fallen very little over the last twenty years or more.

Most of us would like to work fewer hours and enjoy more leisure time. We value a break at the weekend or on our days off. So why do we all work so many hours?

Many business managers think that we should all work less hours each week and, at the same time, share the total number of hours in a working week between more people. This would, they argue, mean that lots more people (including many of the so called 'long-term unemployed') would be able to have a job.

It is, they say, a matter of simple arithmetic. Take a factory which employs 30 people for an average working week of 40 hours. Total labour employed at that factory is 700 labour hours. If the working week were reduced to 30 hours, 40 people could be employed, giving the same total of 700 labour hours, but offering a full-time job to 10 more people and giving more valuable leisure time to 30 others.

In order to make this system a success, everyone at work would have to accept that they would earn a bit less each week as their hours of employment were reduced. Also, the government would have to play its part by making laws about national insurance payments and the like much more flexible. On the other hand, the benefits are worth thinking about very seriously.

1 Summarise the main advantages of a job-sharing scheme as stated in the passage.

2 The article mentions only two problems with the proposal. There are probably lots more. List any disadvantages you can see in the scheme.

3 On the basis of all the arguments as you see them, make a brief summary of your own conclusion and the reasons for it.

IT ▶ **WORDPRO**

This report could be produced on a word processor.

Industry in Britain

The Industrial Revolution
The period of history at the end of the 18th century – 1760 to 1800 – is often referred to as 'The Industrial Revolution'. Historians don't always agree that 'revolution' was the right term to use, but this was certainly the time when factory working became the way of life for many ordinary people. Labourers moved from jobs on the land to the towns and cities where they found work in factories. Machines were developed to mass produce commodities from cotton, wool and steel. Power was supplied at first from water wheels and then from steam boilers, which meant that industries became concentrated where coal could be mined.

The 19th and 20th centuries
The pattern of industry established on the coalfields of Britain, using home produced or imported raw materials, survived into the latter part of the 20th century. The industrial landscape of Britain did not change very greatly in the 19th or in the early years of the 20th century.

Post-war industrial change
The changing pattern of British industrial production began during the years of economic depression in the 1930s, but it was not until after the 1939–45 war that industry and employment really began to change.

The changing pattern of British trade
Much of UK trade was with Empire and then Commonwealth countries. We bought foodstuffs and raw materials from Africa, Australia, New Zealand and India, paying for them with exports of manufactured goods – tractors, cars, electrical goods and clothing.

As countries began to develop their own economies, many became independent and developed their own manufacturing base. They used their own raw materials to produce steel and metal goods, their own cotton to make textiles and, as standards of living improved, they consumed more of their own food. Not only was Britain losing its source of cheap raw materials, but it was also losing its market for exports.

Changes in industry
The pattern of industry began to change. Coal power was replaced by electricity from the national grid, so the need to concentrate manufacturing on the coalfields disappeared and the traditional industrial areas became increasingly less prosperous. A new pattern of UK industry began to emerge in the 1950s,

The Decline of British Manufacturing

The competitive weakness of British manufacturing is brought out clearly when comparison is made with Germany. In many respects the economies of the two countries were quite similar by the middle of the 1950s. They had similar levels of output and capital per person employed and the industrial structure of the two countries – in terms of the sectoral distribution of output, factor inputs and the size of companies and plants – was roughly comparable. Both started out from a similar level of efficiency, while Britain was favoured with a pattern of exports that was relatively concentrated into sectors in which world trade was expanding. Yet during the years 1954–72 there was not one single branch of industrial activity in which this country performed better than Germany. Germany's productive capacity expanded more rapidly than Britain's, and it achieved a much greater improvement in the efficiency with which resources were used, indicating a much greater adoption of new technologies. As a result, Germany's competitiveness improved and its share of world trade in manufactures rose from 19.2 to 22.4% between 1955–73, whereas Britain's share fell inexorably to less than 10%.

Decline of British manufacturing

At the turn of the 20th century, Britain accounted for one third of the world's trade in manufactured goods. In the 1930s it was 21%, but by 1984 it had fallen to only 7.6%.

Read the article above carefully.

Questions

1 How has Britain's share of world trade in manufactured goods compared with West Germany?

2 Can you suggest some reasons for the points you have made?

producing modern electrical goods, light engineering products, synthetic fibres and chemicals, often in new locations.

Increasing competition from abroad

At the same time, new industrial nations were emerging – Japan, Germany and other countries in Europe. One of the main reasons for joining the European Community in 1973 was to develop new trading links to replace the traditional ones in far parts of the world.

Changes in manufacturing

Britain was still a manufacturing nation. In 1960, 36% of the workforce were employed in manufacturing – 8.4 million in total. We contributed 16.5% of world exports of manufactured goods. By 1980 these figures had fallen to 27% of the workforce, a total of 6.7 million and our share of world manufactured exports had halved, to 8%.

Changes in employment

When oil prices rose (by 400%) in the early 1970s, British manufacturing suffered considerably. Between 1966 and 1986 3.5 million industrial jobs were lost (nearly 30%), worse than anywhere else in the world. Industrial output fell by 10% between 1973 and 1980, whilst world industrial output rose by 13%.

The new economy

In the 1980s the whole pattern of the British economy has been changing. Whereas we once paid for imports of food and raw materials with the export of manufactured goods, we are now net importers of manufactures, i.e. we import more than we export. However, the decline in the importance of traditional industry – steel, textiles, motor vehicles, etc., does not mean that modern Britain has no industrial future.

New industrial opportunities

The discovery of North Sea oil has provided an important boost to economic activity, or, at least has slowed down its decline. The electronics industry produced £10 billion of gadgetry in 1984 and has been growing at 20% a year, although its employment is not growing at the same rate. There has been a growth in the number of small businesses and some of these are in new areas of manufacturing. In spite of keen world competition, the UK is successful in many areas of the electronics business, especially information technology. Britain is a successful chemical producer and a leader in European biotechnology – sometimes called the 'bugs' business.

The 'service' sector

Britain is still the fifth largest 'industrial economy' in the capitalist world but it employs twice as many workers in services as in industry. Services account for two out of every three jobs, jumping from 43% to

Chart 2 — % of civilian employment

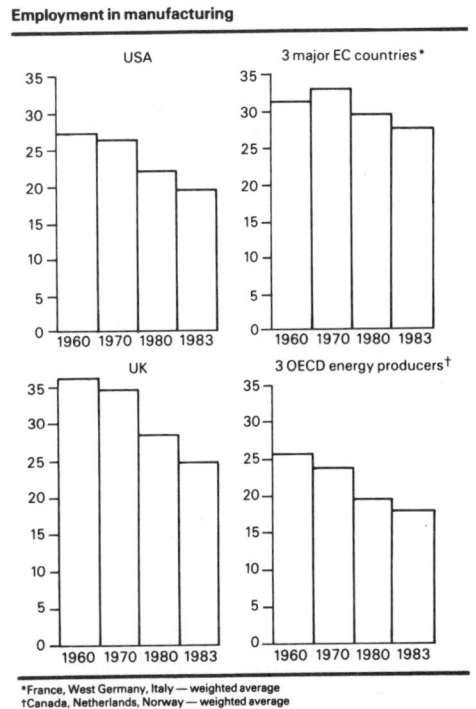

Employment in manufacturing

USA, 3 major EC countries*, UK, 3 OECD energy producers†

*France, West Germany, Italy — weighted average
†Canada, Netherlands, Norway — weighted average

Employment in manufacturing

Questions

1 Look at the figures for the US and the UK. Which country had the higher percentage employment in manufacturing in 1983?

2 How do the UK and US figures compare with those for three EC and three OECD countries shown?

A nation of shopkeepers... and bankers

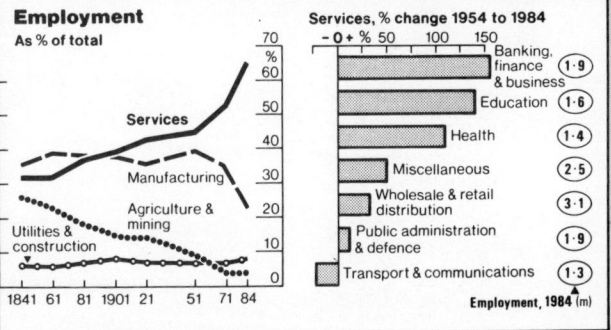

Employment As % of total

Services, % change 1954 to 1984

Banking, finance & business (1·9)
Education (1·6)
Health (1·4)
Miscellaneous (2·5)
Wholesale & retail distribution (3·1)
Public administration & defence (1·9)
Transport & communications (1·3)

Employment, 1984 (m)

A nation of shopkeepers

Questions

1 How does employment in the 'services' sector in the UK compare with other sectors in the economy?

2 Which categories of services account most for the employment changes shown?

65% of the workforce in the last 35 years. Services have generated 1.25 million jobs in the last 10 years. Women account for 55% of service employees, compared with only 28% of manufacturing employment.

De-industrialisation – disaster or opportunity?

The decline in manufacturing industry has been described as 'de-industrialisation'. Many economists view it with concern. Others would argue that change is inevitable and that things had to get worse on the industrial front before they could get better. They point to the new, successful electronics industries which have sprung up right across Southern England, South Wales and Central Scotland and predict a bright future. They are not concerned that we will truly become a nation of shopkeepers and bankers with only foreign goods to sell.

POINTS TO REMEMBER

★ The traditional pattern of industry in Britain was established mainly on coalfield locations and survived from 1760 more or less until 1945.

★ With changes in power, and with newer 'lighter' industries, manufacturing gradually moved to new locations during post war years.

★ Traditional industries like steel, shipbuilding, textiles and vehicle manufacture have declined altogether. To some extent they have been replaced by electronics and new chemical industries, often in new locations, highly automated and employing mainly female labour.

★ The growth of the service sector at the expense of manufacturing is an important feature of this 'de-industrialisation'.

	thousands			
	June, 1978	March, 1985	Absolute change	% change
Agriculture, forestry & fishing	378	321	− 57	−15.1
Energy & water	708	608	−100	−14.1
Other mineral & ore extraction	1,156	780	−376	−32.5
Metal goods, engineering & vehicles	3,314	2,553	−761	−23.0
Other manufacturing industries	2,711	2,034	−677	−25.0
Construction	1,177	942	−235	−20.0
Distribution, hotels, catering, repairs	3,951	4,239	+288	+ 7.3
Transport & communication	1,428	1,263	−165	−11.6
Banking, finance, insurance	1,496	1,926	+430	+28.7
Other services	5,804	6,009	+205	+ 3.5
Self-employed	1,843	2,527	+684	+37.1
All	23,966	23,202	−764	− 3.2

Britain's changing jobs

The table above shows how employment in certain job categories changed between 1978 and 1985.

IT▶ GRAPHICS

Use your graphics package to display the figures for absolute and percentage change in employment in each of the listed categories.

Write a brief passage to summarise what you think the figures and graph show about employment changes in Britain.

Welder wanted: only robots need apply

Question

What types of jobs have been (a) lost, and (b) created by the introduction of robots into factories?

TASK 1

ENTERPRISE ZONES

Read the passage entitled 'Enterprising movers'. It refers to the enterprise zones set up by the government in 1980. It was intended that these towns should have special incentives to encourage industry to develop within them.

Most are examples of industrial towns where manufacturing once thrived but which have declined as the pattern of industry has changed. For example, Dudley was once a prosperous metal manufacturing and engineering town; Corby has been a prosperous steel-making town, using local supplies of iron ore. Both declined in the 1970s and have been identified as areas where special help might encourage new industry to grow.

1 List the incentives which have been offered to firms setting up within an enterprise zone.

2 Examine the map of enterprise zones carefully. Select three of the towns/areas included and try to find out why they have been chosen. You will have to do some research in a library to help you.

3 One of the criticisms of enterprise zones is that they encourage 'boundary hopping', i.e. rather than attracting new firms to the area, they simply encourage existing firms to move a few miles locally to benefit from the advantages. What evidence does the article offer to support or refute this argument?

Enterprising movers

Sir Geoffrey Howe launched the idea of enterprise zones while still in opposition, and put it into practice as chancellor of the exchequer in his 1980 budget. The incentives, which last for 10 years, include:
● Exemption from rates on industrial and commercial property and from development land tax.
● Tax allowances of 100% for new investment in buildings.
● Exemption from industrial training levies and the requirement to supply statistics.

Lest this be seen as regional policy is disguise—easily done given that Wales and Scotland have three zones each, Ulster two and the rest are spread around the English regions—the zones are administered by the Department of the Environment rather than of Trade and Industry.

There are now 25 enterprise zones: 11 were set up between June 1981 and April 1982 (four were subsequently enlarged); and 14 between July 1983 and mid-1984.

Do the zones really create new jobs—and at what price? By the end of 1984, some 48,000 people had jobs in the zones. But this meant the loss of perhaps £250m in taxes and rates. Moreover, one survey showed that in the first 11 zones three quarters of the companies came from the same county as their zone and over 85% from the same region. This suggests that they did not create new jobs—merely shifted existing ones to get financial benefits.

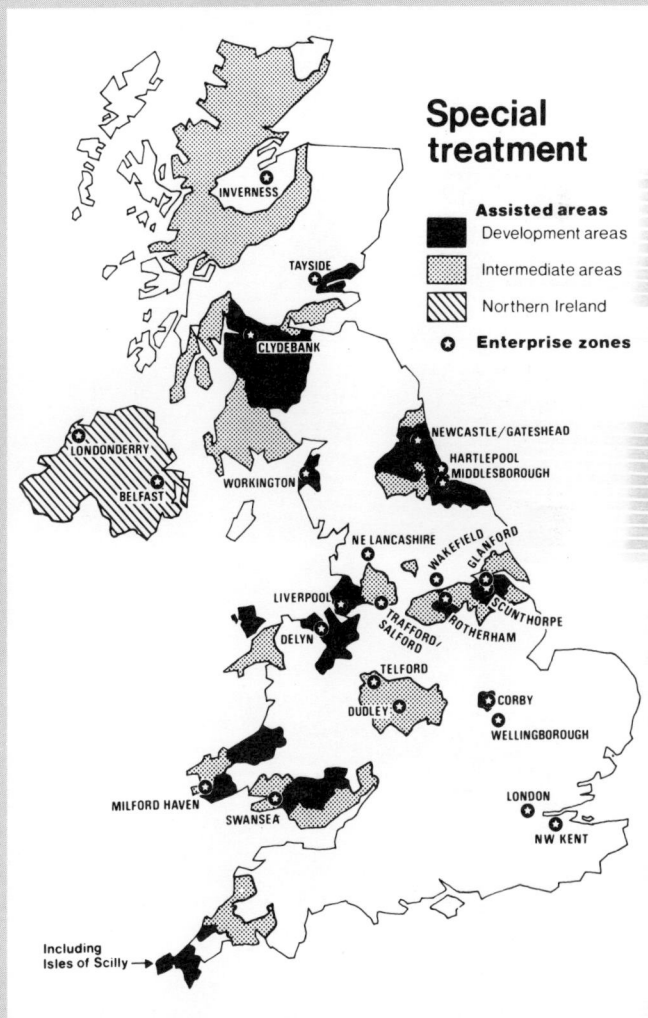

Special treatment

Assisted areas
■ Development areas
▨ Intermediate areas
▧ Northern Ireland
⊙ Enterprise zones

INVERNESS
TAYSIDE
CLYDEBANK
LONDONDERRY
BELFAST
WORKINGTON
NEWCASTLE/GATESHEAD
HARTLEPOOL
MIDDLESBOROUGH
NE LANCASHIRE
WAKEFIELD
GLANFORD
LIVERPOOL
SCUNTHORPE
TRAFFORD/SALFORD
ROTHERHAM
DELYN
TELFORD
DUDLEY
CORBY
WELLINGBOROUGH
MILFORD HAVEN
SWANSEA
LONDON
NW KENT
Including Isles of Scilly →

Areas of the United Kingdom receiving financial help to attract industry

Investigating the
COMMERCIAL
Background

"Maybe Kall kwik can give us some work"

Retailing

All retailers have the same purpose – to sell you goods or services. In high streets, shopping centres, on street corners, out of town sites, boats, airports, through magazines and newspapers, the effort to sell you things seems to know no limits.

This last point is the key to large shops being able to offer low prices – the more you buy from a manufacturer the cheaper you can get it. Large retailers place orders for all their shops around the country, therefore they can buy at very low prices.

Ownership of shops

Shops are owned by individuals, partners or companies and they try to buy finished goods at one price and resell them to customers at a higher price. Once the expenses of the businesses have been deducted, the difference between the price at which they buy and the retail price at which they sell is their profit.

If finished goods are available, why don't shoppers buy them from the manufacturers or wholesaler at the same price as the retailer?

The problem is that manufacturers don't really want to sell one small item at a time. Manufacturers like Mars and Amstrad want to move the output out of the factory by filling large orders so they can keep producing. Production lines are at their most efficient and, therefore, goods at their cheapest, when this happens.

Wholesaling

So what can anybody do with 10,000 Mars bars?

A few retailers could buy this sort of quantity and disbribute it around all their branches, but this is still far too many for most retailers. This is where a wholesaler could be useful. He would buy the 10,000 Mars bars and sell them in smaller quantities to several different retailers – this is known as 'breaking bulk'. The wholesaler might also provide other services, like delivery to the shops or he may let the shops have the goods on credit.

Changes in retailing

There is no doubt that shopping is a major activity these days. Indeed some people actually describe it as recreational activity!

Many high streets have the same shops – Woolworths, Marks and Spencer, Dolcis, and Halfords are found all over the country and each branch has the same layout and the same products.

The unit shop is struggling to survive in this take over of the high street because it lacks many of the

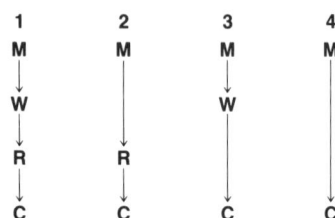

Channels for distributing goods

Question

Shown above are four possible ways of getting goods to the final consumer (C), where:
M = manufacturer,
W = wholesaler,
R = retailer.

1 Which route do you think would be used in each of the following cases?

   a cigarettes to a corner shop.
   b pullovers to Marks and Spencer.
   c glasses to Habitat.
   d cat food sold in Cash and Carry.
   e eggs sold in a farm shop.
   f an aeroplane bought by British Airways.
   g a burger bought in a Wimpy.
   h petrol bought in a garage.
   i a dress bought from a mail order firm.
   j a clearance sale to the public in a wholesale warehouse.

IT ▶ SPREADSHEET/DESKTOP

Question

1 Vintage Cars Limited, a manufacturer of toy cars, offers discounts to retailers for buying in bulk. The more toy cars that retailers buy, the greater the discount. They feel that their customers are not really aware of this deal and want a spreadsheet produced to make the following calculations. The printout should be headed in such a way that it can be included in the next mailing to customers as an A5 leaflet.

Units bought	Unit price	Total price	Percentage discount	Amount of discount	Discounted total price
10	£0.80	?	0%	?	?
100	£0.80	?	5%	?	?
500	£0.80	?	7.5%	?	?
1000	£0.80	?	20%	?	?
5000	£0.80	?	25%	?	?

advantages held by these larger retailers who are often public limited companies.

The larger retailers, like Debenhams and Next, can advertise their shops nationally. They can employ specialists in all the areas of retailing such as accountancy, marketing and display as well as buy in bulk from manufacturers.

Bulk buying

This last point is the key to large shops being able to offer low prices – the more you buy from a manufacturer the cheaper you can get it. Large retailers place orders for all their shops around the country, therefore they can buy at very low prices.

Some small shopkeepers complain that they cannot buy from manufacturers at the same price as large retailers can sell their goods to the public!

The survival of the small retailer often depends on offering something the large shops cannot offer. This might be staying open late at night or trying to be very friendly and polite to customers or even to trade on Sundays, although this is illegal at present for certain goods.

Franchising

One increasingly popular opportunity for people to set up as retailers, and to have some chance of competing with large retailers, is to buy a franchise. Generally, a company develops the idea to sell either a product (e..g. hamburgers) or a service (e.g. drain clearing) and it runs its own business doing these things. When a record of success has been established, the company (the franchisor) sells the right to run the same business in a particular area to another firm (the franchisee).

The franchisor provides the training, equipment, materials and national advertising. In return, the franchisee pays an initial start-up fee and then a percentage of sales. Examples of individuals trading as a franchise are found in every high street and they include Tie Rack, Sketchley, The Body Shop, Pizza Express and Wimpey. MacDonald's have sold only a few franchises and still operate mainly as a company. Whereas about 50% of ordinary small businesses will fail, only about 10% of franchises are likely to be unsuccessful.

Voluntary groups

Alternatively, small retailers have tried to group together as voluntary groups to buy in bulk and distribute the purchases amongst the members, advertising nationally. Examples of shops that do this are Spar, which stands for the Society for the Protection of the Average Retailer, Mace and VG.

Out-of-town shopping

Despite all this competition in the high street, many companies like B&Q, Payless DIY, WH Smith and Texas in the do-it-yourself market see great opportunities in out-of-town sites. Here stores can be very large and offer a wide range of products with ample free car parking. These companies have followed

Clobber

Mr Azid is opening a shop to sell a wide range of clothing which will be very fashionable. He will need to sell the clothes quickly before they go out of fashion.

He intends to employ four full-time staff during the week and four more part-time staff on Saturdays. He is currently considering how to pay them. Generally, the goods take some selling, as customers often look around several shops looking for the best deal. Sales staff need to be persistent but not too pushy, as this puts people off.

Mr Azid is considering either:

a paying them a weekly salary, or

b just paying them commission on the goods they sell.

He has asked you to help him to devise a system to get the most out of his workers at the lowest cost.

Being over keen can put people off!

Questions

1 Suggest what he should offer the full-time and part-time staff. Outline why you think your suggestion would get the most out of the employees.

2 As a potential employee, by which system would you prefer to be paid?

▌▌▌▶ WORDPRO/DESKTOP

Draft an advertisement to be placed in a block 10cm by 6cm in your local newspaper. The advertisement is to offer jobs in Mr Azid's shop. You should state the rates of pay, the hours to be worked and the type of work to be undertaken. Applicants are to phone 0742-66991 for an interview before 10 am on the Saturday after the advertisement appears in the paper.

the lead of the food supermarkets in seeing the importance of increasing car ownership and the desire for a wide range of products.

Telephone sales

Other recent changes in retailing include telephone sales, either by 'cold-calling' of people to sell them products like double glazing and life assurance, or allowing customers to place orders by phone. Several mail order catalogues use this latter method and some accept payment by letting the customer quote their credit card number. In a few parts of the country you can even see what shops are offering on a telephone/TV/computer link in your own home and place orders – some people order their groceries this way every week and the shop delivers them!

POINTS TO REMEMBER

★ Shopping is dominated by the same companies in every high street.

★ Bulk buying leads to low prices.

★ Franchising is increasingly popular.

★ New technology is starting to influence the way we shop.

Changes in retailing

	1982	1984
	no. of outlets	
Unit shops	203157	201633
Small multiples (less than 10 shops)	76346	73670
Large multiples	70153	67850
Co-operatives	6945	5813

Question

1 If you look at the above figures, you will see that the number of outlets in each sector has decreased. Yet all around us we see new shopping centres and out-of-town stores being built. How can the number of retail outlets be falling?

Tesco fights back!

During the 1960s Jack Cohen, chairman of Tesco, ran his chain of supermarkets as a very profitable business. His success was based on 'piling it high and selling it cheap'. During the 1970s Tesco did not respond to the fact that people were looking for better quality and service in their food purchases. Tesco started going downhill, until the fightback started. Small stores were closed; now there are around 400 stores as opposed to 900 in the 1970s. Out-of-town sites with in-store bakeries, car parking and high quality food are the future for Tesco. Others may have to follow suit or perish!

Questions

1 Why do you think there is still a place for small grocery retailers?

2 It is easy to follow current trends, but real success awaits anybody who can spot what the next move should be. How do you think groceries will be sold in the year 2010?

3 List the sorts of jobs you think may have been created in the economy by the changes that have taken place in retailing.

4 Which trend did Tesco not recognise in their marketing of food?

5 Why are large stores more profitable than small stores?

TASK 1

THE INSTANT PRINTER WHO'S EARNED A HOLIDAY

Tally Barash's long haul to becoming Kall-Kwik Printing's franchisee in Kentish Town, north London, is proof that determination can win out in the end. Tally, 38, originally qualified as a graphic designer in her native Israel before coming to England 14 years ago. She spent her first years here working for the VIP section of Israeli airline El Al, developing her talent for mixing and dealing with all sorts of people. "But", she says, "I had always wanted to get back to design."

A friend, one of Kall-Kwik's first franchisees, introduced her to the company and Tally was hooked. She started off five years ago working as a counter clerk at a central London Kall-Kwik outlet. From there she moved on to open a second and later, a third shop for an existing franchisee, experiencing all the pains of starting a business from scratch as a manageress. "But after a while I felt limited in what I could do and no longer wanted to work for someone else", she says. "I had my own ideas and the experience and I felt I could do it on my own. I wanted my own shop."

Being well known by then to Kall-Kwik, Tally had the advantage of a lot of support from head office and its managing director Moshe Gerstenhaber. But, though she had saved hard, she didn't have the initial £70,000 necessary to buy a franchise and finance the start-up.

"Luckily", she says, "I had three friends who believed in my ability enough to put up most of the money." The agreement was that the friends, all of whom had their own businesses, would be sleeping partners while Tally, owning 25%, would be the active franchisee.

With additional money needed to make further improvements to the shop, the total package ended up costing £80,000 by the time she opened the door a year ago. And things took off well immediately. "I made an £8,000 turnover in the first month – the highest ever for a Kall-Kwik franchisee", Tally says. "I had done a lot of work beforehand introducing myself to nearly 500 businesses in the area, walking from one office to another, giving them a folder about the opening and a map to find the shop. That does work and gives you the ability to produce your first mailing list to follow up with additional promotional literature."

She also puts that success down to the team of people she employed in the outlet, most of whom had worked for Kall-Kwik before. "In order to give good service, you need good teamwork. They don't work *for* me but *with* me", she says.

The year's turnover has been over £100,000 "and I'm not far now from breakeven point", Tally says. "We were given overdraft facilities from the bank which I've never had to use. Normally one would expect to be in profit by the third year, but I'm determined to do it in the second.

"It's not just the money that motivates me. It's the wonderful satisfaction I get when customers thank me for the service. I've made a lot of friends through the business. It's being part of community life.

"As far as the franchisor is concerned, I can honestly say there is not one thing I haven't been happy with so far. They give you all the help and support needed. But I don't find working to their line restrictive. They don't control me – I make the decisions on how to deal with customers, choice of suppliers and how to approach a problem. But at the same time it helps to be part of a well known organisation when dealing with suppliers in terms of discount and credit facilities."

Tally is proud to have added "a woman's touch" to the shop with a private seating area and lots of greenery – "not one plant has died yet". She pays Kall-Kwik 10% of her turnover which splits into a 6% franchise fee and 4% towards advertising and promotion budget. "And half of that I can claim back to do my own promotions."

Aiming now to delegate a little more and take a few days' holiday at last, Tally is well on the way to running a profitable small business. "You must be prepared to work very hard and believe in what you are doing", she says. "But the reward is there if you set the goal and go for it."

"Maybe Kall kwik can give us some work"

Ron Kemp describes his and his wife Frances' two years as franchisees as "the most traumatic and awful experience of our lives".

So while on holiday in the UK in late 1984, Ron and Frances took up franchises on two businesses they felt complemented each other covering the Edinburgh and Lothian territory: Safeclean, hand-cleaning of carpets and upholstery run from home, and Poppies, domestic and commercial cleaning services for which they needed an office. Frances was to run the Poppies franchise and Ron would concentrate on Safeclean as a one-man band. "We were both giving up well paid professions and I believed any one franchise would not give us sufficient income to live on."

After buying a house, they put all their remaining money into setting up the franchises, topped up by a £3,000 small business loan. Poppies, says Ron, cost them around £13,000 in all to get off the ground and Safeclean was cheaper at £9,000.

After getting through the difficulty of finding suitable offices for Poppies within Edinburgh's upmarket prices, both businesses were launched in September 1985. Then the real difficulties started.

"The Safeclean work I found doesn't go down well in this area. There is intense competition from cheaper, quicker cleaners who use machines rather than hand-cleaning which is very labour-intensive, laborious and expensive in materials. A large element of the market was denied us – such as guest-houses, restaurants and offices – because it was too time-consuming." With Poppies, Frances had difficulties getting the right staff "and the margins are so fine after all the overheads that it took far longer to get to breakeven point than we were led to expect", Ron says.

The Kemps took overdraft facilities to ease their path and ended up running up a debt of £16,000. In fact, Poppies did reach breakeven point in two years but, for the Kemps, this was too late. "It had cost us a phenomenal amount of money. We were worn out, bitter and disillusioned." Ron now believes it would take three to four years to start making a living profit from either franchise. "My second year on Safeclean was no better than my first, despite hard efforts."

1 What businesses were franchised in the two articles printed above?

2 Who was the franchisee in each case?

3 Who was the franchisor in each case?

4 How much did each franchise cost to start?

5 Why do you think one franchise was more successful than the other two? You should be able to find several reasons for this.

Insurance

People are prepared to pay for insurance (the payment is called a premium) because they fear that something bad may happen. They might die unexpectedly or their business might suffer a robbery or fire.

Statistics

Statistics show that these things do happen – but not to everybody! In insurance a lot of people (called the proposers) pay their premium to form a pool of money and, as only the unfortunate few claim, there is enough money available to pay them for what they have lost. This is called compensation.

The premiums are paid to insurers who are either companies like Commercial Union (owned by shareholders) or Lloyds syndicates which are groups of people with unlimited liability for any insurance they agree to cover.

Insurance can be taken out directly with companies or through their agents (these are often people like bank managers or accountants). Otherwise you can contact a broker who will be able to offer insurance with several companies or syndicates and is himself a specialist in insurance advice.

Taking out insurance

The size of the premium will depend on how likely what you have insured against is to happen. For example, if you live in an inner city area, house contents insurance is higher than in country areas because burglaries happen more often in cities.

On the 'proposal form' you set out all the details of what you want to insure. This could be a car or your life. You must complete the proposal form in the 'utmost good faith' which means that you must tell the truth about yourself and the car – including relevant information which might not even be asked for. If you have already had several accidents, you are a bad risk and your premium will be higher.

It must be clear that you have a 'financial interest' in what you insure – that means you must stand to lose money if you crash the car. This rule stops people insuring things they do not own and then getting compensation for them.

If you do make a claim you will be 'indemnified' – that is you will only be given what you have lost. If you get a rusty car wing repaired and it ends up better than it was before the accident the insurer may not pay all the cost of the repairs. If you pay a higher premium you can have an 'as new' policy where you are given enough compensation to replace damaged goods – this is very useful for items like clothes.

It might never happen but...

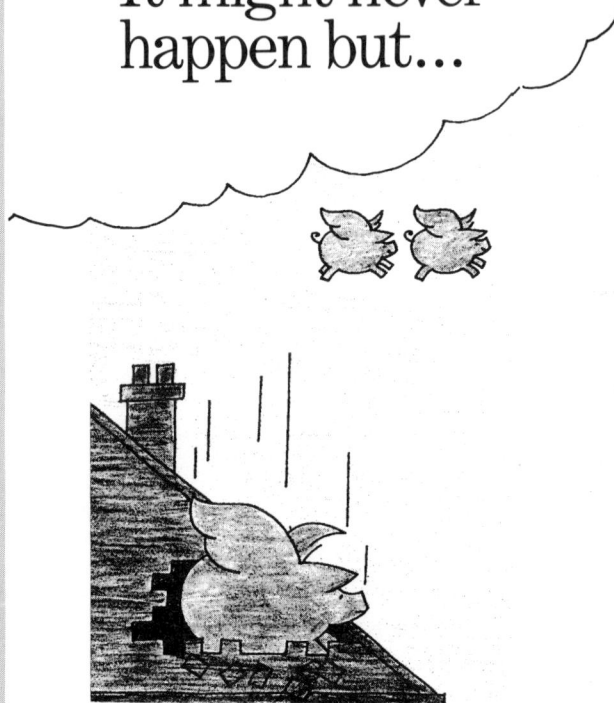

Question

Why would an insurance company find it difficult to set a premium offering insurance against such an incident?

SPECIAL NOTICE TO ALL SHA MEMBERS: DISCOUNTS AVAILABLE ON INSURANCE

Questions

1 SHA is a union for headteachers. Why do you think its members can be offered discounts on various types of insurance?

2 Why do you think non-smokers are offered discounts on life assurance?

How insurance companies make profits

To some extent the premiums charged to policy-holders will mean, after claims have been met and expenses paid, that a company is left with a profit.

When the premiums are collected, it is known how much is needed to meet claims, so the rest is invested, for example in other companies, or lent to British and other governments. Insurance companies collect dividends on the shares they own and interest on money they lend. This helps to increase the profits made by the insurance companies.

Types of insurance: life assurance

You can insure your life for a given number of years (a 'term policy'). If you die, compensation is paid to the person you have chosen to benefit. If you are still alive at the end of this period you get nothing! With a 'whole life policy' you pay premiums until you die and then compensation is paid.

Another choice is to insure your life for a given period and collect a lump sum even if you do not die! This is called an 'endowment policy' and the premiums are higher.

These policies can be 'with profits' so the insurance company shares with the policyholder any extra income they have made from investing the premiums.

Business insurance

Most businesses will want to take out insurance cover against accidents, fires and theft as well as motor insurance to protect their vehicles.

They can also have 'fidelity guarantee' insurance to protect them against dishonest employees who might steal from them.

By law employers have to take out 'employers' liability' insurance to cover them in case an employee has an accident and claims compensation. They may also want 'public liability' insurance to cover them in case a member of the public has an accident when visiting their premises.

Although a fire may be a disaster to a firm, it could also mean that trading cannot carry on. In such cases there may be no money coming in to the business. If the firm had a 'consequential loss' policy the insurance company would compensate the firm for loss of profit after the fire.

Insurance is also possible against a firm's debtors not paying their debts.

An area in which a firm could be involved in multi-million pound claims is when their products are faulty and cause injury to people. Firms can take out 'product liability' insurance to cover themselves against this.

Marine and aviation insurance

Many ships, aeroplanes and oil rigs around the world are insured at Lloyds. Ship owners can insure the ship and its cargo. In certain areas of the world, where ships may be under attack, the premium can be very high.

'We have no insurance'
Shock admission by council

The leader of a county council today admitted that many of the county's buildings were not insured against storm damage. She continued by saying that for events like the hurricane that hit the south east of England, the county had decided that insurance was not good value for money.

Questions

1 Explain why it is sometimes not worth taking out insurance against certain risks.

2 Do you think the county council described above would now take out insurance against hurricanes?

Accidental Window Breakage

An insurance company has offered your school insurance against accidental window breakage by students. The annual premium is £600.

Question

On what information would you base your decision on whether to accept the offer?

Holiday insurance

Insurance can be taken out against having to cancel your holiday due to things like illness or having to serve on a jury. When on holiday you can be insured against losing your luggage or travellers cheques. As medical treatment can be very expensive it is useful to have a policy against needing treatment whilst abroad.

Car insurance

You can have 'third party insurance' – if you have an accident you will get nothing but any damage you have caused to other people will be paid for; or 'third party, fire & theft' – as above but you get compensation if your car is stolen or bursts into flames.

The most expensive is 'comprehensive insurance' – if you cause an accident, damage to your own car is paid for as well as any other damage.

National Insurance

Every employee earning above about £40 per week, and their employer, has to pay National Insurance contributions to the government. This money is used to pay out benefits like unemployment, retirement and maternity pay and it goes towards paying for the National Health Service.

The importance of insurance

Insurance is important to people who take out policies as it gives them some financial security. Many people are employed in insurance as brokers, agents, clerks, computer programmers and statisticians.

Insurance is also important as an invisible export, earning valuable foreign currency when people in other countries insure their ships, planes and lives with British insurance companies and Lloyds syndicates.

POINTS TO REMEMBER

★ Insurance relies on statistics to work out premiums.

★ It is provided by underwriters at Lloyds or companies.

★ The main principles are Indemnity, Utmost Good Faith, Insurable Interest.

★ It helps reduce the risks in business.

★ It is an important invisible export.

HOLIDAY INSURANCE

NORWICH UNION INSURANCE   Members of the Insurance Ombudsman Bureau

Because we consider it essential for our clients to be adequately insured, we have made it a requirement that you accept the special Norwich Union Insurance negotiated by Thomson, or alternatively arrange a policy yourself which is at least as good. Should you decide to accept the Norwich Union cover, the charges per person per holiday for all Air Fare destinations are:–

		Charges (per person)
1.	Up to 9 nights	£12.40
2.	10-17 nights	£14.40
3.	18-23 nights	£15.70
4.	24-30 nights	£17.30
5.	31-40 nights	£18.80
6.	41-51 nights	£20.50
7.	52-60 nights	£22.20
8.	61 nights and over	£23.80

The appropriate charges will be included on your Final Invoice. As cover is immediate, bookings for insurance cannot be cancelled and no refund of premium is possible. This insurance affords you the following cover:–

Cancellation or Curtailment	not exceeding Final Invoice costs
Medical and Associated Expenses including Repatriation	£500,000
Hospital Benefit	£10 per day – £200 maximum
Baggage Delay (after 12 hours)	£75
Baggage and Personal effects (limit £200 for any one article)	£1000
Money	£200
Personal Accident (a) Death (b) Loss of or irrecoverable loss of use of one or more limbs or eyes (c) Permanent total disablement from following usual occupation (other than as provided by (b) above). For children up to 15 years inclusive, the death benefit is limited to £1,000.	£15,000
Personal Liability	£500,000
Missed Departure	£300

Questions

Examine the table above.

1 What is the premium for insuring for 18 nights with Norwich Union?

2 How much compensation would you get if you missed your flight?

3 Why do you think the payments for medical insurance are so much greater than for death?

TASK 1

You are about to set up a business selling a new baby carriage. You will manufacture them in your factory in Birmingham and deliver them by your own vehicles to shops all over the country. You will employ 40 people and expect many visits from retailers to your factory. What insurance policies do you think you should have to cover your business?

TASK 2

HOW EACH POUND IS INVESTED BY INSURANCE COMPANIES

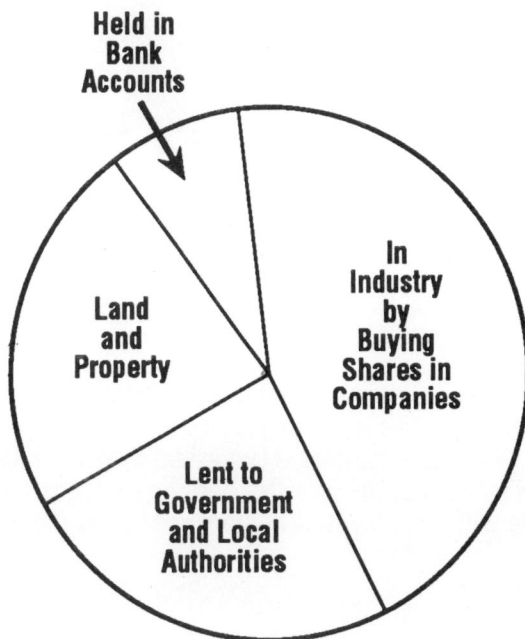

1 Where do insurance companies invest most of their money?

2 Why do you think the insurance companies do not just leave all the premiums they collect in a bank account?

3 Why is it necessary for insurance companies to hold some of their funds in bank accounts?

4 Why do insurance companies often refuse to give life assurance and private medical insurance to people who are seriously ill?

5 Do you think insurance companies should be required by law to cover everybody who wants life assurance and to charge everybody the same premium? What effect would having such a law have on people who are in good health?

TASK 3

Amanda Swizzle was looking forward to her seventeenth birthday as it meant she could at last drive the Cortina she had bought six months before for £600. She had spent another £200 doing it up and she had taxed and insured it.

Insurance seemed a bit of a waste of time because she knew she would be a good driver and would not have any accidents. But she knew the law required it.

When she filled out the proposal form, she did not mention that she had been convicted of driving whilst under age. (She had been caught taking her car for a test run.) She had also stated that it was worth £7500 as this would allow her to buy a new car in the unlikely event of an accident. On the morning of her birthday, Amanda drove alone out of the driveway straight into another car. She claimed for the damage to her own car on her own insurance.

▐▀▐ ⮞ WORDPRO

Try to compose this letter on a wordprocessor without first handwriting a draft.

You work for her insurance company. Write a letter to Amanda at her home address of 12 Killmore Road, Newcastle, stating, with reasons, how you intend to deal with the claim.

TASK 4

1 What is the difference between a term policy and an endowment policy?

2 Why is comprehensive motor insurance more expensive than third party?

3 What is business interruption insurance?

4 Who pays National Insurance contributions? To whom are they paid?.

5 Why is insurance sometimes said to be an invisible export?

Banking

There are many different types of institutions which are keen to look after your money and, if you are the 'right' sort of person, they are also very keen to lend it to you. Only a short time ago, banks were used for a cheque book or deposit account and building societies were used for saving or house purchase. Nowadays banks and building societies offer some very similar services and they see themselves as being in direct competition with each other. The competition between banks and building societies should become more intense when the latter start becoming public limited companies and offer a wider range of financial services.

How banks make profits
You should remember that banks are profit-making companies. One of the ways they make money is by offering you 8% interest when you deposit money with them and charging me 20% interest when I borrow that money from them. After their expenses have been deducted they can be left with very healthy profits. (Rates of interest are changed from time to time and current rates can be checked in banks or newspapers.)

Are all banks the same?
Banks are in the business of offering a range of banking services to encourage custom. They know that, because all banks have essentially the same services, customers can easily move their money from one to another if they are not satisfied. They try to show that each bank is different, but as soon as one bank launches a new service the others follow – so when one bank opened on Saturdays others had to follow.

Competition with building societies
The reason for banks starting Saturday opening was that building societies started to offer similar services to banks – and they opened on Saturdays. The banks had tried to avoid opening on Saturdays (which they had done in the 1960s) by installing cash dispensers which were open 24 hours per day, but the building societies followed suit and they too offered cash dispensers.

The greatest competition came when the banks started to offer people mortgages with which to buy houses. It seems that, as competition increases, the range of services offered to customers by banks and building societies also increases.

The services offered by banks and building societies have different 'brand' names and they

Why should she care which credit card you use?

Children like Jane need your help.
They need it now, and they need it badly. Which is why your choice of credit card could be vital.
Because the new Bank of Scotland NSPCC Visa Card has been created with a particular object in mind.
To help children.
Children in need, in danger, and distress. Last year, the NSPCC helped over 44,000 youngsters.
To some that meant the difference between life and death.
Which is why we've joined forces.
And why we're asking for your support. For every one of these new Visa accounts opened, we'll donate £5 to the NSPCC.

Charity advertising: A very sensitive area in which to work

Competition is intense between banks and building societies to try to get you to open an account. This is based on the belief that you will tend to stick with the bank or building society with which you first start.

Questions

1 Make a list of any incentives currently on offer to persuade you to open an account.

2 Look at the offer made in the advertisement above. Write a paragraph explaining why you think this is, or is not, an acceptable way of getting people to become credit card holders.

⯈ DESKTOP

A consumer advice centre has asked you to produce an attractive A5 leaflet which suggests six precautions to take when using credit cards. The points should help keep people out of long term debt and advise them of the need to keep their credit cards in a safe place.

generally include the following, which are available to both individuals and firms:

A current account

This gives you a cheque book with a guarantee card which covers cheques up to £50 or £100. Sometimes it is possible to get interest on your credit balance – all institutions charge you for going overdrawn. Students are often offered free gifts to open an account because the banks know that customers tend to stay with their first bank.

A deposit account

No cheque book is given but you receive interest on the money you deposit. Sometimes you need to give notice of your intention to withdraw money. The greater the amount you invest the higher the rate of interest you get.

Standing orders

This is an instruction given by you to the bank to get them to pay a set amount of money at stated intervals, e.g. monthly, to another person or company. People often use this to pay rate bills to a local authority.

Direct debits

This is an instruction given to a bank by the person being paid, with the agreement of the person paying, to transfer varying amounts of money on different dates. This is used where the amount being paid can vary from month to month or quarter to quarter, e.g. a gas bill.

Loans

This is when a set amount of money is borrowed. It is repaid over a certain period of time and interest is charged. A mortgage is a loan usually repayable over about 20 years and your house is the security for the loan. That means if you do not repay the loan the bank or building society can reclaim your house.

Overdraft

When you have an arrangement to draw out more money from your current account than you have in it you are said to be overdrawn. You are charged interest daily on the outstanding balance. Many companies operate with permanent overdrafts as this frees their own funds for other purposes and the banks are happy to do it because they charge interest.

Credit cards

These are offered by all the major banks – either a VISA card, e.g. Barclaycard or Trustcard (TSB) or ACCESS, e.g. Lloyds or Midland Banks. These have a preset spending limit, e.g. £1,000 and you have to repay all or part of the balance you owe at the end of each month. 25% is a likely annual rate of interest. It is possible to use such cards without cost to the customer by settling the whole bill at the end of the month.

Examining a cheque

Look carefully at the cheque above.

Questions

1 Who is the money being paid to?
(this person is the payee)

2 Who is giving the money?
(this person is the drawer)

3 On which bank is the cheque drawn?
(this is the drawee)

4 State four reasons why the bank would refuse to settle the cheque.

A mortgage is a long-term loan usually taken out to buy a house. The house is used as security in case the borrower should be unable to repay the loan.

REPAYMENT MORTGAGE				
Amount of Mortgage	Term in Years	Total Amount Payable	Annual Percentage Rate	Monthly Repayments
£20,000	15	£41,400.32	11.8%	£229.37
	20	£50,185.15	11.8%	£208.64
	25	£59,613.24	11.8%	£198.35
£50,000	15	£103,364.82	11.8%	£573.42
	20	£125,331.93	11.7%	£521.59
	25		11.7%	£495.86

Questions

1 If you were to borrow £20,000 for 25 years at a rate of 11.8% per annum, what would your monthly repayments be?

2 If the rate of interest increases would your repayment increase or decrease?

3 If you were to borrow £50,000 for 25 years how much would you repay in total?

Debit cards

In theory, if you buy something using a debit card the till should be connected to a computer which automatically takes the money out of your bank account. Barclays 'Connect' is a debit card. It is operated through the same system as a credit card, except that, when the voucher arrives at your bank, it is immediately debited from your account. There is little advantage in using a debit card rather than a credit card unless you do not like being in debt.

Budget account

With these you agree to pay a fixed amount into the account every month and you are allowed to overdraw to pay your bills. For example, if you pay in £25 per month you could go overdrawn up to about £750. You get interest when the account is in credit and you pay interest when you are overdrawn.

Other services

Other services which you can get include buying foreign currency and travellers cheques, advice on buying shares and insurance and help with making wills.

POINTS TO REMEMBER

★ Banks are in business to make a profit.

★ Banks and building societies are in competition to both look after your money and to lend you money.

★ A wide range of banking services are available.

Question

Which banks and building societies have these signs?

Gold Star Account		
Investments £1 and above	**4.00%**	
Investments £500 and above	**6.00%**	
Investments £5,000 and above	**6.50%**	
Investments £10,000 and above	**6.75%**	
Investments £20,000 and above	**7.00%**	

Look at the interest rates offered by the Building Society Gold Star Account.

Questions

1 How much interest would you earn if you were to save:
   a £500 for a year
   b £3600 for a year
   c £12500 for a year
   d £50000 for a year

2 Why do you think you are offered higher rates of interest for saving larger sums of money?

TASK 1

1 How do banks make a profit?

2 What is the difference between a standing order and a direct debit?

3 What are the differences between a current account and a budget account?

4 What is the difference between a credit card and a debit card?

TASK 3

A new company called Zippy Ltd of 23, Newshire Road, Torbay, Devon, has written to their local bank to ask what services they have available to help a new company that is just setting up business. They have 20 employees and want to pay them without using cash. Many of Zippy's customers will buy on credit. Their sales representatives will spend a lot of time travelling in this country and abroad.

As a bank clerk you have been asked to reply to this letter, outlining at least four services you think might be useful, and offering to arrange a meeting with Mr Dowdeswell, from whom you have received the initial enquiry.

TASK 2

HOW TO CALCULATE INTEREST

To qualify for free banking you must always keep your account in credit. If at any time you become overdrawn, you have to pay all of the following charges

a flat rate charge of £3
30p for each debit entry
interest charges for every day you are overdrawn.

These are worked out as follows:
Interest is charged at 10% p.a. on the overdrawn balance. For example, if you were overdrawn by £200 for 2 days you would be charged:

$$£200 \times \frac{10}{100} = £2/365 \text{ days} \times 2 \text{ days} = £0.11\text{p}$$

This is then added to the flat rate charge and the debit entry charge.

COMPLETE A BANK STATEMENT

The following items should be entered in the correct date order in the bank statement and then, if necessary, bank charges should be inserted.

A standing order for £30 for water rates was paid on 25 August.

A direct debit for £102 reached the bank on 20 August.

A mortgage payment was made by standing order for £230 to the Allied Building Society on 26 August.

Dividends on shares were received by the bank for £27 on 23 August.

The Account holder's salary of £990.87 was paid into the bank by giro transfer on 28 August.

A pools win of £10 was paid into the bank on 18 August.

A charity donation of £10 was paid to Oxfam by standing order on 24 August.

On 17 August the balance in the account was £92.51 and the account holder paid out the following cheques on the dates given (the dates given are the date on which they arrived at the bank).

Cheque Nos	Date	Amount
12345	19 Aug	£11.90
12346	21 Aug	£12.57
12347	22 Aug	£102.91
12348	23 Aug	£111.78

SPREADSHEET

The bank statement can be completed using a spreadsheet.

1 Complete the bank statement.

Date	Details	Dr (money out)	Cr (money in)	Balance
17 Aug	Balance			£92.51
18 Aug				
19 Aug				
20 Aug				
21 Aug				
22 Aug				
23 Aug				
24 Aug				
25 Aug				
26 Aug				
27 Aug				
28 Aug				
29 Aug				
30 Aug				
31 Aug	Bank charges			

2 How could you try to reorganise the dates you receive and pay out money so that you could reduce your bank charges?

3 Show how you worked out the bank charges. Which part of them was the most expensive?

Marketing

Marketing is concerned with getting:
the right product
at the right time
to the right customer
in the right place
at the right price.

To do this successfully a firm has to carry out a wide range of activities like market research, advertising and sales promotion. It must decide on the price and be aware of changes that may be taking place.

Firms that get it right – and wrong!
Some firms clearly manage this well. McDonalds, the hamburger chain, recognised that people wanted good quality food, quickly served. At the time, other shops were offering poor quality burgers and a much less efficient service.

Other organisations like British Telecom are frequently criticised for public phone boxes not working – clearly the needs of customers are not being met.

Finding out what people want
The process of gathering information is usually done either by interviewing people to ask their views or by using information which has already been collected – this is called desk research. The problems of asking questions are well known: people lie; they try to give the answer they think you want; or they simply don't understand the question. Even if the answers you get are accurate you still have to ask the right people. This is usually done by selecting a sample of people who are considered to represent the whole of the population. On the basis of this sample it, may be possible to predict what might happen nationally.

Advertising
Having decided what people want, it is then necessary to inform them about your product and persuade them to buy it. Many firms advertise on TV, radio, billboards and plastic bags, as well as in newspapers and specialist magazines. Generally, there is some 'gimmick' that is used to sell the product. It may be because the product is trendy, cheap, or gives you sex appeal! Also important in this process is the advertising at the point of sale and the image that can be created around the product.

Methods of selling
Having identified the right product, it is now necessary to get it in the right place at the right time. This means that you must think about where it is to be

Brand names

Companies spend many millions of pounds on their advertising – they want you to recognise their name.

Question

Make a list of these brand names and along side each, list the products they sell. The ones you know have obviously made an impact on you.

sold. It could be direct from the manufacturer, via retailers, wholesalers, mail order or telephone sales. The problems of place could also mean you have to concentrate sales in certain parts of the country. In terms of time, some products are 'pushed' at Christmas or in the summer, and some all year round.

Next you have to find the right customers. There is no point advertising in 'The Sun' when the likely buyers of your product read 'The Times'.

How much to charge?

The pricing decision can be taken in a number of ways. Sometimes it can be based on your competitors' price, or on your costs plus a percentage. Some firms just make their products expensive because people believe expensive things are worth having; others make it very cheap because this brings buyers. To some extent the market research will help to determine price. Often the people surveyed will be asked how much they would be prepared to pay for a product. What people say they will pay and what they actually would pay may not, of course, be the same!

The product life-cycle

The 'product life-cycle' will have an influence on marketing tactics. This idea suggests that when a product is first launched its price is usually at its highest. As the product sells more, different prices can be charged in different markets and, towards the end of its life, its price is stable. Finally, as sales start to decline, the price tends to fall. Although this does not happen in every case it is typical of many products.

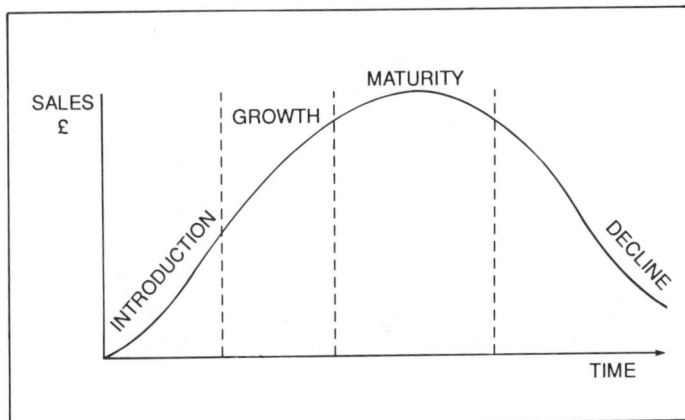

POINTS TO REMEMBER

★ Marketing contains a range of activities designed to satisfy the needs of the consumer.

★ Decisions are based on research.

★ Decisions must be made about the product, its price and its promotion.

MARKET OPINIONS PLC

REPORT ON UMBRELLAS

We have completed our market research in the field and it suggests that people tend to buy a new umbrella every three years, and half of those sold are given as gifts. The graph indicates the levels of sales your shop, Fashion Styles, might expect at each of the prices shown.

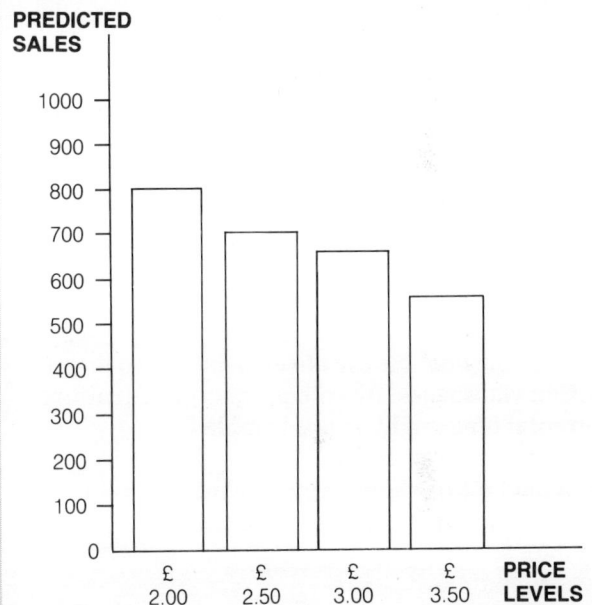

Questions

1 How much sales revenue would there be at each price level?

2 What price should be charged to get the maximum sales revenue?

3 If Fashion Styles can buy the umbrellas for £1 each how much profit is made at each price level?

4 What price should be charged to maximise profits?

5 At the end of the winter season only half the umbrellas ordered had been sold. Can you think of any reasons why these should be sold off at 90p each?

TASK 1

IS THERE A MARKET? – THE FURNITURE BUSINESS

One of the major problems with furniture is that once you have bought it you are stuck with it.

Furniture Rental Limited has been set up to see if there is a gap in the market for a company to rent out furniture for a period of two years with an option to buy at the end of it.

Your group is required to undertake the following:

1 Design a questionnaire to see if there is a market for renting out furniture with a final option to buy it.

2 Try out the questionnaire on parents or friends. Gather the results from the whole class and see if there is a market for this service.

3 Suggest three possible places from where you could sell and rent out the furniture.

IT ▶ DESKTOP

4 Design an A4 leaflet advertising your shop. Point out the particular benefits of furniture rentals.

5 Script and record a thirty second radio advertisement announcing the launch of this business.

6 How else would you advertise your business?

7 The household is the obvious market to target. Can you suggest two other areas this furniture rental idea might be marketable in?

8 What factors should you take into account when deciding the yearly rental charge?

TASK 2

1 What is meant by 'desk research'?

2 What is a point of sale display? Describe one you have seen.

3 Why do you think the price of a product is sometimes lowered as sales begin to fall at the end of the product life-cycle?

TASK 3

CRISPS GET HEALTH CONSCIOUS!

Once upon a time, there were only plain crisps with a little blue bag of salt. These were sold mainly in pubs to get people to drink more. It was some time before they were widely available for sale in shops and supermarkets. Then the market blossomed and different crisp flavours started to appear. Cheese and onion, beef and tomato, salt and vinegar, roast chicken are all favourites. More recently, we've seen hamburger flavour and an enterprising Welshman marketed hedgehog crisps – one shudders to think what might have been in these! Enjoyable though it may be to eat crisps, the salt and the high fat content probably mean that they aren't good for you. No problem – along came the low fat crisp to ease your conscience. Not really healthy food – but an improvement.

1 One of the most important things in marketing is to know to whom you are selling. The market can be segmented by age, social class, part of the country or by the attitudes people have. Look at the six types of snack and say at whom you think each is aimed. Based on your answer, suggest one place where each could be advertised.

2 It could be argued that the hula hoops could be in another market apart from that for food. In which market do you think they could also be?

3 The range of flavours of crisps seems always to be increasing. Why would this make it very difficult for a new company with only one flavour to exist in the crisp market?

TASK 4

MARKETING FOOTBALL

The Football League is concerned about the poor image the game has and the way attendances at matches have been affected over the years. Your group has been asked to prepare a report, based on evidence you have gathered, showing how you would market a local league club in such a way as to increase the number of people in the 12–16 age group who attend matches.

Group work

Your group should consider:
a an analysis of the problem.
b pricing policy.
c the way the club could be advertised and promoted.
d other ideas to attract 12–16 year olds.

Finally, the results should be presented to the rest of the class.

TASK 5

Protect your family and your home...

this could be your child!

fit **SAFECOAT** safety film to glass for under £10.00 (960mm x 2mts.)

For further information and free sample send an 18 pence stamp with name and address to:

Plastic Safety Coatings Ltd.

Solar House, New Street, Petworth, West Sussex GU28 0AS

Please quote ref: GH

The content of advertisments is usually either 'informative' or 'persuasive'. Some adverts contain more of one than the other.

1 Look at the advertisement above and list those points which are persuasive and those which are informative.

2 Look through newspapers or magazines and try to find one which is wholly informative and one which is wholly persuasive.

TASK 6

BOOKS FOR KIDS

As a pair of teachers who were fed up with teaching, Fred and Alice were about to leave their schools. The problem was they had no experience of any other jobs, so they had to find something which would allow them to use the experience they had developed in teaching. They decided to set up an educational book shop. They knew that most parents were concerned about their children's education and study aids and guides were selling well. In addition to this there were a great number of reading schemes and maths schemes for primary children. They felt they could offer specialist advice as well as offering, in one shop, a very wide range of educational books.

They obtained shop premises in a newly built shopping precinct in Stafford and, with the aid of bank loans, obtained a very good selection of books. They then found that they were not allowed to offer reduced price books, so they had to sell them at the same price as their competitors. It was therefore essential that they considered the marketing of their shop and its services very carefully. You have been asked to help.

1 At first, they thought they would call the shop 'Books for Kids'. Explain why you think this is a good or bad choice.

2 Design another name for the shop, suitable for display outside.

3 You want to make the first day of opening a special event. You have decided to offer cheese and wine to all adult customers and orange squash and a chocolate biscuit to all children. You estimate about 300 adults and 200 children will come into the shop. Approximately how much would this promotion cost? Show your calculations. (You will need to make estimates on problems like how many pounds of cheese you will need and how many glasses you can get out of a bottle of wine.)

4 You have contacted the headteacher of the local comprehensive school who has agreed to place your advert in the school magazine. This will cost you £30. You agree to do this. How can you decide whether this is an effective form of advertising?

5 It is always important to know in which markets you are operating so that you can provide appropriate services. As well as selling books, which other services or products do you think parents and children would want from such a shop?

Consumer Protection

No problems – most of the time!

When you buy a product like a radio or purchase a service like a new hair style, there is a chance that something may go wrong. Consumer protection sets out to help consumers with problems and tries to show them what to do if something does go wrong. You must remember that many millions of purchases are made every day without problems. Even when there is a difficulty, many shops will replace goods without argument. When you buy cheap items and find them faulty, it may not be worth taking them back as the bus fare may come to more than the item – although your legal rights are the same as they are with expensive goods.

Research before you buy

Many problems can be avoided if you do some research before you buy goods or services. One way is to ask friends or neighbours to recommend traders to you – this is particularly useful if you want to use services like builders or plumbers.

Which?

About one million people subscribe to a monthly magazine called *Which?* This is published by the Consumers' Association and it tests a wide range of goods and services each month. It accepts no advertising and is completely independent of all traders. It does not even accept from manufacturers the products to be tested but buys them in the normal way. In each product area it will recommend a 'best buy'. Copies of these magazines are available in your local library for reference.

Trade associations

Another way of checking that your trader is sound is to see if he/she is a member of a trade association. For example, many travel agents are members of the Association of British Travel Agents (ABTA) and they contribute to a fund which is used to pay the debts of any of its members who stop trading. This is a safeguard for holidaymakers and makes them more confident about using travel agency services in general. Such associations also have 'codes of practice' which have set ways of dealing with disputes between customers and traders.

As you can see, it is often possible to avoid problems before you start but sometimes things will still go wrong.

What have you the right to expect?

If you buy goods like clothing, records or computers they should be:

Which?

of merchantable quality – this means 'good enough to do the job for which they are designed'.

as described – a leather jacket should not be plastic.

fit for the purpose made known to the seller – if you ask for a glue to fix plastic, it should do so.

If the goods you buy fail under any of the above then you may be able to get your money back, have a replacement or a repair. Exactly what will happen does vary from case to case but remember you are not entitled to claim if:

you have just changed your mind and now don't want the item.

you have damaged the item.

If you buy a service like a TV repair or a new hair style, then you are entitled to expect that it is done:

with reasonable skill.

within a reasonable time.

for a reasonable fee.

The problem is, of course, what is 'reasonable'? It is usually best to state exactly what you are expecting to be done, by when, and for how much and get the trader to agree.

Still got problems?

The Office of Fair Trading (OFT) has encouraged many organisations to set codes of practice which establish how disputes can be dealt with. These often involve going to arbitration. The arbitrator is an independent person who will look at both sides of the case and give a decision which both parties then have to accept.

If you don't want to go to arbitration you can take your problem to the County Court. Claims of less than £500 can be settled quite quickly by a court registrar rather than a judge. Claims up to £5000 will have a full court hearing.

Other help is available from:

your local council's environmental health officer if the problems are to do with unfit food or dirty shops.

the Trading Standards Officer if prices are misleading or goods are not described properly.

the Citizens' Advice Bureau (CAB) for general help on what to do or who to contact.

Watch out for these signs

'We take no responsibility for your goods whilst they are being dry cleaned'. This is an exclusion clause. These may not be valid – traders must take reasonable care of your belongings.

'No Refunds'. This is actually illegal – tell your trading standards officer about it.

'20-year guarantee'. Do you think the firm will last that long?

Pressure groups

As well as publishing reports on goods and services, the Consumers' Association also tries to put pressure on the government to pass laws which will help the consumer. In the same way, manufacturers may try to stop the government passing a law which might increase their costs and reduce their sales.

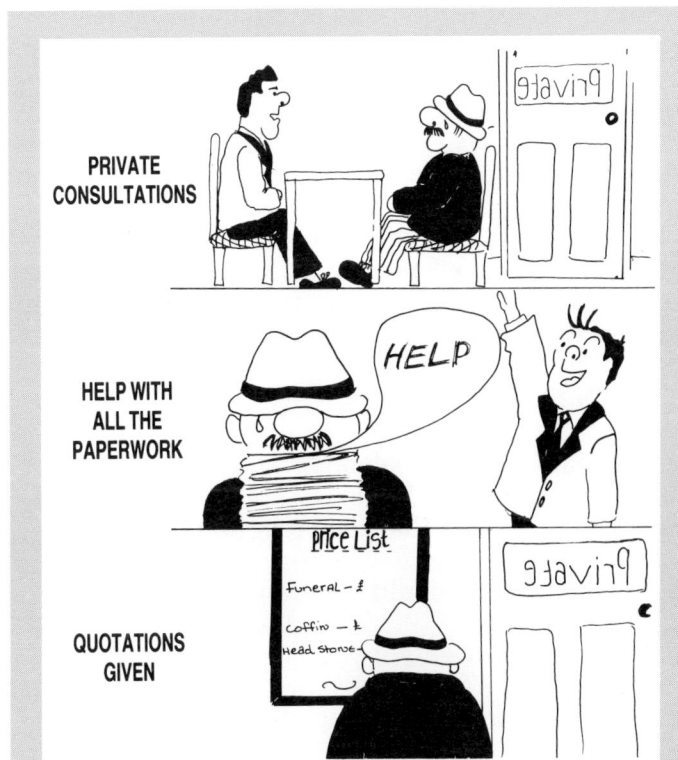

Code of practice – funeral directors

The Office of Fair Trading is keen to develop codes of practice to protect the consumer. Shown above are some of the points covered by such a code for funeral directors. When people die there is a tendency for relatives to forget to look for value for money in a funeral. Many people would not bother to get estimates. This code should help people get a better deal, even when arranging a funeral.

Questions

1 Think about the problems you could have if you employ a firm of carpet cleaners. List six points you think should be covered by a code of practice for carpet cleaners.

IT ▶ DESKTOP

2 Present on a piece of A4 your code of practice for firms selling franchises.

If you think about the issue of inflammable foam in furniture you can see the problems. The Consumers' Association wants the government to impose standards to improve safety. Manufacturers, whilst concerned with safety, know that large price increases will reduce sales. Both groups put pressure on the government to consider their point of view.

In this area of consumer protection, TV programmes like 'Watchdog' and 'That's Life' act as pressure groups in trying to get manufacturers and retailers to behave responsibly.

POINTS TO REMEMBER

★ Do some research before you buy.

★ Give the retailer the chance to help.

★ Remember you could be wrong!

★ Enforce your rights if you need to.

★ Pressure groups can bring about change.

Outline the rights you have in the following situations.

1 You buy a pullover but when you get home you decide you do not like the colour.

2 You go into a self-service shop and buy a glue to repair a damaged vase. You do not speak to anybody in the shop. When you get home the glue does not work.

3 You buy a new watch. As you go out of the shop you take it off your wrist to show it to a friend. It accidentally falls on the floor and stops working.

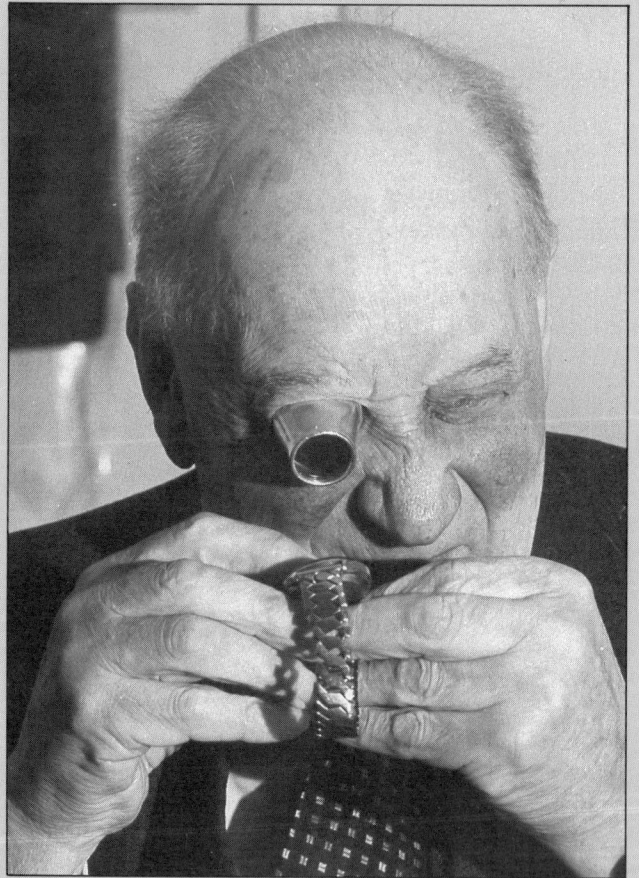

Group activity

1 Discuss, in groups of three, what you think is 'reasonable' for the following:
   a The time taken to repair a watch.
   b The cost of repairing a pair of shoes.

IT ▶ WORDPRO

2 Your group is responsible for providing a training leaflet for students who work only on Saturdays in a hardware shop. What main points of advice would you give them so that you could reduce the number of customers who return goods?

TASK 1

Convictions under the Trade Descriptions Acts year ending 30 September 1986

Reported cases 1985–86	Trade Descriptions Acts					
	False description of goods		False price claimed		False statements about services	
	Numbers	Fines £	Numbers	Fines £	Numbers	Fines £
Goods						
Food and drink..............................	97	46,600	26	9,650	—	—
Footwear, clothing and textiles..	199	93,329	6	3,615	—	—
Furniture and floor covering.......	20	14,060	2	860	—	—
Household appliances...................	43	24,985	8	4,670	—	—
Toilet requisites, soaps, detergents.....................................	12	4,565	2	465	—	—
Solid and liquid fuels......................	20	5,755	7	1,455	—	—
Motor vehicles and accessories .	523	298,075	8	5,830	—	—
Others..	318	158,261	31	12,450	—	—
Services						
Home repairs and improvements	—	—	—	—	5	1,520
Repairs and servicing to motor vehicles...	—	—	—	—	17	10,805
Other repairs and cleaning...........	—	—	—	—	7	2,950
Holidays, entertainment and accommodation..........................	—	—	—	—	5	5,150
Public utilities, professional and general services...........................	—	—	—	—	142	44,365
Totals..	1,232	645,630	90	38,995	176	64,790

Look at the table above showing criminal prosecutions achieved under consumer protection law in 1986.

1 How many successful prosecutions were there for people falsely describing:
   a food and drink?
   b household appliances?
   c home repairs and improvements?
   d holidays, entertainment and accommodation?

2 In which category were there most prosecutions?

3 What was the total amount of fines paid by people who described goods and services incorrectly?

4 What was the average fine imposed on people who incorrectly described motor vehicles and accessories?

5 What was the average fine imposed on people who incorrectly described repairs and servicing to motor vehicles?

6 Why does the table not show the full extent to which goods are being wrongly described?

IT ▶ SPREADSHEET

7 a Present the above table as a spreadsheet showing the average fine in each category.
   b On average, which offence attracted:
      i the lowest fine?
      ii the highest fine?
   c Can you suggest two reasons for these differences?

TASK 2

1 What sort of information can be found in *Which?* magazine?

2 What is an exclusion clause?

3 With what does a trading standards officer deal?

4 What should a code of practice offer a consumer?

TASK 3

Imagine. . .
   You have recently had a new chair delivered after a delay of two months. This was to be expected as you were told the furniture was made to order. As you were out when it was delivered it was left with a neighbour. When you unwrapped it you found there was a small chip in one of the legs.
   Write a letter to Furniture World of 78 Sembledown Road, Newcastle-upon-Tyne, saying what you would like done.

IT ▶ WORDPRO

Try to compose your letter straight onto a word processor, without handwriting a draft first.

Transport

Alternative forms of transport

In business, we need to understand the importance of transporting goods or people from one place to another. Business managers will need to find the most appropriate method – this may not be the cheapest or the quickest, but the most 'cost-effective', i.e. the best value for money. Often, moving goods or people will require more than one form of transport to be used. For example, aeroplanes are very quick but they do not offer a door to door delivery service as does road transport. Before choosing which method of transport to use, the business manager will consider the following:

The cost: This depends on the type of transport and on some of the points below.

How urgent the delivery is: Fresh food, flowers and medical supplies often have to be moved very quickly, whilst it may not matter if tinned food or machinery is delayed because a cheaper method of transport is used.

How far the journey is: For short journeys road transport is often the cheapest; for longer journeys other methods of transport may be better value.

Where suitable terminals are: For example, are there railway stations, airports or ports available to use?

The type of goods being moved: Are they perishable, dangerous, bulky, heavy? It may be thought wise to move dangerous goods like poisonous chemicals by the quickest possible method, even if it is the most expensive.

Published timetables or charters: Using a service with a published timetable, like a daily road delivery, may be quite cheap because a load will be shared. On the other hand, if you hire a special vehicle this may be more expensive but more flexible.

Road transport

Road transport offers a door-to-door service and is often used to complete the final part of a journey. It is the most flexible method because it offers a wide range of specialised vehicles, like coaches, cement mixers, oil tankers and car transporters. It is particularly quick over short distances.

There are, however, several problems faced in road transport. The loads which vehicles can carry are limited both in weight and width. Delays can be caused by roadworks, traffic jams and bad weather and lorry drivers' hours of work are limited by law.

The cost of a single journey from London to New York by Concorde is about £1400 and the journey takes four hours to cover the 3000 miles. Concorde carries about 100,000 people per year.

Question

IT ▶ SPREADSHEET

1 How much does British Airways take in fares on Concorde in a year?

2 How much does one passenger pay per mile travelled.

3 Calculate the cost per mile of a local journey you have taken by bus or train.

4 How does the cost of this compare with travelling by Concorde?

Question

Barges on canals are a slow method of transport. If you had to promote the use of canal transport to industry, what would you suggest are its three main advantages?

Air transport

Air transport offers a fast service with a high level of security but it can be disrupted by bad weather and sometimes it is too expensive to be economic. Despite this, the demand for air transport is increasing.

Nowadays, it is quite common for people to fly between places within the United Kingdom and 'shuttle' services operate between many cities. In addition, many thousands of people take package holidays abroad, making airports very busy during the summer months.

Probably the most important market to the airlines is the business class. Most airline advertisements on TV are trying to attract business managers away from other companies. The problem would seem to be that one airline is much the same as another. They have to advertise the width of seats or the services provided by the cabin staff rather than point to any really important benefits of flying with them.

Water transport

Sea transport is very important to international trade as most of our visible imports and exports are carried by ships. A wide variety of sea transport is available which includes oil tankers, container ships, roll-on-roll-off ferries and fishing vessels.

Inland canals are not widely used by industry because it is relatively slow form of transport and the network of canals is limited. However, there is a growing leisure market for canal boats and this is causing more canals to be brought back into use.

Rail transport

Rail transport in Britain is provided by British Rail (BR) and by Passenger Transport Authorities (e.g. Merseyside, Tyne and Wear).

The main BR services are provided by separate divisions:

Passengers: Inter-City, Provincial and Network SouthEast.

Railfreight: e.g. moving coal.

Parcels: e.g. Red Star Parcels and Post Office contracts.

Freightliner: movement of goods in containers.

Travellers fare: selling food at stations.

As in many countries, the railways are subsidised by the government and in 1988 about £809 million was given to improve efficiency and the quality of service.

Railways continue to have the problem of deciding whether to provide trains in rural areas where there are few passengers. The network has declined gradually but there is now evidence of a new lease of life for railways in areas like the London Docklands, and the Channel Tunnel project indicates that there are still profitable investments in railways.

The problem of congestion

A major issue facing Britain's transport system in the 1990s is that of peak-time congestion of our road, rail and air networks.

The changing size of buses

Pictured above is a common sight in many of our cities and towns. The familiar double decker buses working alongside, or being replaced by, a minibus service.

Questions

1 When do you think double-decker buses are more useful than the mini-bus service?

2 Why do you think that more mini-buses are being brought into use?

Write a report on the quality of local bus services on one route in your area. You should include the types of buses used, how frequent they are, whether the service is reliable, and what the policy is on fares (is it a flat rate?). Finally you should make suggestions as to how the service could be improved. Remember that in writing a report like this you will need to gather information or ask other people their view, because your experience of what the buses are like may not be the same as others.

No sooner have new roads like the M25 around London been built than they are overcrowded. Rail travel into many cities at rush hours is made unbearable by the crowds who cram into trains. During the summer delays are frequent at airports as aeroplanes try to gain access to the crowded air space over Europe.

As the rail network has a great deal of spare capacity off peak, it would make sense to move much of the heavy freight off our roads and move it by rail. However, loading and unloading goods for their final destination can increase costs.

To reduce the problems in towns, some councils make it very expensive to park and encourage park and ride schemes. Although they do reduce congestion they can be inconvenient for shoppers.

However, the solution of just building more and more roads or airports must be looked at very carefully. This is because some consideration should be given to the people who have new airports or roads built near them. They often have to put up with the noise and other forms of pollution which are associated with improving transport systems.

It is interesting to see whether people's travelling habits can be altered by what they have to pay. For example, does increasing car parking fees or introducing motor tolls or increasing train fares keep people off these forms of transport?

Evidence would seem to suggest that such moves do have an initial effect but, gradually, people adjust to the higher costs and soon return to their usual forms of transport. Often these cost increases are just passed on in the form of higher prices for everybody.

POINTS TO REMEMBER

★ There are a number of factors to consider before choosing a method of transport.

★ Each method of transport has its own advantages and disadvantages.

★ Transport systems often link with one another.

TASK 1

Network SouthEast's share of the London commuter market

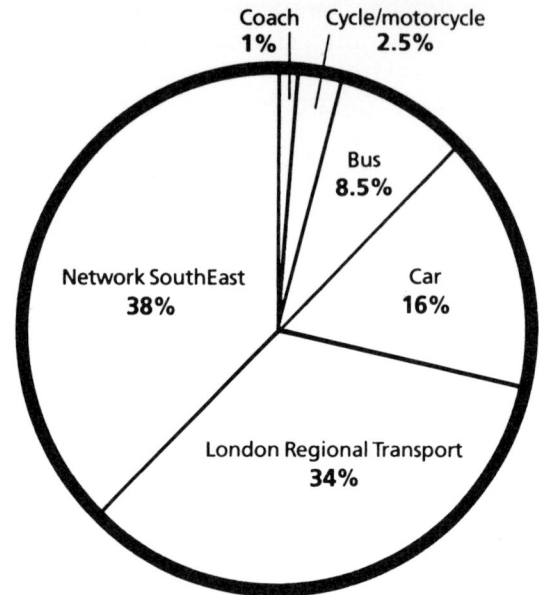

1 How do most of London's commuters get to work?

2 What percentage of commuters do not use cars?

3 16% of commuters still travel to work in London by car. This often causes traffic congestion. Suggest three things that could be done to stop people driving their cars into central London.

4 In 1986/87 the government gave £196m to Network SouthEast to operate train services. If this support was cut, what effect do you think it would have on:
a train fares?
b the use of cars?

TASK 2

ALL ON THE BUSES

IT ▶ WORDPRO

Your local council is considering making bus travel free and introducing park and ride schemes by increasing the local rates by 30 per cent per year per household. Business rates will also increase. In addition, car park charges in the city centre will be increased to £5 per visit. As the streets are congested parking meters will be discontinued and on street parking will be prohibited.

You have been asked to write a letter on behalf of the local chamber of commerce pointing out the problems these measures will cause for local businesses, delivery vans and sales representatives.

TASK 3

	ADVANTAGES	DISADVANTAGES
ROAD		
RAIL		
AIR		
SEA		
PIPELINE		

Draw up a grid as shown above and briefly outline the advantages and disadvantages of each method of transport. This should be done on a sheet of A4.

TASK 4

Which methods of transport would you consider most suitable for the following deliveries? You may have to use more than one method in each case:
a oil from the North Sea to Scotland.
b fresh flowers from Holland to Leeds.
c a human heart for transplant from Middlesborough to Harefield hospital.
d 20 tons of clay from Cornwall to Stoke on Trent.
e 200 new cars from Dagenham to Glasgow.
f oil from Kuwait to Milford Haven.
g diamonds from Amsterdam to London.
h steel for the Thames Barrier from the North East of England to London.
i grain from the USA to the USSR.
j flour from Manchester to Hull.

TASK 5

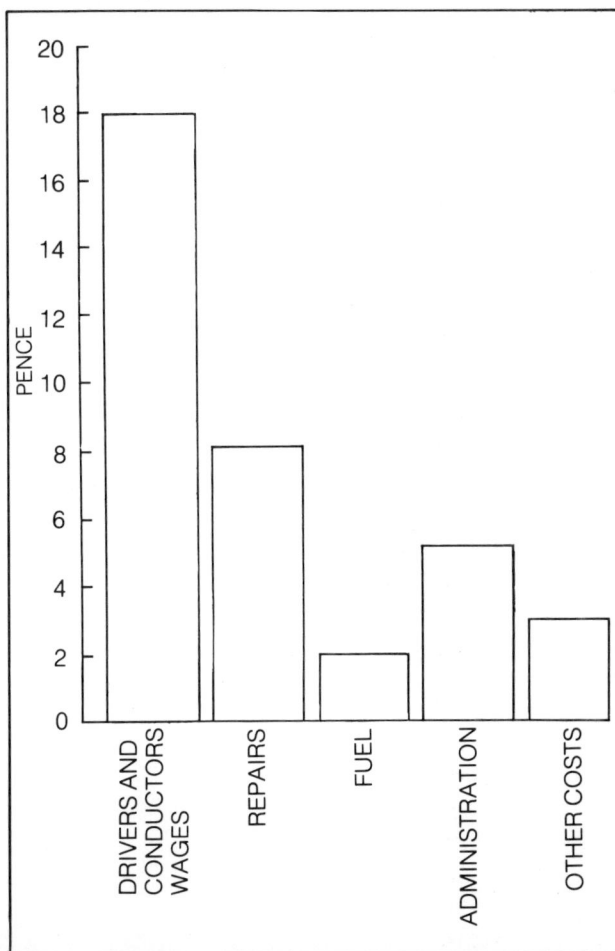

The cost of an average bus journey in a town is 36p per passenger. 30p is paid by the passenger and 6p is given as a subsidy by the local authority. The bar chart shows what the 36p pays for.

1 What percentage of the total fare is paid to drivers and conductors?

2 If fuel costs were to double, by how much would the fare have to go up to cover this increase?

3 If the cost of repairs was to increase by 25% what new fare would have to be charged to cover costs?

4 Give two reasons why a local authority should subsidise bus travel.

IT ▶ GRAPHICS

Taking into account the changes in questions 2 and 3 redraw the bar chart.

Investigating the ORGANISATIONAL Background

Business Objectives

Types of business: small firms

There are many different types of business, whether we classify them by size, by ownership or by what they do. You will know of lots of small firms – corner shops which sell everything and stay open late, window cleaners, local driving schools and many others. Some quite small premises are not really 'small businesses' at all. We use this term to describe who owns the firm, so a small shop or business unit is often really owned by a big company. For example, public houses are often owned by a brewery, estate agents are part of a local or national group, as are jewellers, betting shops and milk rounds.

Large companies

There are, of course, lots of well-known large companies. Supermarkets are usually owned by the large retail food chains like Sainsbury, Tesco, Safeway, etc. The House of Fraser owns many department stores; Shell and BP are major oil refiners and garage owners. Some of these firms are internationally owned and don't really belong to one country more than another. These are often referred to as 'multi-nationals'. All these business types have one thing in common – they set out to make a profit, by ensuring that total costs are less than total revenue.

Business costs

Costs comprise a whole range of things like interest charges on capital borrowed, costs of labour employed in wages and salaries, costs of goods bought in as stock to sell or process (often called 'raw materials' in manufacturing industry) and then the cost of fuel like coal, gas or electricity.

Sales revenue

Revenue is earned from the sale of goods or services. In retailing it comes from the sale of stock to a customer. In manufacturing, it is the money raised from the sale of component parts or finished goods. In commerce, revenue comes from payments for the service you provide. Banks make money from their lending and British Rail obtains revenue from its fares.

Maximising profits

If a firm is to make as large a profit as possible it must try to raise as much revenue as it can and, at the same time, try to keep its costs low.

Raising revenue

It will raise its revenue by trying to sell its goods (or services) at a high price and to sell as many as

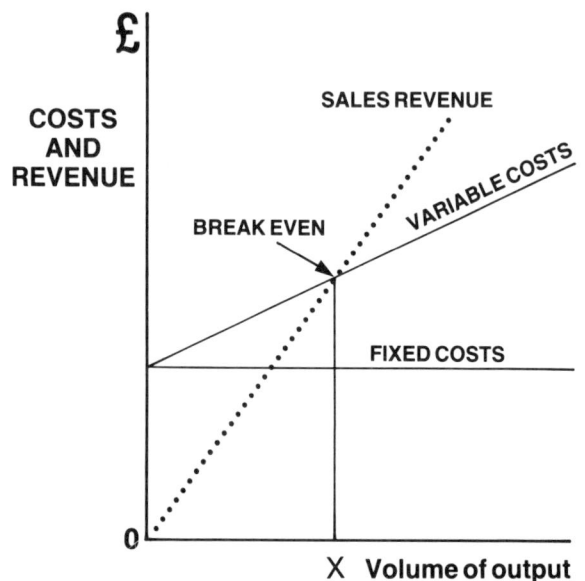

Break-even chart

The chart shows the fixed and variable costs for a firm plotted against its sales revenue. Point 'X' indicates the 'break-even' level of production.

Questions

1 What is meant by the term 'fixed costs'? Why do these not change as output increases?

2 Explain the shape of the curve for 'variable costs'.

3 How is 'sales revenue' found?

4 A company may not be operating at its 'break even' level of output. Explain why a firm might be operating:
   a to the left of point 'X' – i.e. below break-even.
   b to the right of the break-even point.
   In each case, what should the firm seek to do about its trading position?

it can. It will advertise to increase sales but, of course, advertising will raise its costs. Only some advertising will be worthwhile. Competition with other firms will tend to keep prices down. A firm must find the right balance between the amount it sells and the price it charges to maximise its profits.

Cutting costs

Cutting costs is also a matter of balance. A retailer must have enough stock to sell to attract and satisfy the customer. Manufacturing and distribution also need efficient handling of stocks and resources. Cutting the number employed is all very well to save costs but there must be enough labour to make the good or to serve the customer. An experienced business manager will know how to reduce costs through efficient management of resources without damaging the business.

What to do with the profit

We can regard profit as the payment which the business manager takes from the company as a reward for running the company. In a company, the shareholders, who are the owners, receive the profits as a payment on their shares called 'dividend'. There are other types of business which don't set out to maximise profits in this way but we will examine these in a later unit.

Re-investment in the business

In all cases, the owner(s) will set out to ensure the future success of the business. It is wise to ensure that some of the profit is kept back to improve the business in some way or, at least, to keep in the bank for a rainy day. If the profit is 're-invested' in the firm it will be used to buy new machinery, to replace or expand premises or to add to the capital employed. All sensible and successful businesses ensure that they re-invest in this way and only take the profit out of the firm when they are sure that adequate provision is made for the future.

POINTS TO REMEMBER

★ Many businesses set out to maximise profits and to distribute these profits as payments to the owners – in the case of a company, to the shareholders.

★ They do this by maximising their revenue and minimising their costs. It is a skill of management to get these balances right.

★ Most firms don't distribute all their profit to the owners; they 're-invest' in the future of the business.

£144m profit- yet another Cookson record

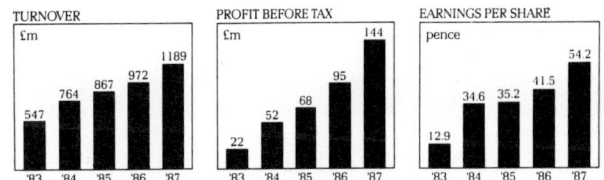

TURNOVER £m	PROFIT BEFORE TAX £m	EARNINGS PER SHARE pence
547, 764, 867, 972, 1189 ('83–'87)	22, 52, 68, 95, 144 ('83–'87)	12.9, 34.6, 35.2, 41.5, 54.2 ('83–'87)

a company which dominates every market to which it sets its mind and grows at a dazzling rate.

QUESTOR COLUMN, DAILY TELEGRAPH, MONDAY, FEBRUARY 22ND 1988.

	1987	1986
Turnover	£1189m	£972m + 22%
Profit before tax	£144m	£95m + 52%
Profit after tax	£93m	£59m + 58%
Earnings per ordinary share	54.2p	41.5p + 31%
Dividends per ordinary share	12.00p	8.75p + 37%

Cookson C

Copies of the annual report will be available from 25th April and may be obtained from the Company Secretary, Cookson Group plc, 14 Gresham Street, London, EC2V 7AT

Cookson Group plc

This advertisement was placed in national newspapers to tell members of the public and company shareholders how well the Cookson Group had performed in the trading year 1987.

Questions

1 Explain the terms:
   a Turnover.
   b Profit before tax.
   c Dividends per ordinary share.

2 How did these figures compare with 1986?

3 What can you conclude about the success of the company on the basis of the figures shown?

4 What other information would you like to have about the Cookson Group in order to give a full picture of their trading success?

TASK 1

BUSINESS OBJECTIVES

It is probably the case that a significant number of businesses do not have the maximisation of profit as their main aim.

1 Can you suggest alternative objectives for:
   a a sole trader who owns a plumbing business?
   b the Post Office?
   c a company which has just started business?
   d a multinational company like Unilever?
   e a retail co-operative shop?

TASK 2

CREATION AND DISTRIBUTION OF WEALTH

The diagram shows how a typical company in the food industry might create and distribute its profit. The company has 'total sales' of £308.8m. This figure has been broken down into:

Raw materials: these are all the things which a food firm might buy in order to manufacture the finished foodstuffs, e.g. flour, sugar, meat products, etc. Also included here are the cost of its electricity, fuel for its delivery vehicles and some of the taxes it has to pay. Total: £229.6m.

Added value: when the firm has manufactured and sold its finished food products, it has added a lot of 'value' to the raw materials it started with. Some of this value is its profit but, of course, a lot of it is absorbed in other costs of production – wages and other employee payments, interest on its loans, and the updating and replacement of equipment. Total: £79.2m.

Net profit: this is the figure which remains from the total sales revenue after all the costs of the firm have been covered. Total: £14.2m.

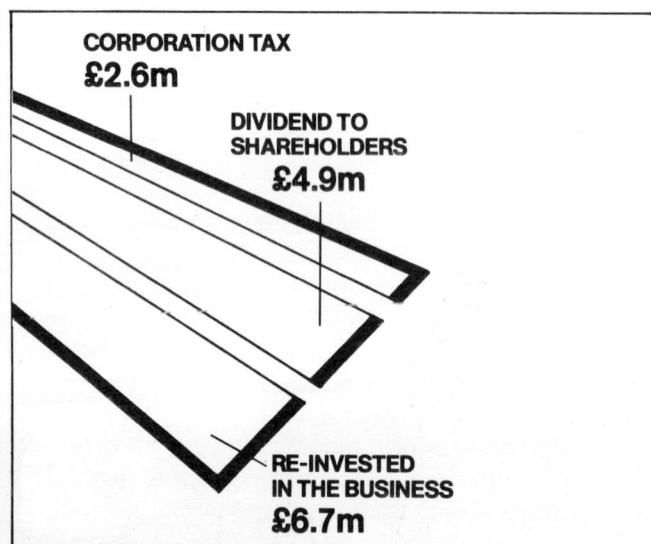

Wealth: its creation and distribution by a company

RAW MATERIAL, SERVICES, RATES, TAXES ON VEHICLES AND FUEL ETC. £229.6m

ADDED VALUE £79.2m

TOTAL SALES £308.8m

Salaries	£39.2m
Pensions	£6.2m
National Insurance	£3.8m
Welfare, including redundancy contributions	£1.5m
Interest paid on borrowed money	£10.7m
Replacement of worn-out equipment	£3.6m
Net Profit	£14.2m

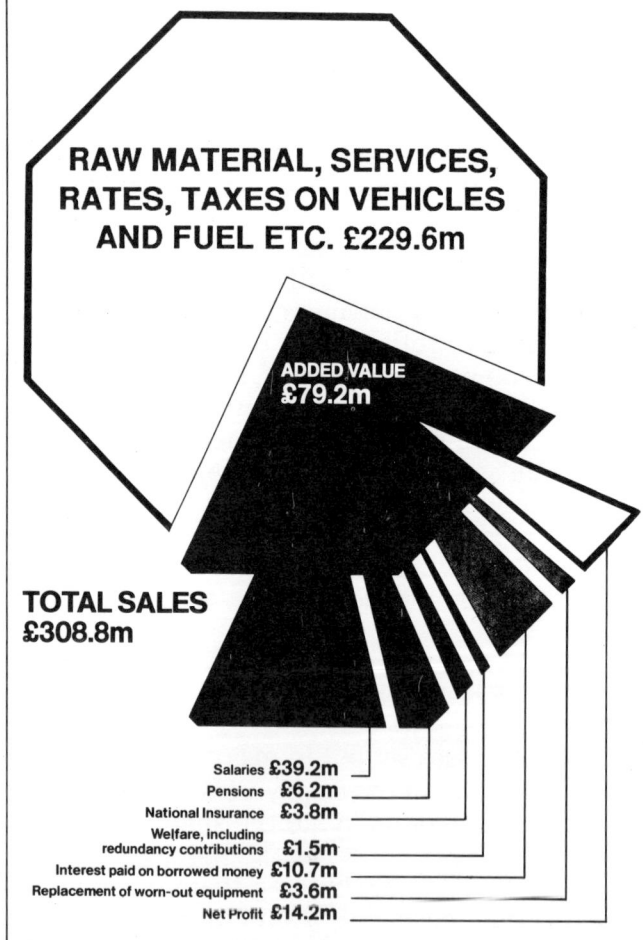

CORPORATION TAX £2.6m

DIVIDEND TO SHAREHOLDERS £4.9m

RE-INVESTED IN THE BUSINESS £6.7m

What happens to the net profit?

1 What were the total sales of this company?

2 How much did shareholders receive in dividends?

3 How much did the government take in tax?

4 What is the purpose of reinvesting £6.7m in the business?

TASK 3

'TREE LOPPERS'

Two YTS trainees have enjoyed a course in basic forestry at their local college. They decide to set up in business as experts in tree 'surgery' – the felling, lopping and pruning of trees. Although they are sensible people neither feels able to make many business decisions and, at the end of their first successful year, they come to you for advice.

During the year they concentrated their service on private houses in the wealthier part of town. They did some farm work but are unsure about the potential of this. The local council gave them no work at all.

They provide the following figures:

EXPENDITURE:
Open lorry (second-hand)	£ 1800
Powered chain saw	£ 300
Other saw and equipment	£ 200
Running costs	£ 600
Interest charges on bank loan	£ 200
Personal living expenses (both)	£10000

INCOME/REVENUE (after tax):
Payments from customers	£12500
Sale of wood	£ 3000

You are also told the following:

They calculate fees at £10 per hour, including the removal of all wood and branches.

They spend nothing on advertising and get all their custom at present from personal calls.

Their fees to farmers are £8 per hour but the jobs are much larger and so involve less travelling and wasted time looking for custom.

A larger lorry would greatly increase their speed of working. At present they are slowed down by their slow rate of removing wood and branches.

A second chain saw would occasionally be helpful.

IT ▶ WORDPRO

As a business consultant, you are asked to offer professional advice to the two trainees.

1 Look at the figures and calculate the profit made in their first year.

2 Produce a suitably headed report on the word processor, which offers sound advice on their business.
Classify your report under the headings of:
pricing policy.
advertising policy.
re-investment of profits.

3 In order to make final recommendations for next year, you need some further information. What other questions do you wish to ask to help with the second part of your report?

Managing a Business

Ownership and control: the shareholders

In a large company there is often a great difference between the ownership and the management of a business. The ownership is in the hands of the shareholders. In a private company these are often members of one family. In a public company, there may be many thousands of shareholders, unknown to each other. Indeed, quite often, the shares are held by institutions like insurance companies or investment trusts. The policies of the company are usually determined by a board of directors, elected by a majority of the shareholders. The directors are usually major shareholders and sometimes have a controlling interest in the firm.

The managers

In a company, the management is in the hands of senior officials appointed by the board of directors. There may be a managing director who has a major say in policy and in general management. Sometimes the other directors also have a management role – the financial director, the sales director, etc.

In a small firm, one person may be owner and manager, responsible for day-to-day activities and all decision-making. This is a demanding responsibility but at least there is no need to share the profits!

The role of the manager

It is possible to think of the role of the manager under several headings:

Financial management: deciding on prices to charge in order to maximise sales revenue; deciding on how to reduce costs without destroying the working of the business; organising loans and overdrafts; handling profits, dividends and investment; keeping accounts.

Managing people: getting the best out of the workforce; paying them fairly without awarding unaffordable wage increases; ensuring that working conditions are good; looking after general employee welfare; recruiting and training new staff.

Production management: in an industrial firm, making sure that production is steady and uninterrupted; ordering materials; meeting delivery dates; maintaining machinery and equipment; forward planning.

Management of sales and marketing: deciding on marketing policy; organising appropriate advertising; running a sales team; meeting customers.

The purpose of a business

To know what a business is we have to start with its *purpose*. There is only one valid definition of business: *to create a customer*.

It is the customer who determines what a business is. It is the customer alone whose willingness to pay for a good or for a service converts economic resources into wealth, things into goods.

What the customer thinks he or she is buying, what he or she considers value, is decisive – it determines what a business is, what it produces, and whether it will prosper. And what the customer buys and considers value is never a product. It is always utility – that is, what a product or service does for him or her.

Customers are the foundation of a business and keep it in existence. They alone give employment. To supply the wants and needs of a customer, society entrusts wealth-producing resources to the business enterprise.

Management
Peter Drucker

The article above states clearly the view that business does not exist just to make a profit. It argues that business exists to sell goods or services to customers. If this is successful, then the firm will make a profit.

Questions

1 In a small group, discuss this view of the purpose of a business. Find some examples where you think that the success of a firm has depended on pleasing the customers and satisfying their wants.

2 Can you think of successful businesses which do not seem to bother much about what the customers want?

3 Do you think that firms set out to make profits or do they set out to 'create a customer'? Does this really amount to the same thing?

How managers make decisions

All these jobs vary from business to business. They would be different in an insurance company and a steel works. However, the basic requirements of management are broadly the same. The six stages of decision-making:

The first stage of the decision-making process is to identify the nature of the problem you need to solve. What outcome is required? Whom will it affect?

The second stage is to get hold of all the relevant information and then to sort it into some kind of sensible pattern. Which bits are important? What else do you need to know? This may involve a lot of consultation.

Stage three probably requires the manager to analyse the issues involved – to take the problem and the relevant information and to begin to think out alternative solutions.

Stage four is to make the decision on the basis of the problem, the information and the analysis.

The fifth stage is the implementation of the decision. Putting it into effect means that various people must be consulted and people lower down the mangement scale instructed in their own role in making the required changes happen.

Finally, a good manager will evaluate his or her decision. Did it work? Could it have been improved? Was it put into effect well?

Management styles – what is a 'good' manager?

It is sometimes thought that good managers are clear thinking and ruthless. On the contrary, many very successful managers care about people a great deal. They have to make decisions and solve problems, but very few do so without being sensitive to the problems of people.

Lessons from abroad

Perhaps this has been the greatest lesson which we have had to learn in Britain as we compete with firms in Germany, Japan and elsewhere overseas, where management styles are often quite different. Managers dress like their employees, share canteen facilities, and they consult and listen to advice from others in the company. They are not a class apart. They see themselves as employees like everyone else, but employees with particular management skills.

Profit-sharing

One way in which managers may wish to involve their employees more in the affairs of their company is through a 'profit-sharing' scheme.

This means that the workforce is given a share in the profits of the company when the trading results are announced at the end of the year. In some cases they are simply given a bonus in the wage packet or salary cheque, in others they are given 'free' shares in the company.

Question

One of the charts shows the man's blood pressure is rising. What three pieces of advice would you give him to help him make decisions and keep his blood pressure low?

Are you a good decision-maker?

Think of a decision you have made recently.

Questions

1 Was it a decision to spend some money? Or perhaps it was a decision on how to organise a disco or plan a holiday?

2 How did you set about your decision? Did you set yourself an objective and then plan accordingly? Did you discuss your ideas with others and listen to their objections and their advice? Were you happy with the decision you made or will you change your mind next time?

3 Make a brief list of some of the things you think you have learned about being a good decision-maker.

In either case, the employees are made to feel part of the organisation and they have a shared interest in the company doing well.

Large companies like the John Lewis Partnership, ICI, Kodak and Boots have done this for a number of years. New firms in Britain are now joining them, including Habitat, Marks and Spencer, Bulmers and several of the banks.

POINTS TO REMEMBER

★ All businesses, large and small, need to be managed. Decisions have to be made regarding long term policy and day-to-day problems.

★ Management decisions come under several different headings – financial, people, production, sales and marketing and others.

★ Management often involves the skills of decision-making – stating the problem, getting hold of good information, working out alternative solutions, making the decision, implementing it and evaluating the results.

TASK 1

Conder International is a privately owned engineering group based near Winchester. Its 1976 turnover was £50.3m, its wage bill £7.3m, to which its profit sharing scheme added £1.3m. Shareholders' funds were £4.8m.

Each quarter, every company in the group (there are about a dozen) separately calculates its own trading profit, defined as the profit earned after paying wages and all other costs, depreciation included.

From the trading profit is deduced interest on shareholders' money at a commercial rate, normally 15%. The resultant figure (after a further small deduction to finance profit-sharing for the central services staff) is genially known as "smog" profit, and split 50:50 between the company and the employees.

The company's share (half the smog profit plus the 15% on shareholders' money) is its pre-tax profit, available after tax, for distribution or retention.

The employees' share (half the smog profit) is divided among employees and paid in cash at the end of the second month after the trading quarter. The division is in proportion to basic salary, subject to a factor that increases the share of those for whom some extra effort is not directly reflected in wages: the factor is 1 for employees paid overtime, 1½ for those not paid overtime

even if they work it, and 2 for directors, whose extra effort is reckoned to include ulcers.

The direct benefit of the scheme to the company is that the relatively high proportion, 50%, of the smog profit that goes to employees gives them a powerful reason to increase efficiency and avoid waste – the company has a slogan "you pay half".

Even so, the scheme falls well short of the ideal of those who claim that profit should be split in proportion to the relative inputs of capital and labour. These can reasonably be measured by the respective costs of hiring the two factors of production; and at Conder labour's wage bill is over £7m, capital's "wage bill" – i.e., 15%, on shareholders' funds – a little over £700,000. So, given that depreciation is deducted before the smog profit is arrived at, employees could argue for a split 90:10 in their favour. But, says chairman Mr Robin Cole, the 50:50 split "is generally accepted as fair". The 18% that it adds to wages is certainly more than is common in profit-sharing schemes.

CONDER INTERNATIONAL

1 Note down the main elements of the scheme outlined in the article above.

2 Write a summary of your view of the scheme, its benefits and possible pitfalls.

I☰T ▶ WORDPRO

Use a word processor to present your summary.

TASK 2

WESTERNBOX LIMITED

Westernbox is a limited company with 1100 employees on three factory sites – Taunton, Shrewsbury and Carlisle. The company is privately owned by the Turner family, who started the business in Taunton over 50 years ago.

The firm makes corrugated cardboard containers for sale to all sorts of firms as packaging – what we all know as cardboard boxes. They buy brown paper from paper mills all round the country and turn it into corrugated cardboard and then form it into flat box shapes for sale to customers according to their order. Everything is sold to order and to the customer's specification. It is the job of the sales representatives to go out to get these orders, which the factory must deliver on time.

This 'pyramid' shows the senior management positions in the company. The next line of management might be called 'upper-middle' and then 'middle' management.

1 Try to place the following in the management structure: credit controller, cost accountant, training officer, factory managers, progress planners, design manager, services manager, transport manager.

2 Draw the complete management pyramid and, for each management position, write a brief note to explain what role you think each might perform.

MANAGEMENT STRUCTURE			
	Company President : John Turner BOARD OF DIRECTORS William Turner Chairman and Managing Director		Senior Management
Jane Turner Financial Director	George Turner Company Secretary	Tony Stevens Production and Sales Director	Upper-Middle Management
Accountant Company Solicitor	Personnel Officer Marketing Manager	Production Manager	Middle Management

TASK 3

WESTERNBOX – A PROBLEM WITH EASTER EGGS

Westernbox have a customer who wishes to order a container in which to pack 27 easter eggs. The materials and chargable costs for this box price it at £370 per 1000, which is the smallest order Westernbox will do. In order to make the Easter market, the boxes must be delivered to the customer by 1st October.

The production manager says that this is absolutely impossible. The schedules are already planned and the earliest delivery time from the factory would be 1st November. The marketing manager says that the order will lead to more business with the firm in the future. The customer is arguing for a price of £350 per 1000, which he says he can get elsewhere. The financial director would be prepared to cut the profit on this order and supply it a bit cheaper, if she can be sure that it will lead to more business, but she wants guarantees.

Role-play

Imagine that you are the managing director of Westernbox. You have called a meeting of the senior management team to discuss this order. Other members of your group are playing the roles of production manager, marketing manager, financial director and customer (who is not at the meeting, but can be called in).

Each 'actor' in the team should jot down the main points to argue. Play out the situation and see if you can resolve the problem. Someone should record what you agree. Did you take the order? At what price?

Raising Finance

Business managers need money when they are about to start a business and also when they are ready to expand. The first is sometimes called 'startup capital'. It will usually be required when the firm is small – big companies rarely start from scratch. However, large companies also need to raise funds when they want to get bigger – usually because they are successful, but sometimes because they are struggling to survive and need to borrow in order to make changes.

Entrepreneurs

When we refer to the 'owner' of a business we often think of a particular person. Sometimes there is really a group of people who are joint owners. We have a special term for them – 'entrepreneurs'. The entrepreneur is the person who is behind the business, whose job is usually to find the money, set up the premises and undertake the legal activities. It is also the privilege of the entrepreneur(s) to take the profit. As you can see, in a big company, the entrepreneurs are the shareholders, but the business probably didn't start that way.

Starting up

Most businesses start with a business idea. Either someone leaves a job to start out on his or her own in the same line of busines or perhaps they want a fresh challenge. It is likely that only four sources of money are open to them:
personal savings.
a bank loan.
a loan from a friend or 'backer'.
some kind of government grant or loan.

Obtaining loans

Most people will need a bank loan to start. Almost always, the bank will want to know a lot about the business idea and the person behind it. You will almost certainly need to put up some money of your own, even if only as a guarantee of your commitment to the venture.

In the US there is much more private backing of new businesses (called 'venture capital') but this is relatively unusual in Britain. The entrepreneur may be able to interest friends and relations in putting some money forward to add to the capital available.

The government is quite keen in some areas to make money available to those wishing to start a business of their own. In some parts of the country, many people who have been made redundant from traditional industries like steelmaking have been able to use their redundancy pay to start a small

Who is the entrepreneur?

Sometimes all is not what it seems. The friendly street corner grocery store may not be owned by the jovial chap in the white coat. Your local newsagent may be part of a regional or national chain. The local pub is almost certainly owned by a brewery and you may already be a shareholder in your local supermarket.

Questions

1 Suggest four ways in which 'Small Fry Ltd' may have raised capital when it first started trading.

2 When would the firm be allowed to advertise for shareholders?

3 Can you find out the names of companies which are owned by Unilever plc, or any other large company?

business and the government has helped with further grants.

Business expansion

Once a business is up and running it may want to expand. It may need new machinery, bigger or more premises, or it may want to branch out in a new direction. There are really three ways of doing this:
re-investing its own profits,
issuing (more) shares,
borrowing from a bank.

Re-investment

No well-run business fails to put some funds into reserve when it is making profits. It would be very silly to pay out all profits to the owners of share-holders. This money can be used to finance ex-pansion and a carefully-run firm will ensure this goes on all the time.

Share issue

Sometimes a major expansion scheme will require more capital than the firm can afford. If the business is not run as a company, this will often be the time to issue shares. These will be sold to people who are known (a private company) or to the general public (a public company). If an existing company wishes to expand, it may issue more shares to raise capital. It may sell more shares to its existing shareholders ('rights' issue) or it may simply advertise to the public at large (public subscription).

Government financial assistance to firms

The government tries to increase national product-ivity by encouraging firms to invest and create new jobs. In regions of high unemployment, grants are offered. Some of the measures are specially targeted at small businesses and some of the funding is provided by the EC.

Rural industries

Help is provided for firms who wish to set up in rural areas – mainly through small factories and workshops. The Council for Small Industries in Rural Areas (COSIRA) provides advice and loans to small businesses.

Small firms

The government is keen to encourage small firms and has introduced measures to provide incentives and reduce the burdens of taxation and red tape. Tax relief is offered to people who will risk investing in new firms and to those who are unemployed who wish to start a business.

Regional Policy

The problem of economic imbalance between regions is partly due to the steady decline of older industries like coal, steel, shipbuilding and textiles and partly due to the tendency of newer and expand-ing industries to develop elsewhere. This has left the traditional industrial areas with higher rates of

---

PICTURE FRAMING FRANCHISE £42,000

Group discussion – then make your own decision

Many advertisements for people to take out loans, after taking advice from their bank manager, often seem to have a happy ending – but how many of us have the courage to give up a job and make the effort to start our own business? Consider the following case.

Barbara and Kevin Paige are both aged 30. They have two children, Heather and Jamie who are six and eight years old. Barbara is expecting another child in five months time. Kevin has had a fairly successful career to date as a biochemist earning £13,000 per year. Barbara earns slightly more than him selling advertising space in a local newspaper. It took her three years to find this job, which she enjoys.

Kevin is particularly fed up with his job but, if he leaves it his knowledge is likely to become out of date and he is not likely to be able to return to it at the same salary level.

Kevin and Barbara have been considering taking up a franchise on picture framing in Edinburgh, where they live. They have managed to save £2000 and would have to use this and borrow £40,000 to obtain the franchise. This would cover all their training, setting up and running costs for the first six months. They have been told by existing franchise holders that they can expect to be earning £25,000 per year after two years, if all goes well. This figure could double in the following years as the shop gets a good reputation.

In order to do this, both of them will have to give up their jobs. To get the bank loan, they will have to put up their house as security. If the business fails they will lose the house.

Questions

1 List all the advantages and disadvantages of taking the franchise.

2 If you were in their position what would you do?

IT ▶ DESKTOP

3 Imagine that you have been commissioned as a graphic designer to design a block advertisement for a half-page advertisement in the *Edinburgh Daily Press* newspaper. This is to illustrate the picture-framing business and the excellent service it offers. Use A4 paper, landscape.

unemployment – South Wales, the North, Central Scotland and the West Midlands.

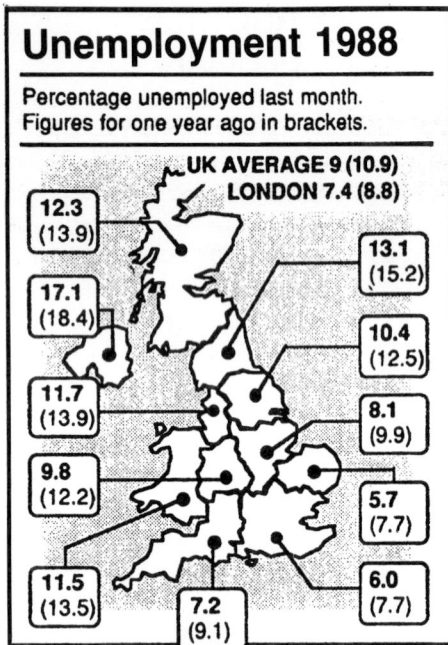

Unemployment 1988

Percentage unemployed last month.
Figures for one year ago in brackets.

UK AVERAGE 9 (10.9)
LONDON 7.4 (8.8)

12.3 (13.9)
13.1 (15.2)
17.1 (18.4)
10.4 (12.5)
11.7 (13.9)
8.1 (9.9)
9.8 (12.2)
5.7 (7.7)
11.5 (13.5)
7.2 (9.1)
6.0 (7.7)

To encourage firms to develop in these areas, grants are available for 'development' areas and 'intermediate' areas. All manufacturing industries and some service industries are eligible for regional development grants. The government will provide factories and workshops where firms are unsure about investing in them.

POINTS TO REMEMBER

★ Small firms starting up will need to have some initial funds available but will then use bank loans and other borrowed funds to raise the capital they need to start out.

★ Larger companies may also borrow from banks but are more likely to use their own profits for re-investment and to raise most of their capital for expansion from the issue of (more) shares.

★ The government assists industry with finance in several ways.

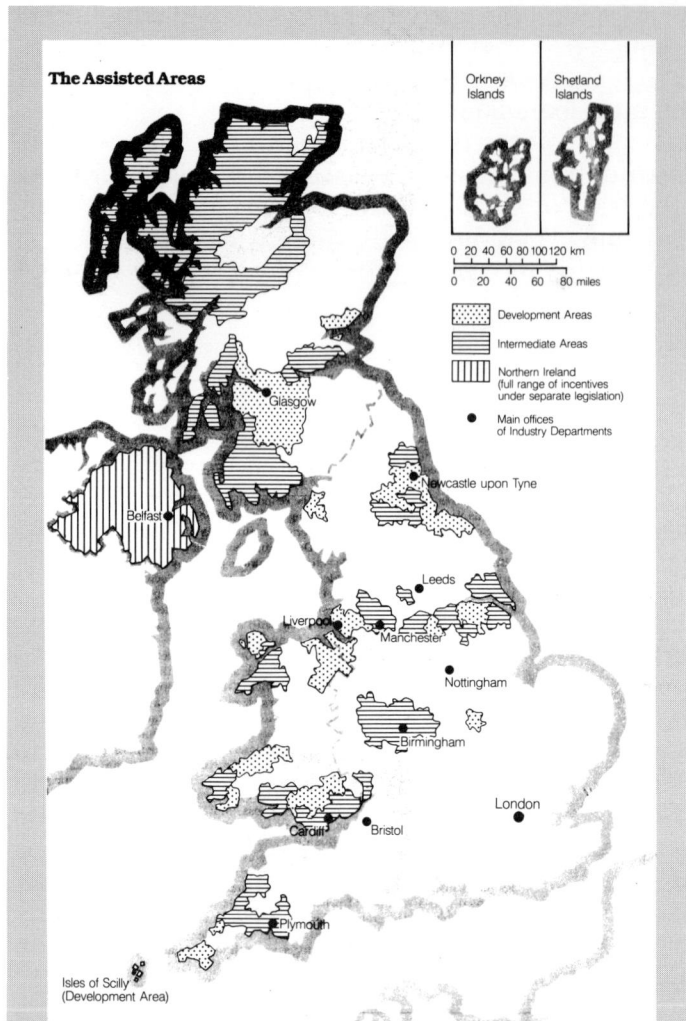

The Assisted Areas

Orkney Islands   Shetland Islands

0 20 40 60 80 100 120 km
0 20 40 60 80 miles

Development Areas
Intermediate Areas
Northern Ireland (full range of incentives under separate legislation)
● Main offices of Industry Departments

Glasgow
Newcastle upon Tyne
Belfast
Leeds
Liverpool
Manchester
Nottingham
Birmingham
London
Cardiff   Bristol
Plymouth
Isles of Scilly (Development Area)

The assisted areas

Some financial help is still offered to firms which locate or expand within the shaded areas on the map.

The development areas receive most benefit and the intermediate areas rather less. Government policy is moving away from the support of these regions towards specific targeting of their aid.

Questions

1 Despite the aid available to set up in these assisted areas, many firms still set up in the South East of England. Can you suggest five reasons why they should want to do this?

2 Give two reasons why an insurance company could easily move its head office from the south east to an area of high unemployment.

TASK

Hills, moors, bogs and jobs

The highlands and islands of Scotland are thinly populated, and remote from major markets. What kind of business can survive there?

IN THE lore of the airport duty-free shop, Scotland's products are whisky, the kilt and smoked salmon. Actually, north of the industrial heartland, the local bread seems to be made from three things—tourism, North Sea oil and tax-free forestry. American fears of Libyan terrorism and the fall in oil prices hit the first two in 1986. Just as they are now reviving, the third is at risk from nature-lobbyists who want to do away with the tax breaks on trees, which they say are ruining the blasted heaths of the far north. If they win, forestry will suddenly become unprofitable. Where next will the jobs come from?

Some 365,000 people live in the highlands: nine, on average, per square kilometre. The big markets of south-east England and continental Europe seem far, far away. Fast trains from the south go no further than Inverness and Aberdeen. Nor do flights from London: southerners who want to do a day's work in Wick must expect to charter a private propeller-plane from Inverness. The road network—sparse in the east and worse in the west—is picturesque for tourists, no fun for heavy lorries. Other countries have made up for such deficiencies with good telecommunications. Not Scotland; few telephone lines are good enough for computer data—and there is no cellular telephone network.

But the highlands are beautiful, too. Property prices are among the lowest in Britain; the oil boom apart, so are wages. The workforce is well educated in traditional schools, and innocent of industrial militancy. Many managers would give up a lot if they could think of a round of golf or a salmon beat only ten minutes' drive from the office. And there is a healthy chauvinism, a determination to show the Sassenachs (lowlanders, that is, and those from unspeakable places yet further south) how things ought to be done.

Bringing them in

Some enterprises have an obvious place in the highlands, as anywhere else: those that serve a local need (retailers) or use local raw materials (salmon-smokers, chipboard-makers). How can others be pulled in? The Highlands and Islands Development Board (HIDB), a quango, provides cheap factory-space, low-interest loans and capital grants. This is small-scale stuff: half its money is doled out in grants of between £10,000 and £100,000. That is not necessarily a drawback. Communities that once put their faith in a single big employer (a builder of oil-rigs, for instance) are now more wary.

The board has its showcase of pocket success stories. Osprey Electronics, the world's biggest maker of underwater cameras, turns over £4m a year from the small town of Wick. Gaeltec Research, with 29 Highlands staff in Dingwall, sells a computerised chart recorder to foreign hospitals. Zonal, one of Europe's few profitable manufacturers of magnetic tape, has just set up a finishing plant in Invergordon employing 20 locals. In Brin, Furness Controls has a niche in the market for precision measuring instruments, and makes pre-tax profits of £700,000 a year on a turnover of £2½m. Caithness Glass has introduced to Wick the alien art of glass-blowing, and sells £1½m-worth of glass paperweights and whatnot a year.

The common feature of all these firms is the small size and high price of their products. The underwater cameras start at £2,000; the hospital equipment at more like £15,000. One firm sells for £400 a computer device containing components worth £80 which cost £5 to assemble. So bad communications matter less, and anyway some can get round them. One firm has found a way of sending its products from Scotland to Essex for less than it costs to get them from Essex to London.

REGIONAL DEVELOPMENT

In complete contrast to the densely populated towns of South-East England, there are remote and beautiful parts of Britain which need and deserve new employment opportunities too. Although the population is not large, there are many people out of work in these remoter areas of the country, including Northern Scotland. You may feel that government has a responsibility to encourage industry and employment into regions such as this.
Read the article carefully.

1 Summarise the main points of the article in a list under three headings: geography; the traditional local economy; modern economic development.

IT ▶ **WORDPRO**

You can use a word processor to complete this task, taking care to ensure careful layout under the three headings.

2 What do you think the government should or should not do to promote economic prosperity in Northern Scotland.

This may be a good idea for group discussion and some further project work.

Small Businesses

What is a 'small' firm? – the 'one-person business'

There is no easily agreed definition of a 'small business'. In some industries, like motor vehicle manufacture, a firm employing less the 1000 would be regarded as small. In office cleaning, a firm employing 50 would be large. Even a 'one-person' business could employ a lot of people but we will settle for this as a definition.

Support for small business enterprise

The government is keen to promote small businesses. For example, there is a shortage of skilled trades-people in some parts of the country, notably plumbers and electricians. It is argued that many semi-skilled workers made redundant from the steel or textile industries could take training courses in appropriate skills and make a good living. If enough do so, there would be healthy competition and the high prices householders now pay for a the services of a tradesperson would be reduced.

It is this approach which the government wishes to promote through training support, loans, grants and tax concessions. Banks have been encouraged to support small business ventures by looking favourably on loans and by offering business advice and general support. This has been slow to develop in Britain but the government believes that this is an important route to economic recovery.

Arguments against small firms

The arguments against this view of the future for the UK economy are also quite strong. Small firms do not benefit from what we call 'economies of scale'. That is, a small firm cannot employ specialists very easily, they cannot benefit from buying materials in bulk at discount prices. Any 'overhead' payments they make for premises and equipment must be paid for from quite a small amount of income. It is argued strongly that this is not the way to make Britain competitive on world markets. It may be adequate for local plumbers but not for modern manufacturing and new production technology.

The problems of the small business

The owners of small businesses have certain obvious problems:

they must find their own finance and offer their own guarantees to the bank.

they must rely on their own expertise in lots of directions. They may not be quite a 'jack-of-all-trades' but it is more difficult for them to build a team of specialists and experts.

they bear all the worry and responsibility for the

Manufacturing – Size of Businesses by Employment		
Employment size	Number of businesses 1986	Employment 1984
1–9	97,527	306,720
10–19	17,072	234,448
20–49	12,397	382,783
50–99	5,512	382,335
100–199	3,331	464,028
200–499	2,348	714,159
500–999	829	573,707
1,000 and over	576	1,816,933
Total	139,592	4,875,113

Size of manufacturing business

Look at the figures in the table.

Questions

1 By far the largest category is that which includes very small firms – those employing fewer than 10 people. What percentage of total employment in manufacturing does this represent?

2 There are fewer than 600 firms in British manufacturing industry which employ over 1000 employees but, in terms of total employment, they are the most important single group. How do you account for this?

GOING IT ALONE

If you have been made redundant or are unemployed, now could be your great chance to become your boss, go it alone. You probably have a skill, a background, that can be developed into a viable business proposition – given the right help and advice. The MSC can give that help.

ENTERPRISE ALLOWANCE SCHEME – which allows for a taxable allowance of £40 a week, for a maximum of 52 weeks, for unemployed people who wish to set up their own businesses, is available throughout Britain. Places for 25 000 people will be available from August 1983 until March 1984 allocated broadly in line with the numbers of unemployed in each area. The MSC administers the scheme – with help from the Department of Industry's Small Firms Service, whose counsellors provide advice and guidance to those entering the scheme.

Questions

1 What is the opportunity cost of taking a place on the enterprise allowance scheme?

2 What is meant by a taxable allowance?

success of the business – this probably discourages more people from setting up on their own than any other factor.

There are two significant advantages:
They are their own bosses and are free to make their own decisions.
They do not have to share their profit.

Once a small business has been established successfully, there are opportunities for it to grow. Indeed, most companies started in this way and their development can often be traced to one founder who developed a business idea which happened to be successful – sometimes at the third or fourth attempt.

POINTS TO REMEMBER

★ The government feels that a sound economic future can be built by encouraging the growth of small businesses in Britain.

★ This may not be appropriate in all forms of enterprise.

★ The development of successful small companies requires some management expertise, especially if it is to expand and to create extra jobs.

The decline of the corner shop

The corner shop used to be a feature of cities, towns and villages in every part of the country. It is part of retailing tradition.

Much of the trade in such shops is done out of 'normal' shopping hours – such shops often stay open until quite late in the evening and open before people set off to work.

The future of such shops has been threatened for a long time. People's shopping habits have changed. Home freezers mean that many families now shop once a month rather than every week. They have cars to take them into town centres or out to shopping precincts. Many corner shops have closed. They cannot compete with the prices which supermarkets are able to charge, nor can they carry a large range of stock.

Consider the future of such corner shops.

Question

1 List five factors which you consider have caused the decline of the corner shop.

2 How are corner shops adapting to the changes which have occurred?

3 Think of a corner shop known to you. What is it like? What does it sell? Why is it able to survive? How might it be improved?

IT ▶ WORDPRO

A survey of local views

It would be a good idea to try to find out local views about the future of 'corner shops' in your local community.

Think of the questions you would wish to ask and set up an appropriate questionnaire on the word processor.

In order to conduct your survey, you will need careful planning. Think carefully about how many samples your survey would require.

IT ▶ GRAPHICS

Processing results

Once your survey is complete, you will need to process the results. This could involve the use of a database to classify views and/or a graphical presentation of your findings.

A display of your findings might also be a good idea.

TASK 1

THE BUSINESS PLAN: A GUIDE FROM MIDLAND BANK

Imagine that you are about to set up in business. You may think that the first thing you have to do is to book next year's holiday on a South Sea island. Forget it. You might manage a weekend for two in Southsea! The first years of a new business will be full of hard work and little financial reward. Most new business enterprises which fail, do so in the first eighteen months.

Cash flow is the main problem. It takes a long time to bring in the first return of cash as the business builds up – and loans have to be repaid from the first month. The bank manager may be very sympathetic to new business ventures but she is not offering charity. She will want to know that you are in control of things and can honour your obligations.

Before you set out in business, especially if you want a loan from the bank, you will be expected to draw up a 'business plan'. This will sketch out a lot of detail of your business idea:

What experience do you have?
Where is your finance coming from?
How much do you intend to sell?
What costs will you incur?
Etc.

Your own ideas

In your group, you can set up a business idea and set out an imaginary plan for it.

Perhaps there is something you think you could make and sell?

Perhaps there is a service you can provide?

Look at the outline questions which the Midland Bank have asked. Draw up outline answers to them for a business which you have dreamed up.

Midland Bank
BUSINESS SERVICES

FIRST STEPS IN SETTING UP A BUSINESS

BEFORE YOU START

S O YOU THINK you can run your own business? Provided you know what it takes and can give what it needs, then you are on the first rungs of the ladder towards success.

But starting a business is always a risky venture. For, even with the most detailed planning and best professional advice, unforeseen problems and setbacks can arise to trap the unwary. The more thought you can give beforehand to the problems you are likely to face, the more you will be able to anticipate and prevent some of the worst from happening. In addition, thinking and talking about your business plans will give you, as the proprietor, a better appreciation of your business sense, your management abilities and your deficiencies.

YOU AS A BUSINESSPERSON

1. Are you the kind of person who really can start a business and make a success of it?

2. Think what it means to you. You'll work long hours for uncertain returns, is that what you expect?

3. Have you any practical experience of the business you want to start?

4. Have you any experience as a supervisor, a foreman or a manager?

5. Have you had any formal business training?

6. Have you any money you can put into the business?

7. Do you understand the legal requirements placed upon you as a small business?

THE BUSINESS PLAN

A LL BUSINESSES, NEW or existing, need to plan. You need to know:

☐ Where you are
☐ Where you are going
☐ Have you the ability to get there?
☐ How are you going to do it?
☐ How much will it cost?
☐ How much will you get out of it?
☐ Is it all worthwhile?

Much of this information is probably in one's head, so now is the time to get it down on paper. Then the information can be used to put ideas into action and act as a benchmark upon which progress can be monitored.

The Business Plan will also be useful if you need to approach the bank manager for financial assistance or guidance since the information required will be readily available within the plan.

SOME BUSINESS IDEAS

TASK 2

BUSINESS FAILURE

You will see from the table that small firms are much more likely to fail than larger ones.

Can you suggest five different reasons why this is likely to be the case?

Turnover size in 1980 (£'000)	Number of businesses	Failures	Failure rates (%)
1–13	172,976	43,321	25.0
14	19,870	3,209	16.1
15–49	424,106	50,955	12.0
50–99	237,230	17,185	7.2
100–499	277,239	12,299	4.4
500–1,999	64,769	2,306	3.6
2000+	22,389	871	3.9

Table 1 Failure Rates by Size of Turnover

TASK 3

GOVERNMENT POLICY TOWARDS SMALL BUSINESSES

The UK government sees the growth in small businesses as a major source of wealth and job creation and has introduced many new policies to help them.

Critics point out that not enough attention is given to make people who start small businesses better managers. Not enough money is re-invested in small businesses to help them expand safely. Not enough attention is given to the need to create jobs in small firms – and the effect on unemployment figures has been very small.

How could the government target its policy measures:

a to make sure that small business managers recognise the need to re-invest their profits to expand their business?

b to make sure that its help for small firms is actually creating more jobs?

TASK 4

Small Businesses in Britain

In the UK there are approximately 1.3 million businesses registered for VAT, but it is not easy to reach a satisfactory definition of which can be classified as small, medium or large.

The most widely accepted definition of a small firm is one which has a small share of the market, is owned and managed by the same individual or small group of individuals, and is legally independent, i.e. not owned by a large enterprise.

THE PERFORMANCE OF SMALL FIRMS IN BRITAIN: SMALL BUSINESS IN BRITAIN 1981

Of all the firms in the small business category shown in table, most are in retailing (25%).

1 Draw a divided circle (pie chart) to show how firms with a turnover of less than £1m per year are grouped by category.

Turnover in 1981 (£'000)	Manufacturing	Construction	Road transport & transport services	Wholesaling and dealing	Retailing	Finance	Catering	Motor trades	Other services	TOTAL
18–49	35,997	80,395	23,331	23,932	94,621	32,621	48,160	24,479	65,337	428,853
50–99	23,746	29,630	7,764	17,337	73,896	12,283	37,955	11,356	21,567	235,534
100–249	27,522	23,392	7,380	22,145	52,458	11,785	19,067	12,606	17,078	193,433
250–499	14,240									14,240
500–999	10,092									10,092
TOTAL	111,577	133,417	38,476	63,414	220,975	56,689	105,182	48,441	103,982	882,157
% of Total	(12.6)	(15.1)	(4.4)	(7.2)	(25.0)	(6.4)	(11.9)	(5.5)	(11.8)	(100.0)

Table 2 Sectoral Composition of Small Businesses in Britain, 1981

2 Why do you think the number of very small firms is higher in the construction industry than in manufacturing?

Companies

A company for Saba and Taya – 'Superprogs'

Saba and Taya knew that they could start a successful business, devising and selling computer programs. They had made some rough calculations:

Lease of office	£3000 p.a.
Computer hardware	£2000
Software	£ 500
Fixtures and fittings	£1000
TOTAL	£6500

That came to a lot of money and they certainly did not have it to hand! They thought about borrowing it from a bank but Saba was very gloomy at the thought of the business failing and spending the rest of her life paying this back. Taya thought a way round this might lie in becoming a company. Saba thought this quite ridiculous as companies like ICI, the Midland Bank and BP were huge and there were only two of them!

Getting advice

Uncle Vanya was a solicitor and they decided to tap him for some free advice! Yes, he explained two people could start a business but the law required you to do certain things in order to become a company.

Deciding on a name

Saba suggested that they start with a name and she quite liked the sound of 'International Superprogs'. Uncle Vanya then immediately poured cold water on this name because, he said, to use words like International, Royal or British needed special permission from the Secretary of State for Trade and Industry. Eventually Superprogs Limited was agreed upon.

Saba and Taya then set about forming a 'private company'. They found out they needed at least one director and a company secretary. Taya was to be the director and Saba the secretary – the person to be responsible for making sure the paperwork of the business is in order and accounts are properly kept.

What are shares?

Uncle Vanya explained that they should put some of their own money into the business and this would give them a 'share' of the ownership – Saba immediately worked out that this was what 'shareholders' were. Superprogs started with share capital as follows:

Saba	1000 shares at £1 raised	£1000
Taya	800 shares at £1 raised	£800

This meant that, together, they put £1800 into the business. Taya asked what would happen if the business went bankrupt. Would she lose the car she

SAINSBURY'S

Company profile: J. Sainsbury Plc

Business: Food Retailing. 56% of sales are 'own brand', UK's largest butcher and wine seller.
Main markets: South of England.

Pattern of development:
1914 115 branches selling groceries.
1973 Went 'public'. Most shares still held by members of the Sainsbury family, 69,000 employees hold 30% of the shares.
1979 Launched 'Homebase' – a chain of DIY stores. Started to use computer checkouts with laser scanning of bar codes at checkouts.
1987 Bought controlling stake in Shaw's Supermarkets which has 41 stores in New England, US. Sainsbury's now has 272 stores in the UK.

Questions

1 What happened to the control of J Sainsbury when it was floated on the Stock Exchange?

2 Why do you think some companies encourage their employees to hold shares?

3 Why do you think laser scanning was introduced at checkouts?

4 Why do you think Sainsbury's moved into the DIY market?

5 When Sainsbury's announced that they were going to buy shares in Shaw's Supermarkets in the US, Sainsbury's share price fell. Can you suggest one reason why this should have happened?

had just bought for £1300? Uncle Vanya explained that this was perhaps the greatest advantage of being a private company – they both had 'limited liability'. This meant they could only lose the money they had put into the business – her car was safe!

No advertising – yet

£1800 was not enough to set up the business. They needed more people to put money into the business and become shareholders. Saba suggested they advertise in the local paper. Uncle Vanya was horrified! He explained they were only a private company and advertising to the general public for shareholders was only possible for public companies. They might one day become a public company but as yet they had to ask only people they knew.

Obviously, this was a hint, so Saba and Taya promptly sold 1000 shares at £1 each to Uncle Vanya. Another £5000 was raised by selling shares to other members of the family and close friends.

Who owns a company?

Saba then noticed that something odd had happened. They had raised capital of £7800 but she and Saba owned only £1800 worth of shares. Who owned the business?

Uncle Vanya explained that this was quite normal; all the shareholders owned the business and in Superprogs each share carred one vote. They would appoint executives to manage the business and these would be Saba and Taya.

Annual general meeting

Each year they would have to hold an Annual General Meeting and present the accounts and suggest the dividend that should be paid. In this way the people who had put money into the business (the shareholders) could keep a check on what was going on.

Dividends

Saba was alarmed at the thought of giving her hard earned profits away. Uncle Vanya said this was only reasonable. The shareholders had lent their money (which they could have put on deposit in a bank and been given interest) therefore the company, Superprogs, had to pay some of its profits out as dividends to the shareholders.

Before they could start trading, Superprogs would have to be officially formed as a company – Uncle Vanya suggested the easiest way to do this was to buy an 'off-the-peg' company from companies that specialise in forming companies. This would cost about £150. Saba found it rather strange that the actual business of a company could be forming other companies!

Going public

After several years trading Superprogs had become a very successful business. There were now ten other employees but financing the business remained a problem. All the time better and better computers were available which the company needed to buy in

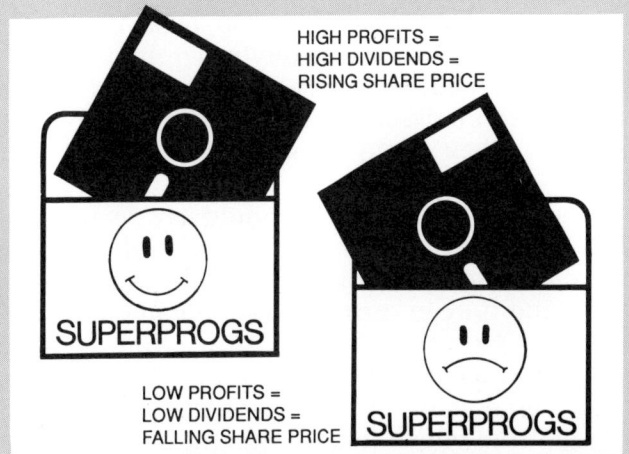

A company can decide not to retain its profits to finance further investment in things like buildings and machinery. Then the increase in profits can go to the shareholders in the form of dividends. This can lead to the company's share price going up. Sometimes the share price will rise if people expect that future profits will be higher than they are the present. Of course, if profits fall, share prices can also fall.

Question

Look at the following news headlines about Superprogs after it became a public limited company. Explain the possible effect on its share price of each headline.

Superprogs win export order

Main programmer at Superprogs leaves to join IBM

Workers at Superprogs go on strike!

Superprogs announce breakthrough in games programs

Shortage of trained computer programmers in UK

Government announced that all schools are to be given 10 computers!

Cost of computer chips to double!

Computer games programs 'dumped' in UK

order to develop their programs.

Saba and Taya had ploughed back most of the profits they had made into buying equipment but the existing shareholders, who were their relatives and friends, had no more money available to put into the business. They again sought the advice of Uncle Vanya.

He suggested that they should try to become a 'public limited company'. This would mean that they could advertise shares for sale to the general public and they in turn could sell them on the Stock Exchange. However, Uncle Vanya pointed out that they would have to show that they were a company which had a good record of profits, which was well managed and which had a bright future. They would have to show all their past accounts and try to predict what their future profits might be.

Having done this they would be able to issue a prospectus inviting people and institutions like pension funds and insurance companies to buy their shares.

The money raised from the sale of shares could be used to finance the development of the business. These new shareholders would expect to be paid dividends from the profits made and to vote at the Annual General Meeting when decisions were made.

POINTS TO REMEMBER

★ Shareholders own companies.

★ Shareholders elect the directors to run the company.

★ Dividends are paid out of profits to shareholders.

★ Only public companies can advertise for shareholders.

★ Companies hold Annual General Meetings to look over the running of the company.

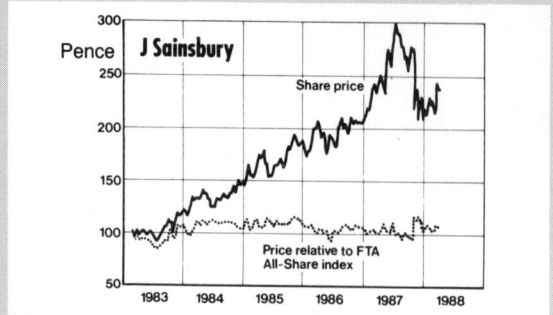

Questions

1 How much would one share in J Sainsbury have cost to buy at the start of 1983?

2 What was the maximum value of a share during the period 1983 to 1988?

3 Find out the value of one share today.

4 What does this mean people think about the company?

5 What caused the fall in the share value in October 1987?

6 How well has this share done in comparison with all other shares?

Is J Sainsbury Plc a large company?

UK companies in order, from number 16 to 20, by total value of shares:

		Share price	Value
16	Barclays Bank	490p	£3601m
17	Beecham	472p	£3556m
18	J Sainsbury	234p	£3434m
19	Cable & Wireless	328p	£3381m
20	Prudential	868p	£3170m

IT▶ SPREADSHEET

Questions

1 Approximately how many shares are there in each company.

2 What would happen to the total value of J Sainsbury if its share price fell to 225p?

3 Check the current share price of all the above companies in a newspaper. What is the current value of each company? Show the new rank order.

4 Can you suggest three other ways in which it would be possible to measure the size of a company?

TASK 1

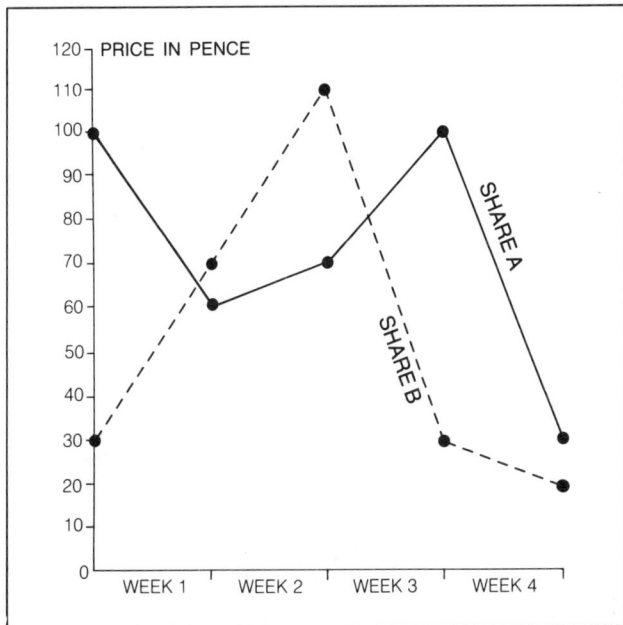

BULLS AND BEARS

Some people do not buy shares as a long-term investment on which they can earn dividends, but buy and sell shares in order to make a quick profit.

· A 'bull' is a speculator who expects share prices to rise. She might buy a share for £1.00 wait for the share to rise to £1.20 and then sell it – she then makes 20p profit per share.

A 'bear' is a speculator who expects share prices to fall. She makes a deal to sell a share for £1.00 in two weeks time. During that two weeks she hopes share prices will fall, so she can buy the share at £0.80. She then sells them for £1.00 on the date she previously agreed.

Look at the graph showing the share price of two shares A and B over a period of one month.

1 If a bull bought one share 'A' at the start of week one, what would it be best for her to do? How much profit or loss would this lead to?

2 If a bull bought one share 'B' at the start of week one, what would it be best for her to do? How much profit or loss would this lead to?

3 A speculator agrees to sell one share B at the end of week three for 10p. When would it be best to buy it? How much profit or loss would she make on this share?

4 Explain why speculation in share buying and selling can be a risky business.

TASK 2

TYPES OF SHARES

There are three main types of shares which companies can issue. These are:

ordinary shares,
preference shares,
cumulative preference shares.

The most common type is probably ordinary shares which carry voting rights and which entitle their holders to a share in the profits of the company. Generally, the more profit that is made the greater are the dividends received by the ordinary shareholders.

Preference shares carry a fixed percentage dividend and get their share of the profit before the ordinary shareholders are paid. It might be expressed like this:

7% £1 Preference Share

This means the holder would be entitled to a dividend of 7% of £1, that is 7p.

In some years companies may not give a dividend, so if you are a cumulative preference shareholder, you are entitled to have your claim for a dividend held over to the next year.

A company has the following share capital structure.

1000 £2 Ordinary shares
2000 10% £2 Preference shares

1 If all profits are distributed as dividends how much would one preference share and one ordinary share receive if:
    a a profit of £500 was made?
    b a profit of £5000 was made?

2 What is the main advantage of preference shares over ordinary shares?

3 What is the main advantage of ordinary shares over preference shares?

Business Competition

Does competition keep prices down?

In a 'market' economy, you will remember that it is competition between firms which keeps prices under control. If one firm tries to put its price up, consumers can turn to another supplier for more or less the same good at a cheaper price. This is why having lots of small firms in competition with one another is thought to be healthy. However, you will also have noticed that lots of apparent competition does not always keep prices under control. Often, several local firms put their prices up all at the same time – petrol stations are a good example.

Advertising

Most companies spend a lot on advertising to persuade customers that their products are uniquely good – that there is no competitor for them. We have already looked at Coca-Cola and Pepsi-Cola. If they were absolutely identical, we would always buy the cheaper. Whether there is any difference or not, both firms spend a lot of money each month to tell us that there is, so if the price of one were to go up we would stick with it and not change to the other. You may or may not think that this is successful – clearly both companies think it is very important.

Rational spending

Competition also breaks down because we, as consumers, do not always make sensible spending decisions and buy the cheapest of similar goods. This is partly because we believe lots of the advertising we see and partly because we don't always shop around to find out what is the best buy. We often buy from habit but sometimes we want a change.

Big Business

The economy is certainly not made up of lots of small firms cutting each other's throats. There are over 80,000 firms which employ less than 20 people, but these employ only 20% of the workforce. The other 30,000 larger firms employ the other 80%. Firms have always tried to buy up their competitors to give themselves a stronger market position.

Government policy

Governments try to control such 'mergers' (where two companies join) and 'takeovers' (where one company buys enough shares in another to take control) to ensure that competition takes place. The laws governing such activities date back over 40 years and there have been many cases where mergers and takeovers have been refused. On the other hand, 1986 was a year in which more took place than in any year since 1972.

Competition on the petrol forecourt?

The two petrol stations shown in the photographs above are within 200 metres of each other. They are owned by different petrol companies – Texaco and Mobil – and they are in direct competition.

Questions

1 What do you notice about the prices they are charging?

2 How do you account for the pricing policy of the two service stations?

3 They are competing with each other, but this competition is in forms other than the prices they charge. What forms does this competition take?

Recent mergers and takeovers

Some of these made press headlines: Guinness bought the Distillers Group and Bell's Whisky; Elders (who brew Foster's lager) acquired Courage breweries; ICI bought the American paint giant Glidden for $580m; Habitat Mothercare merged with British Home Stores. Others were refused by the Secretary of State for Trade and Industry: GEC were not allowed to take over Plessey, one of its main rivals in electronics with a £1.2bn bid, because this would have reduced competition in an important industry.

Why firms wish to merge

Getting rid of competition is only one reason why firms are often keen to merge with one another or why one company wishes to buy out another. Being a large firm allows the benefits of 'economies of scale' – cheaper buying, better spreading of 'fixed' costs like premises and equipment, better research and development and many more. Some firms wish to move into slightly different markets – Waterford Glass took over the Wedgwood Pottery group to diversify their interests. Perhaps even more important has been the wish to establish bigger firms in Britain to compete with the foreign giants in international markets. Ford, for example, tried to take over Alfa Romeo but failed when Alfa merged with Fiat to compete in the luxury car market with BMW, Porsche and Jaguar.

Multinational companies and world markets

The biggest firms of all are those which operate in many different countries. It would be hard to say which country one of these 'multinationals' belonged to. Some of the international car giants, for example, may have originated in America but now manufacture parts for cars in different countries and assemble the finished product in one of a number of plants all over the world.

The problem of the multinationals

It is possible for such giants to exploit the tax advantages of different countries and to benefit from the grants which different countries offer for industrial location. Perhaps the biggest danger of these multinational companies is that it has become very difficult for individual governments to control them. A decision by one of them to re-locate a major plant or to change a company policy may threaten the whole economy of some smaller developing nations.

POINTS TO REMEMBER

★ Competition, in a 'free' market, keeps prices down.

★ Unless government policy is strict, firms tend to combine and this reduces the benefits of competition to the consumer.

Proposed Bank Merger: Barclays, Lloyds and Martins

In 1968 a merger was proposed between Barclays, Lloyds and Martins Banks. The banks claimed that two main kinds of advantage would result from the merger.

First, there would be direct benefits to customers in the form of the improved service, including a wider geographical coverage, that a larger bank could give. Insofar as this would include increased overseas coverage, this would enable the bank to compete on better terms with American banks.

Second, there would be savings in running and capital costs, – mainly on the use of computers and by eliminating over-lapping branches. These savings might amount to almost £10 mn. a year, and would be important in holding down charges to customers in the future.

The Commission were not very impressed by the arguments about improved service. They found, from a survey of large companies, little demand for a bigger bank to meet their borrowing needs. On the other hand they agreed that savings of roughly the magnitude suggested by the banks were likely, although the members of the Commission differed in their views as to how long it would take before they were achieved.

However the Commission felt that the most important point was the likely effect on competition and efficiency. They commented upon the existing lack of competition and efficiency

Lloyds Bank

Barclays Bank PLC

Bank merger turned down

The article above refers to a proposal which is now part of the history of banking in Britain. Whereas there were once well over 100 banks in operation there are now just six major ones. If the merger had been permitted, there would have been only five. Very soon afterwards Barclays were able to take over Martins Bank.

Questions

1 What arguments did the two banks put forward to justify their proposed merger?

2 What arguments were put forward by the Monopolies Commission against the proposal?

IT ▶ WORDPRO

Imagine that you are a shareholder in the 'Midshire Bank'. Write a letter to the Chairman and Board of Directors explaining your own view about the merger of your bank with one of the 'big four'. Include the reasons for your view.

This should be a formal letter and can be produced on a word processor.

TASK 1

MULTINATIONALS are not so widely vilified these days as they were a few years ago, but as one of Britain's few true multinationals, BAT Industries will attract whatever opprobrium is going. Add to that the fact that its staple business is tobacco and a large number of ethical investors are immediately deterred.

The group is so huge that currency movements hit profits by £192 million — more than the total pretax earnings of companies like GKN or Cadbury Schweppes. BATs' sales, even after being reduced by over £2 billion on translation into sterling, run at around £73 million per day — similar to the annual sales of a company like Pentos.

Tobacco still accounts for the biggest chunk of the group, as the chart shows, but it is huge in its three other sectors of retailing, financial services and paper. Trading profits from each of these sectors is over £200 million. Compare that with pre-interest profits from Woolworth yesterday of £183 million, and £242 million this week from the Pru.

These non-tobacco interests have been built up since 1970, not entirely without pain, but without the disasters encountered by most other major tobacco groups seeking to diversify from their dying base. If Imperial Group were still in existence it would only be necessary to look there for how not to do it, but in fairness to Imperial, BATs is one of the few to have bought fairly wisely and managed its buys pretty well.

True, there was a clear-out of poor US retailers in 1986, along with the German home improvement business and some investments picked up with Eagle Star. Previously BATs had sold International Stores in this country, and Beecham took the cosmetics business off its hands, while Mardon Packaging was the biggest buyout of its time.

Paper and pulp had something of a hard time last year because of pressure on margins, but profit at constant exchange rates was up 6 per cent nevertheless. Wiggins Teape continued its growth path and profits increased despite significant reorganisation costs. Brazil, Portugal and Spain are growing in importance, helping to widen the group's geographical diversity even further.

In retailing, Argos was a star performer. Its profits last year increased by a third to £47 million, although that rise is flattered by hefty reorganisations costs in 1986. Even so, the catalogue showroom business is still booming, with a growing number of superstores and the new Best Sellers chain.

News from the US shops was less positive, where the market crash (and the consequent currency effect which figured so largely throughout the results) hit retail sales generally in the fourth quarter. Saks Fifth Avenue increased sales but margins sufferred and total profits fell. Elsewhere there was an improvement in the Breuners furniture business but it still operated at a loss.

Eagle Star's contribution was hit by the market crash, which wiped over £100 million off its investments. But premium income increased by 10 per cent and the loss on underwritng was reduced, despite the net £16 million cost of the October hurricane.

Allied Dunbar also continued its rapid growth as the UK's largest unit-linked life company, although of course interest in unit trusts has been pretty low since October.

The group's immediate concern, of course, is the mega-bid for the Farmers insurance group, which is the result of the long-signalled need to add a US financial services arm following the UK and Canadian acquisitions.

BAT INDUSTRIES

British and American Tobacco (BAT) is described as 'one of Britain's few true multinational companies'. It has interests all over the world in tobacco, paper, retailing and insurance. It is a true 'multinational' in that it belongs to no particular country – for example, it controls a quarter of Japan's imported cigarette market.

Read the article and answer the following questions:

1 What is meant by the term 'multinational'?

2 Why have 'currency movements' affected BAT by £192 millions?

3 BAT have sold some companies as well as bought some. Find examples of firms in both categories.

4 Which was the most successful BAT company in 1987? What were its profits?

5 What was the state of its two insurance companies last year?

6 BAT is now diversifying into the US market with a bid for Farmer's Insurance. What does the term 'diversifying' mean and why might it be important to BAT?

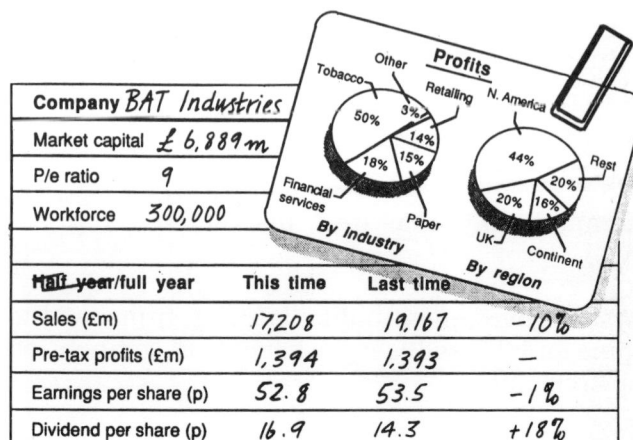

Company BAT Industries		
Market capital	£ 6,889m	
P/e ratio	9	
Workforce	300,000	

Half year/full year	This time	Last time	
Sales (£m)	17,208	19,167	−10%
Pre-tax profits (£m)	1,394	1,393	—
Earnings per share (p)	52.8	53.5	−1%
Dividend per share (p)	16.9	14.3	+18%

Profits

By Industry: Tobacco 50%, Other 3%, Retailing 14%, Financial services 18%, Paper 15%

By region: N. America 44%, Rest 20%, UK 20%, Continent 16%

TASK 2

PRICE AND PRODUCT COMPETITION: WILKINSON SWORD vs GILLETTE

More men in Britain still shave with a 'wet' shaving system than anywhere else in Europe, where electric razors are generally preferred.

The two main manufacturers of razor blades and shaving systems – like the 'GII' and the 'Twin Fixed' – Wilkinson Sword and Gillette, are fierce competitors in the market. Everything one firm develops has been countered by the other.

The consumer has benefited from all this competition. Products have improved and prices have fallen.

Read the article carefully and then try to answer the questions.

1 What form does competition take in the production of razor blades?

2 How has competition in the razor blade market benefited consumers?

Try to find evidence in local shops of the competition between these two firms.

BATTLE OF THE BLADES

Mr King C Gillette started the production of disposable razor blades in 1895. Fifty years later little had changed – until stainless steel was invented.

The small English family firm of Wilkinson, makers of ceremonial swords and garden tools, first produced the stainless steel razor blade. At the end of World War II, Gillette had 85% of the razor blade market. They soon copied the Wilkinson 'stainless' blade and actually patented it first. There was no goodwill between the companies, either then or now, and the razor blade market became extremely fierce.

Competitive advertising was costing the companies £1.4m when the total joint market sales were only £14m. Profit margins were very low as competition kept prices down.

As each company developed a new product design the other followed. Gillette developed two new shaving 'systems' – Techmatic and GII. These were aimed at 'young, modern people'. Wilkinson Sword was seen as a more traditional and brave British competitor. They responded with their own products in the disposable razor market. Both developed a 'swivel-head' blade.

Gillette stole a lead with their 'Platinum' blade. Wilkinson were scathing about this, claiming that the product is an alloy, 87% chromium, like theirs, and only 13% platinum. Gillette were equally critical of the claim that more Wilkinson 'Bonded' razors were bought than any other system.

Competition reached a peak in 1970. Razor blades were getting better without becoming more expensive. Gillette caused a minor sensation with their double edged blade system – GII, now knows as 'Blue II'. Wilkinson, of course, responded. They market the 'Twin Fixed' system and the customer is now faced with a bewildering array of choices in a market dominated by the two leaders, but increasingly infiltrated by newcomers like Bic who can claim to have invented the very cheap throw-away razor. As they say, 'watch this space'.

People in Business

Despite the arrival of high technology there is little doubt that people are the key to success in every business enterprise. In large companies the recruitment and welfare of staff is often left to the personnel department who may employ a recruitment agency to find highly qualified and specialist staff for them. This process is sometimes referred to as 'head-hunting'!

Recruiting staff
In general, people are employed when they can contribute more to the output of a firm than it costs in wages to employ them.

The process of recruiting staff has often been criticised for being too hit and miss and often dependent on the whims of the interviewers rather than on the merits of the candidates.

Employers have vacancies either because somebody has just left or because they have expanded and need to take on more staff.

Job specifications
The firm should be able to give an indication of the sort of job to be done. This can vary from a vague idea that a secretary is needed, to a firm producing a very precise list of tasks they expect the new person to do. This list is called a job specification.

Job advertisements
Some people never see advertisements for jobs they would like to do because they don't know where to look.

Possible sources are local or national newspapers, job centres, privately run employment agencies and specialist magazines. You can even apply to a firm that has not advertised a job – they may just have a vacancy coming up and want to save the cost of an advertisement.

After the advertisements have been placed, a firm would wait to receive all the applications – either their own preprinted forms which people have completed or letters of application which would usually have a curriculum vitae attached.

Curriculum vitae
The curriculum vitae (CV) should contain details of a person's name, age and address, schools, colleges and universities attended, previous employers, salaries earned and details of referees. Referees are people, often your previous employers or people who know you very well, who are prepared to write a report about your character and work.

"THE MAIN ADVANTAGE OF INCENTIVE PAYMENT SYSTEMS IS THAT THEY LINK PAY TO PERFORMANCE"

Some people are paid an agreed wage each week whilst others are paid an amount which relates to how much they have produced. This latter system is called 'piece work'.

Questions

1 What are the advantages and disadvantages of:
   a paying people a piece work rate?
   b paying people a fixed wage?

IT ▶ WORDPRO

2 Interview an adult about their job. Then on a wordprocessor create a job specification. Ask the adult to check the list and order the points starting with the one they like most and finishing with the one they like least. Reprint this order by using the text movement facility on your word processor. All the job descriptions of the class can then be presented as a wall display.

Short-listing

At this stage the employer has to decide who to interview. Often, it is not possible to interview all the applicants so the employer will read the applications to find out which applicants have the skills, qualifications and experience needed.

Having made the initial selection, the referees will be approached to check what sort of person the applicant is. Those who have been shortlisted to come for an interview will be sent a letter stating the day, time and place. Usually, the applicant will write or phone to confirm the details or perhaps to alter the day or even to reject the offer of the interview.

The interview

What happens on the day of the interview can vary. Some employers will give you a tour of their premises and introduce you to various people you might be working with or they might give you various tests on maths, English or something relating to the job. When you confirm the interview it is worth checking what is going to happen on the day, so you can prepare yourself.

There may be more than one interview for you to go through and each interview panel may have several people on it. They will be trying to find out whether you can do the job that was advertised, whether you will be able to fit in with them and what potential you might have for the future. At the end of the interview you will normally get the chance to ask questions – it is important that you do because you have to be happy with the job you are offered.

You might want to ask about the training you will get, your chances of promotion, holidays, salary, recreational facilities or sports clubs.

You should also discuss any fringe benefits that might be on offer – these could include a company car, interest free loan for season tickets, free medical insurance and discounts when buying goods.

Having taken all these things into account you should, if you can, consider whether you will enjoy the job. Job satisfaction helps make the day pleasurable. However, when jobs are hard to find, it might be the least of your worries.

You may be told on the day whether you have the job or you may have to wait several days while they interview other people.

Who to appoint

When making their decision the employers must not discriminate against people because of their sex, race, colour or nationality. If they do they are breaking the law and the person they have discriminated against would be entitled to compensation.

Training

Training or opportunities for further study should be very much in your mind when you join a firm. None of us can expect the skills we currently have to last us the rest of our working days. This is because technology changes very rapidly and we need to

You are the owner of a small retail record and cassette shop and want to employ somebody part-time to help you in the shop. You have only had two people apply for the post, Amy and Albert.

Albert is 55, very reliable, and in good health. He knows nothing about pop music.

Amy is 19. Her school report shows she was often absent and late. She knows a lot about pop music.

Questions

1 Write a list of the sorts of jobs Albert or Amy might be expected to do.

2 List five questions you would ask Amy and Albert to find out if they were suitable for your shop.

3 On the basis of the little information you have about Amy and Albert, whom would you appoint and why?

4 Explain why it is possible that a reference written on a person may not reflect their potential ability.

develop a range of skills.

Nowadays, for school leavers, much of the training is done through YTS courses, and apprenticeships are becoming less and less common. Although people do spend many years working for the same firm, there is much to be said for broadening your experience by changing jobs. This gives you new ways of looking at problems and often allows you to improve your salary.

The method of paying employees varies from firm to firm. Very often you are required to open a bank account so that you can be paid by Giro transfer straight into your account. You will receive a pay-slip showing how much you have been paid, and how much has been deducted for income tax and National Insurance. You might be paid a flat salary or you could work for a commission. This is particularly common in selling jobs, it is quite simple – the more you sell the more you earn! Some people in manufacturing work on piece rates. In this case they are paid for every unit they produce.

Appraisal

Nowadays many employees have their performance assessed, often by their manager. This is done to help people improve their performance in doing their job. In about 40% of firms it is used to determine whether they should be paid more.

POINTS TO REMEMBER

★ People are the most important element in running a successful business.

★ It is worth taking time and effort in appointing the right people.

★ Modern jobs are more attractive where continuous training is available.

Some 9 per cent of the American workforce change occupations in the course of a year...

Questions

As you go through your working life many of you will have to consider changing jobs.

1 Give two reasons why you might have to change the type of job you do.

2 Why is it likely that we will continue to need chefs and road diggers?

3 Do you think it would be easy or difficult for a road digger to become a chef? Give two reasons for your answer.

4 What benefits do you think there are in changing the sort of job you do?

5 Suggest two ways in which managers can help to prepare their employees to accept job changes within their own firm?

IT ▶ GRAPHICS

Survey of job changing

Interview 20 adults and record the different full-time jobs they have done. Use a graphics package to illustrate the number of different jobs each has done. You may need to think carefully about how this can be displayed if you cannot get 20 along the horizontal axis.

TASK 1

Look at the jobs shown in the pictures.

1 Write in each job at the top of a column. List under each job which of the descriptions opposite may apply to it. You can use each description more than once if you want to:

2 Check your list with a group of three other students. Do you agree?

3 Suggest reasons why each person is paid the amount they are.

4 Present your reasons to the rest of the class and see if they agree.

high academic qualifications
long hours
dirty job
short working life
job security
good working conditions

respected by society
no qualifications
training needed
great talent required
trade union member
employed by a local authority

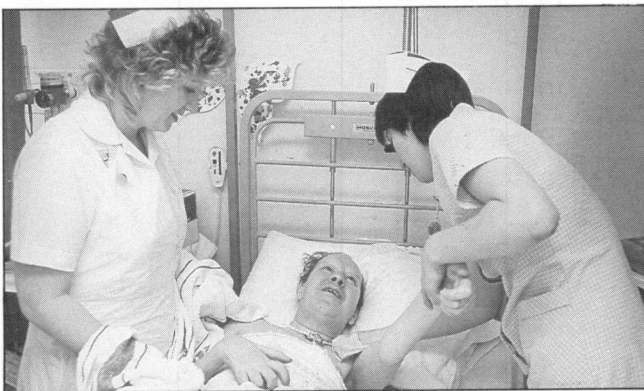

Nurse
Salary £9000

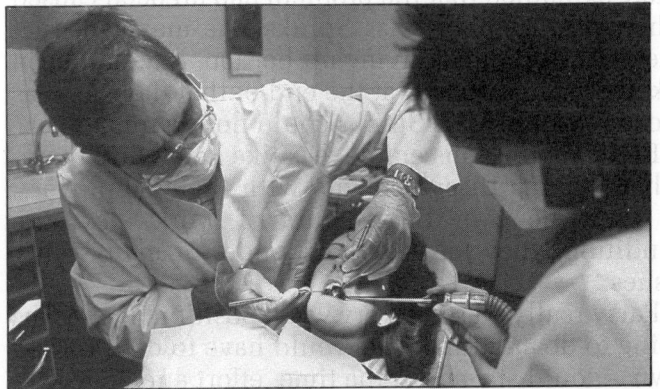

Coalminer
Salary £13 000

Footballer
Salary £30 000

Dentist
Salary £25 000

Police officer
Salary £14 000

Production line worker
Salary £13 000

Trade Unions

Being sacked!

Patsy explained that the problem had all been caused when she had told Miss Spinks, the manager, that she was thinking of giving up her job. She had been taken at her word and at the end of that day she was sacked. Surely Miss Spinks could not do this to her?

For many reasons employees like Patsy find themselves having disagreements with their employers. It could be over their hours of work, pay, the conditions they have to work under or many other issues.

Patsy really was in a very weak position. If she was going to do anything, she would have to do it on her own – could she afford the time, effort and energy to appeal to an employment tribunal?

Obviously Patsy was in need of help. Many people get this help by being members of a trade union. It may seem old-fashioned to talk about 'trades' but nowadays trade unions are available in many different jobs: shopworkers can join the Union of Shop, Distributive and Allied Workers (USDAW); office workers and managers can join the Manufacturing, Science and Finance union (MSF); while doctors can be members of the British Medical Association (BMA).

Safety in numbers

The reason why people join together in unions is to make sure that there is support from others when a difficulty arises. In Patsy's case, she was on her own and would have found it very difficult to do anything about being sacked.

Members pay a subscription so that the union can employ officials to run the union and provide services. The services include legal advice, representation in negotiations over pay and conditions of work and even arranging compensation in cases where members are made redundant. Many unions also run welfare schemes to which members contribute so that they can have financial help when they are absent from work due to illness or injury.

In each workplace members elect their representatives to speak for the members in discussions with management. For example, teachers belong to different unions and each union elects a teacher to act for its members in discussions with the head teacher – who is often a member of a union as well.

Collective bargaining

Many unions enter into 'collective bargaining' with employers. This means they have talks about the pay and conditions of work on behalf of all their

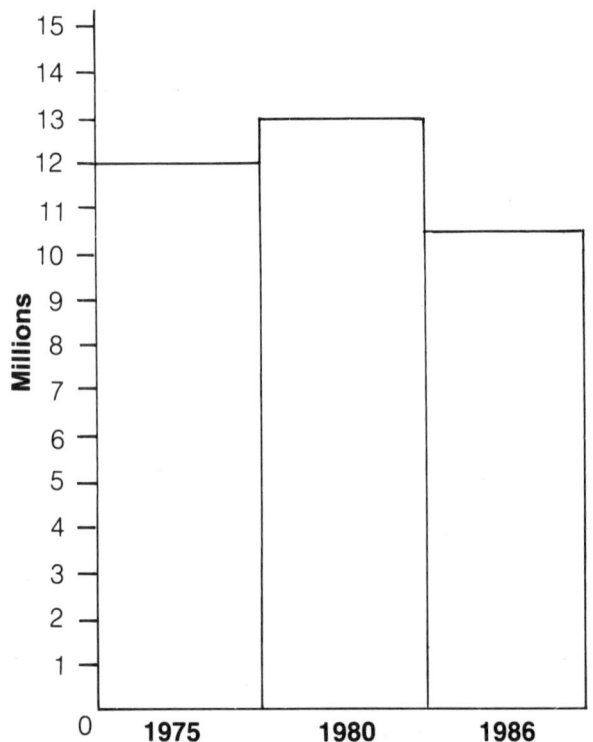

TRADES UNION MEMBERSHIP IN MILLIONS

Questions

1 How many people were members of trade unions in 1975?

2 By how many did trade union membership fall between:
   a 1975 and 1986?
   b 1980 and 1986?

3 If the working population of Britain in 1986 was 22 million, what percentage were members of trade unions?

4 Give one reason why you think trade unions are losing members.

5 Redraw this bar chart, altering the scales, to make it appear that union membership decreased drastically between 1980 and 1986.

members. Where unions do not exist, employers have to negotiate with each employee as an individual.

Strikes

In many people's minds unions are associated with strikes and disruption. It is, in fact, very costly to go on strike and not something that union members undertake lightly. In recent years the number of working days lost due to strikes has been decreasing. This is partly because of the costs to the union members and their families and to a change in the law which requires unions to hold a secret ballot of members to ask if they want to go on strike. Before this, a strike could be called after a show of hands at a mass meeting of the membership.

ACAS

When unions and their employers cannot reach agreement they often use the services of ACAS (Advisory, Conciliation and Arbitration Service) which is an independent body. This service, independent of both sides, tries to find common ground which can lead to a settlement.

TUC

Many unions are members of the TUC (Trades Union Congress) which tries to promote the general interests of unions and sort out problems between them. In the same way as many large companies give money to the Conservative Party, many unions give financial support to the Labour Party.

No-strike agreements

A recent issue amongst unions has been the introduction of 'no-strike' agreements. The benefit of this to employers is a guarantee of no disruption. Union members have to give up their sanction of withdrawing their labour if they do not like what the employer is doing. Some unions like EETPU (Electrical, Electronic, Telecommunications and Plumbing Union) have signed such agreements in return for improvements in pay and conditions.

POINTS TO REMEMBER

★ The strength of a union is achieved because its members act together.

★ Unions provide a range of services for members.

★ Union membership is declining.

People usually join a trade union which represents those who have the same things in common. For example, 'craft' unions represent people who have a particular skill or specialism. 'Industry' unions exist where all the people in an industry can be represented by the same union. There are also the 'general' unions which represent people who work in a wide range of industries.

NUM
NUT • COHSE
MSF • EETPU
TGWU • USDAW
NUPE • BMA • AEU
UDM • NUBE
ISTC

Questions

1 What are the full names of the unions shown above?

2 Head three columns 'craft', 'industry' and 'general' and list each of the unions under the appropriate heading.

3 Which of the unions shown above would it be most appropriate for each of the following to join?
a a computer operator.
b a bank clerk.
c a nurse.
d a foundry worker.
e a shop assistant.
f a teacher.
g a mineworker.
h a refuse collector.
i an electrician.
j a hospital porter.
k a hairdresser.
l a school cook.

TASK 1

1 What services does a union usually provide?

2 Which union do you think Patsy could join?

3 What are union subscriptions used for?

4 Why are strikes less frequent these days?

TASK 2

WELLBELL ENGINEERING – MANAGERS MEET SHOP STEWARDS TO CONSIDER DISCIPLINE

IT ▶ **DESKTOP**

Prepare an A4 leaflet for distribution to all employees stating the outcome of the discussions on each point. Remember this is a serious matter and the leaflet should reflect this.

This task should be undertaken in groups of four. Two of the group managers of Wellbell Engineering, who manufacture parking meters, and the other two are shop stewards representing the workers. The group has to decide which of the actions below should lead to instant dismissal and which should result in a warning to the employee concerned. If you wish to state how many times each incident should be allowed before action is taken you should record this.

a not phoning in when ill.
b fighting with other employees.
c being late five times per month.
d making private telephone calls.
e taking 50 company envelopes.
f poor quality work.
g smoking in the paint store.
h arriving for work drunk.
i clocking in for another employee.
j swearing at a supervisor.

TASK 3

WAGE NEGOTIATION GROUP WORK

You should form teams of three members. One team is composed of union representatives, the other represents management.

All team members should take part in negotiations but you will need a timekeeper to time strikes, a secretary to record your position and a main negotiator.

At the end of the negotiation one member of each side should report to the rest of the class what they managed to achieve and what cost their side had to suffer.

Thirty minutes will be needed to look at the conditions surrounding the negotiations.

Background on the firm

The firm under discussion is Novatex plc which employs a workforce of 150 people of which 120 belong to the union. In the last two years Novatex's profits have been steadily increasing but that was only after five very bad years when large losses were incurred. During those years 50 union members lost their jobs and there had been a strike in each year protesting about the job losses. In each of the last three years the annual wage negotiations had produced pay increases of 2.5%, 4% and 3.5%.

The need to break even

To break even this year, orders worth £100,000 must be secured. The company will go out of business if it does not achieve this.

Future prospects

Future prospects for the company are far from certain. A major customer, Plyrite, which places an annual order for £20,000, is threatening to withdraw if a lower price cannot be offered. Any pay increase above 5% would mean this order would be lost. The local council has just imposed a large rates increase and it is inevitable that 10 people will have to lose their jobs to meet it. As the company believes it is already overstaffed by 10 people, there will be no loss of output because of this.

On the brighter side the national economy is improving and three large orders could be won if delivery dates can be guaranteed. These are valued at £50,000 each. However, the company will lose £12,000 of orders for every 1% the pay rise is above 5%. It is not certain whether these orders will be repeated in future years. In the past the unions, despite the strikes, have been co-operative, though reluctant, in recognising the problems of the firm.

TASK 3 CONTINUED

However, its members are becoming increasingly concerned that their standard of living is falling because their pay increases are less than the rate of inflation.

The annual pay round

The crunch has come. The members of the unions are demanding a 10% pay increase and expect no job losses. Having taken a ballot, the union is able to call a strike for one minute if any offer of less than 8% is made by the company or if any job losses are threatened.

The costs of a strike

The company sees 10% as totally unreasonable. Strikes are the alternative to talking – but they are costly to both the firm and the union members. However, they might just make somebody shift their position. 20 minutes are allowed to complete the negotiations and find a settlement. Every one minute of strike during negotiations loses four union jobs and orders from customers worth £10,000.

The conditions for each side

For the trade unions:
a trying to get a 10% wage increase.
b if they are offered less than 10% they can strike if they want to.
c if they are threatened with job losses they can strike for one minute – this will, however cause the loss of four jobs.

For management:
a need £100,000 of orders to break even.
b need to lose 10 workers to pay for the rates rise.
c maximum possible orders is £170,000.
d for every 1% the pay rise is above 5% they will lose £12,000 of orders.
e if the pay rise is more than 5% they lose the order for £20,000.
f each strike of one minute causes £10,000 of lost orders.

After negotiations are complete management will need to calculate its orders.

MAXIMUM POSSIBLE	£170,000
Loss due to strikes	....
Loss due to wage increase above 5% (£20,000)	....
Loss for every % above 5% £12,000 for each 1%	....
FINAL TOTAL OF ORDERS =	_____

If less than £100,000 you go out of business

OVERALL SUMMARY CHART

Team	Wage Increase	Job Losses	Orders Gained	Strike Minutes
	%		£	mins

De-briefing points

1 Which team has negotiated most successfully?

2 What were the styles of negotiation (co-operation or confrontation)?

3 Could ACAS have helped?

4 What happened to non-union members?

Business Law

One of the important things to remember when looking at business law is to realise that each individual situation must be looked at in great detail before a final conclusion can be reached. After all, if everybody was completely certain about the law cases would not have to go to court to be decided!

Making a contract

Every day many people make legal contracts. For example, paying for a bus ride or buying lunch both have all the ingredients required to make a contract.

Firstly, you make an 'offer' which can be made by word of mouth and somebody 'accepts' the offer. For this to be a contract in the eyes of the law there must also be 'consideration'. This means that there must either be some gain taken by one person or some loss suffered by another.

For example, if a person sold a car, he loses the car and the buyer gains the car so there is consideration on his side. The buyer gives up his money and the seller gains the money so there is consideration on both sides. Because all the ingredients of a contract are present, the contract can be enforced in law.

Enforcing a contract

Many contracts are made in business every day and are carried out with no problems, but sometimes things do go wrong. For example, suppose you agreed to buy 1000 boxes of oranges for your whole-sale shop and the seller did not send them. What can you do? If you can get no satisfaction by contacting the seller and sorting out the problem, you could take him to court. You may be able to claim an amount of money from the seller in 'damages' or the court may order the seller to carry out the contract and deliver the oranges.

Invitation to treat

Whilst an offer may be by word of mouth or in writing, it should not be confused with an 'invitation to treat'. When you see goods for sale in a shop this does not mean the shopkeeper is making you an offer. It just means he is inviting you to come in and make him an offer! This explains why a shop does not have to sell you any of the goods on display because they are not actually there as an offer for sale.

Ways of accepting an offer

The acceptance of an offer can again be oral, in writing or by what is called 'by conduct'. For example, if a bus stops at a bus-stop, that is the offer. When you get on the bus you are, by your conduct, accepting the offer.

Questions

1 Does the price ticket indicate that the knife is being offered for sale at £18?

2 What is the 'consideration' if a sale is made?

3 Write a paragraph which could be put in an Act of Parliament which would restrict the sale of knives to 'undesirable people' but would still let people buy them for normal use.

If you were to reply to an offer by post, the law states that you have accepted the offer when you have posted the letter – not when it is received by the person who made the offer.

Terms and conditions in a contract
When you make a contract you may find that it is subject to certain terms or conditions. For example, if you rent a flat, there may be a condition which prevents you from keeping any pets in the flat.

Exclusion clauses
In business, some firms have tried to hide behind such exclusion clauses – the most common being ones which say the firm is not liable for any damage caused. Whether or not this can be upheld depends on whether the claim is considered to be reasonable. If, for example, a dry cleaning firm damages a coat, a court may have to decide if they took reasonable care. This would depend on the facts of the individual case.

Negligence
An increasing concern for manufacturers of goods is the possibility that their products might cause damage. This takes us into an area of law called negligence. In 1932 a case was heard in the House of Lords where a person had drunk from a bottle of ginger beer which had somehow been bottled with a snail in it. The person drinking it became ill and the manufacturer was held to be liable to pay damages.

Such cases do crop up from time to time. For example some years ago pregnant mothers were given a drug to help with morning sickness. It was claimed that the drug had a serious side effect which led to deformed babies. You can imagine that the potential claims against a company could be very large. Claims in this area can take a long time to settle and the legal cost can be very high. Some people think that it is unfair to expect individuals to have to take on large companies in the courts in cases of negligence and that another solution should be found.

Product liability insurance
Most manufacturers take out product liability insurance to meet such claims. In the US claims can run into millions of dollars whilst settlements in the UK tend to be much lower.

Acts of Parliament
Parliament is constantly engaged in the process of looking at the law to see if it needs altering to improve it or to reflect changes which have taken place in society. This leads to the drafting of Bills, which are then discussed in parliament. When they become law, these are called 'Acts'. Some of the provisions of various Acts are given below.

Trades Descriptions Act 1968
This Act makes it an offence to describe wrongly goods and services which are being sold. Action can

Questions

1 Do you think that the sign states a reasonable exclusion of liability by the car park owners?

2 Would your answer be different if the charge was 10p per hour?

■IT▶ DESKTOP

Much of our law is decided when cases are heard by courts. These decisions give rise to a 'precedent' which is a decision which is often followed in later cases.

Try to advance your study of law by some research.

Questions

1 Find some law books in your local or school library and find out what happened in each of the following cases, which all come from the law of contract. Your group should divide up the research work.
Carlill v Carbolic Smoke Ball Company 1893
Fisher v Bell 1961
Chappell v Nestlé Company Limited 1960
Appleson v Littlewood Pools
Eastham v Newcastle United Football
   Club 1964
Jackson v Horizon Holidays Ltd 1975
Doyle v White City Stadium Ltd 1935
Raffles v Wichelhaus 1864

2 Use a desktop publishing package to produce newspaper reports on each case with a suitable headline.

3 Produce a wall display showing the research and desktop publishing your group has done.

be taken by the local Trading Standards Officer who is employed by the local council.

Fair Trading Act 1973

This Act gives the Director General of Fair Trading the power to refer to the Monopolies and Mergers Commission any merger between two firms which may not be in the public interest. For example, two companies who are in competition may try to merge to avoid having to compete against each other – this could lead to a lack of choice or higher prices for the consumer. The final outcome could be that the merger is stopped.

Consumer Credit Act 1974

This limits your liability for lost credit cards to £50 and gives user rights against the credit card company, as well as the seller, if goods are faulty.

Unfair Contract Terms Act 1977

The Act stops suppliers of goods avoiding their legal duties by hiding behind unreasonable conditions in contracts.

Sale of Goods Act 1979

This requires goods to be of merchantable quality, that means in a fit condition to be sold. For example, if you bought a new car the seats should not be torn or dirty. This, however, may not be necessary for a second-hand car even if it is to be of merchantable quality. The goods should also be fit for their purpose. This means that, if you buy a bucket, it should not leak.

Supply of Goods and Services Act 1982

The Act gives protection against faulty work when you have goods repaired. The general rule is that repairs should be carried out to a reasonable standard.

Data Protection Act 1984

This requires users of personal information on computers to register what use they are making of the data. It is a criminal offence not to comply with this requirement.

Companies Act 1985

This Act controls the setting up and running of companies.

Company Directors Disqualification Act 1986

In recent years there has been much concern about people who set up companies with limited liability and then go out of business owing a lot of money. The effect of limited liability was that they did not have to pay back what they owed before they started up another company. Under this Act such people can be disqualified from becoming directors of companies again and could be made personally liable for the debts of the company.

Porky-Pies Ltd let off!

A company selling pies was let off without any fine after they had been prosecuted by a local council because one of its pork pies was found to contain some oil. It is a criminal offence, under the Food and Drugs Act, to sell food which is unfit for human consumption. The court heard that the company cleaned the mixing machines at the start of each day, but in this instance some oil must have got into the mixture.

Question

Can you explain why no fine was imposed in this case?

Questions

Look at the picture of the man eating a biscuit with a maggot in it.

1 You have been engaged to defend the biscuit manufacturer. Write a paragraph explaining why you think no fine should be imposed.

2 Having answered question 1 write a paragraph explaining why this defence is not sufficient to avoid a fine.

European law

As the UK is a member of the European Community it has to follow laws which the Community makes. One such law to come into force in 1992 will allow the free movement of people, goods, services and money between European Community member states.

POINTS TO REMEMBER

★ Laws help to control business activity.

★ Laws change to meet new situations.

★ European law is becoming more important.

TASK 1

BUYING SHEEP

On 1st November you were offered a contract to buy 50 sheep. As you cannot personally visit the seller, on 17th November you post a letter accepting the offer.

The letter is delayed in the post and the seller receives it on 25th November. However, on the 24th November he sold the sheep to somebody else because you had not replied to the letter.

1 Explain what rights you have in this matter.

TASK 2

UNFAIR DISMISSAL?

If an employee is going to be sacked, then the firm should make sure that:

the dismissal was reasonable.
other solutions to the problem were considered.
the person was treated in the same way as other employees.

Read the two reports of an incident presented to an industrial tribunal claiming a dismissal was unfair.

Group discussion

In a group of four decide whether or not you think the employee was fairly dismissed. Note down the reasons for your decision. When you have done this you can compare your answer with other groups.

IT ▶ WORDPRO

Wordprocess a letter to the employee outlining the reasons for your decision.

Report from employer

The employees had already been warned for lateness on five occasions. We usually dismiss employees if they are late four times. She arrived for work 15 minutes late and was told to report to the manager. The manager warned her that if she was late again she would be dismissed. On hearing this she swore at the manager and left the office. No action was taken on this, but the following day she was one hour late and was dismissed.

Report by employee

I had been late on several occasions but most have been due to my husband, who is unemployed, being ill and my having to take my three children to school. The manager swore at me during our last interview. On the day I was dismissed, the bus did not turn up on time and I had to walk to work. I tried to explain this to the manager but he just told me I was sacked.

Privatisation

'If you see Sid – tell him'

You may remember this slogan. It is an example of what the advertisers call a 'whispering campaign' and, although eventually many people became tired of hearing it, it will always remain associated with the sale of shares in British Gas.

The sale of nationalised industries

The government was the owner of British Gas, which was a nationalised industry, until it decided to turn it into a public company. This meant that the individuals and institutions (like pension funds and insurance companies) who bought shares became the new owners. All the money which was paid for British Gas shares went to the government who thus gave up ownership. This process of changing a nationalised industry into a public company is called 'privatisation'.

Government policy

This policy has been promoted very strongly by the government in the 1980s. They believe that if shares in companies are owned by many people there is an incentive to work hard for a successful economy. Opponents of the process of privatisation would argue that very important industries like gas supply should not be owned by shareholders but by everyone in the country – through the elected government.

Are these industries different?

British Gas is expected to make a profit. As a 'nationalised industry', it was able to charge lower prices to consumers like British Rail and accept lower profits. Some nationalised industries have often made losses and these have been 'subsidised' by payments from tax-payers.

In order to consider your own view on this issue you will have to think carefully about why some industries should be thought of as different and why they might not exist simply to make profits.

The government has sold its control of several large organisations including British Aerospace, Jaguar Cars, British Gas and BP. Sometimes the government decides to keep some shares and therefore some control over how the companies are run. For example, the government still owns 50% of the shares in British Telecom.

Raising revenue for the government

As the new companies can no longer rely on financial help from the government, they have to charge competitive prices and aim to make profits. The government also obtains large sums of money from

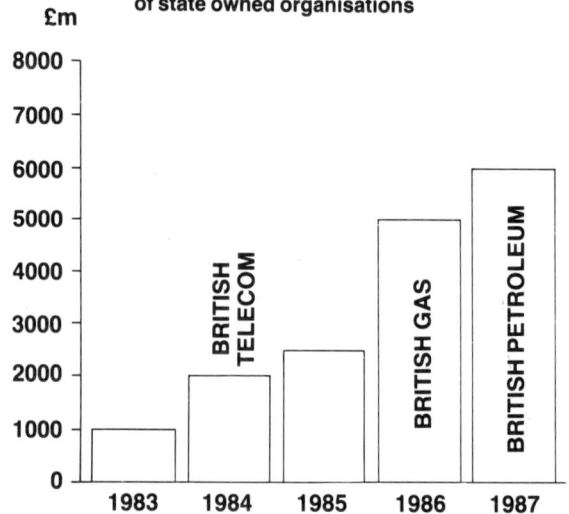

Money raised from the privatisation of state owned organisations

£m — 1983, 1984, 1985, 1986, 1987 — BRITISH TELECOM, BRITISH GAS, BRITISH PETROLEUM

Money raised from the privatisation of state-owned organisations

Questions

1 How much did the sale of shares in British Gas raise for the government?

2 Approximately how much has the government raised from privatisation issues since 1988?

3 If British Petroleum shares cost 330p each, approximately how many were issued?

4 If the government had not privatised these industries, how else could it have raised this amount of money?

5 The government is preparing to sell the Water Authorities. Do you think it is a good idea to do so? What effect do you think this would have on the consumption of water?

selling shares. This means that it does not have to borrow so much to pay for all the things on which it spends money.

Quick profits or an investment

The government has tried to make sure that as many people as possible can buy the shares in these new companies and, when people apply to buy the shares, the number they can buy is often limited. Some have bought the shares, not because they want to invest in the new companies, but because the want to make a quick profit when the newly-sold share prices rise.

Generally, lots of people want to buy shares in these new companies – often more than are available for sale. Unsuccessful investors may be able to purchase shares as soon as they are re-sold. If lots of people want the shares, the price will start to increase – in some cases prices have doubled. The people who just want a quick profit are called 'stags' and they sell their shares for more than they bought them and make a profit. About 1.6 million people bought shares in British Telecom and on the same day as they were first issued they could be resold for almost twice the amount for which they had been bought.

For those shareholders who hold onto their shares there is the prospect of getting dividends every year. There are sometimes other benefits available, such as the vouchers which British Gas shareholders can use towards paying their gas bills.

Effects of privatisation

Although many people see privatisation as a way to make quick profits, there are other points that need to be looked at to see if it is really worthwhile. One of these is the effect on consumers.

Obviously, if the new companies are efficient, prices may fall and the quality of service improve. On the other hand, the need to run at a profit could mean that prices rise and services are cut.

POINTS TO REMEMBER

★ Privatisation takes place when an organisation owned by the government becomes a public limited company owned by shareholders.

★ People buy shares sometimes to make a quick profit and sometimes as a long-term investment.

★ There are arguments for and against privatisation.

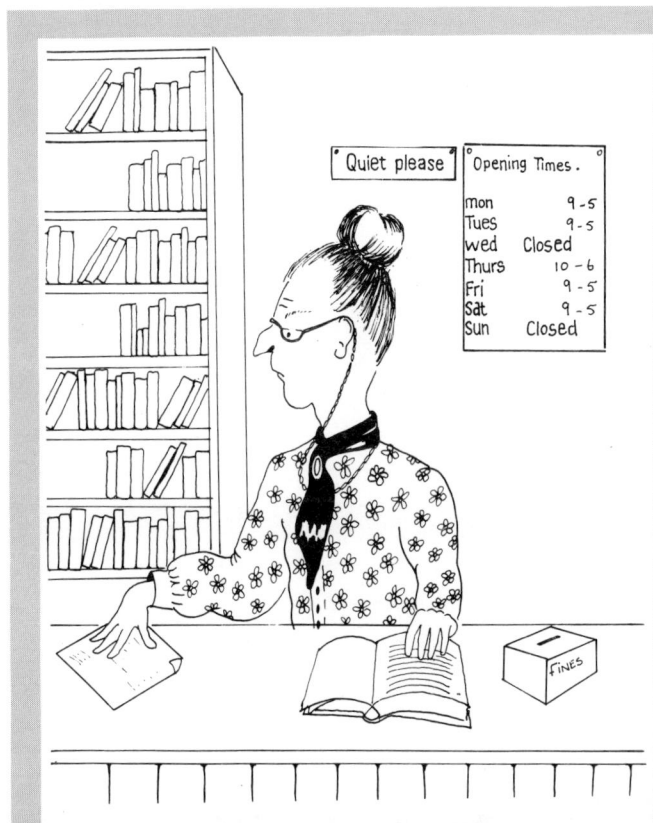

Group activity – debate

The arguments for and against privatisation have been extended to include all sorts of services. These can include any of the activities underdaken by your local authority. It may not involve the issuing of shares but it means that services such as school meals or refuse collection could be provided by companies.

One side should present the argument that libraries are kept under the control of local authorities and the other should argue that a complete rethink is needed to get rid of the library image as portrayed in the picture.

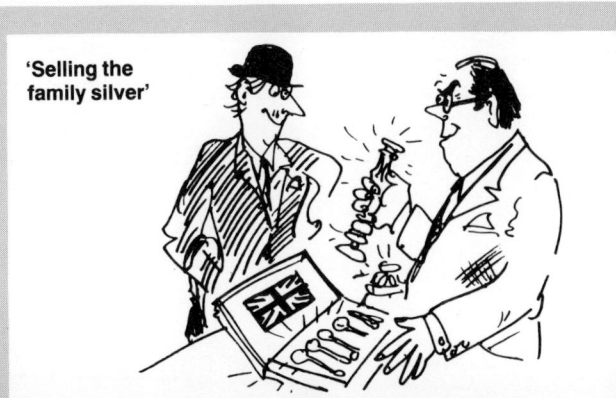

'Selling the family silver'

Question

Privatisation has been called 'selling the family silver'. Can you explain why some people take this view?

TASK 1

1 Name three industries which have been privatised.

2 What advantages does privatisation have for the government?

3 What are the benefits of privatisation for the new shareholders?

4 Explain how a 'stag' makes profits out of new share issues.

TASK 2

Some nationalised industries have been 'got ready' for privatisation by turning them from unprofitable to profitable organisations. Explain how each of the following would have helped or hindered British Airways when they were about to be privatised.

a replacement of senior management.
b staff reduced by 17,000.
c services withdrawn on some routes.
d fears over terrorism grow.
e fewer American visitors to UK following Chernobyl disaster.

TASK 3

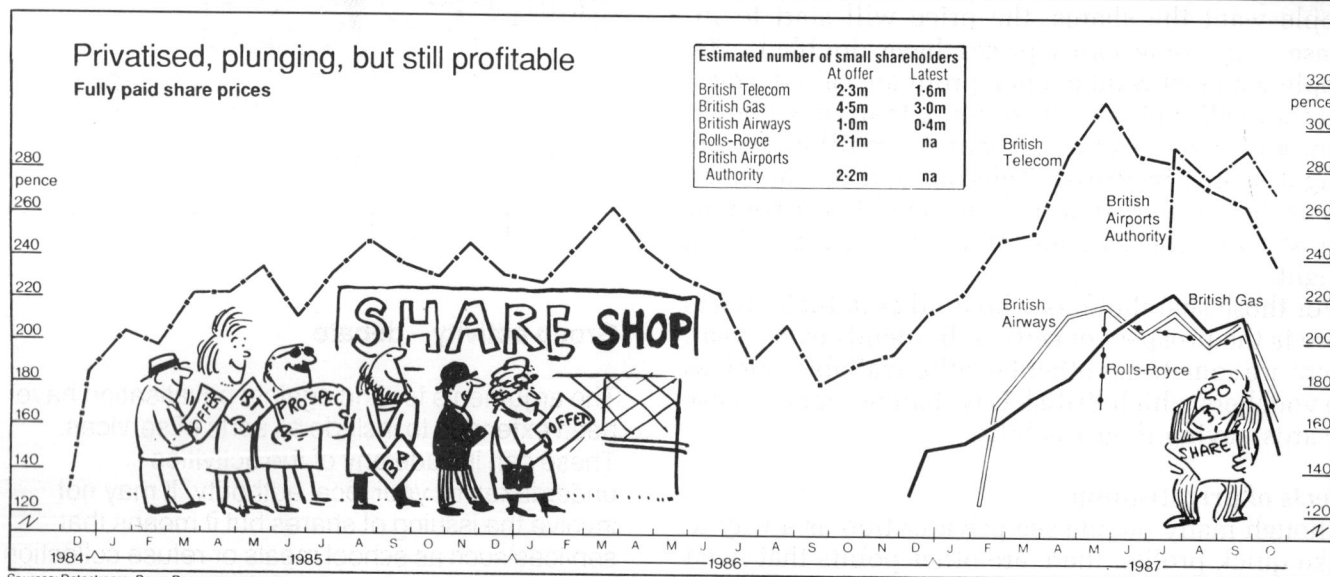

Privatised, plunging, but still profitable
Fully paid share prices

Estimated number of small shareholders		
	At offer	Latest
British Telecom	2·3m	1·6m
British Gas	4·5m	3·0m
British Airways	1·0m	0·4m
Rolls-Royce	2·1m	na
British Airports Authority	2·2m	na

Sources: Datastream; Dewe Rogerson; company reports

1 How many small shareholders in British Gas have sold their shares?

2 What percentage of small shareholders in British Airways have sold their shares?

3 Explain what has happened to the price of Rolls Royce shares since May 1987.

4 What evidence is there to support the view that most people buy privatisation issues only to make a profit by a quick re-sale of them?

TASK 4

BP

What happened to the British Petroleum share issue?

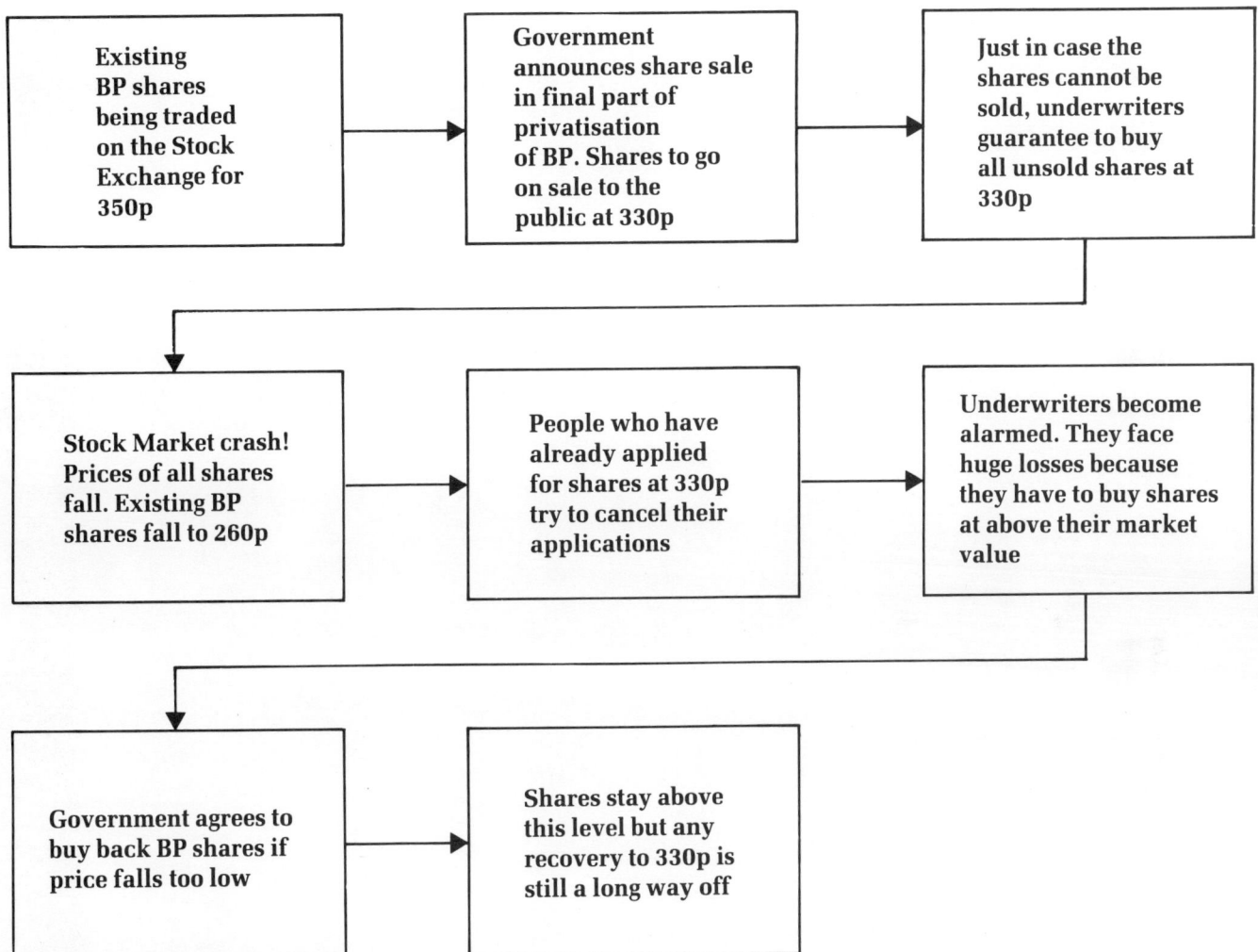

Existing BP shares being traded on the Stock Exchange for 350p	**Government announces share sale in final part of privatisation of BP. Shares to go on sale to the public at 330p**	**Just in case the shares cannot be sold, underwriters guarantee to buy all unsold shares at 330p**
Stock Market crash! Prices of all shares fall. Existing BP shares fall to 260p	**People who have already applied for shares at 330p try to cancel their applications**	**Underwriters become alarmed. They face huge losses because they have to buy shares at above their market value**
Government agrees to buy back BP shares if price falls too low	**Shares stay above this level but any recovery to 330p is still a long way off**	

1 Why did the government not try to get 350p for each share, if that is what they were worth on the Stock Exchange?

2 People who applied early for BP shares, before the price fell, were not allowed to cancel their applications. Do you think this was a fair decision?

3 The underwriters, who had been paid fees for guaranteeing to take up all unsold shares, wanted to cancel their obligations to buy the shares. Do you think they should have been allowed to do so?

4 What advice would you give to investors before they make an application for shares in the next industry to be privatised?

Investigating the
GOVERNMENT
Background

Government and Business

The mixed economy

In earlier units we considered the issue of a 'mixed' economy, in which some things are run by private enterprise for profit and others are controlled by the state. We also said that things are now more and more run by private firms because the government believes that competition is a good motive for efficiency and that it gives consumers more choice.

Problems of the 'free' market

We know that this kind of 'free' market system does not always work fairly. Sometimes competition forces firms out of business leaving a very few producers as 'monopolists' – the only suppliers. They can often charge high prices since the consumer has no alternative market in which to buy. Another problem of the free market is that firms may find it difficult to invest in major projects without government financial support – especially where schemes involve new technology which will not pay the money back for many years.

The present government view is that firms should be made to stand on their own feet and find their own funds for investment. It is for this reason that so many firms have been 'privatised' in the last five or so years. However, there is more to government economic policy than running nationalised industries, or selling them off.

Policy objectives

It would be impossible to list every economic objective for a government and, in any case, they vary from year to year and depend on which political party is in power. The views of one conservative government may differ from those of another. We can try to group the business policies in order to understand them.

Business policies

The control of nationalised industries. At the time of writing, these are electricity supply, British Coal, British Rail and the Post Office. The last to be sold off to public shareholders was British Gas and it is likely that electricity supply and parts of the Post Office will be sold off too.

These have remained in state ownership so far because they have been considered very important to the whole economy. They benefit from the large investment which public money has made available for them. It must be said that they are now subject to much tighter controls and the government takes the view that they must all be considered for privatisation.

Monopoly policy. In a free market system, firms

British Gas

Control of prices – British Gas

The Director General of Fair Trading, Sir Gordon Borrie, has asked the Monopolies and Mergers Commission to investigate British Gas's pricing policy to large industrial customers. These companies do not pay a standard tariff rate but they are able to negotiate individual contracts. This leads to a wide variation in the prices paid by different customers.

Questions

1 Why might this practice be unfair to some companies?

2 Why should the government wish to intervene through the Director General of Fair Trading?

British TELECOM

It's you we answer to.

British Telecom

A similar concern to the British Gas problem above has been expressed by 'OFTEL' the British Telecom industry 'watchdog'. The director, Brian Carsberg, has called for an enquiry into what will happen to telephone charges when the present agreements between the government and BT run out in 1989.

Questions

1 Why should the government continue to monitor the charges levied by a private firm like BT?

2 Should it do the same for Cadbury Schweppes or Ford Motors?

will expand by merger and takeover. Competition will force out the less competitive firms. Some of this competition is healthy – large firms benefit from economies of scale and are better able to compete in world markets. On the other hand, less competition may mean less choice for the consumer and higher prices. For this reason the government regulates monopolies, mergers and unfair trade policies through the department of the Director General of Fair Trading and a number of Acts of Parliament.

Financial support for industry. In the past, governments have spent a lot of money on the support of industry in depressed areas through regional policy – grants, loans and concessions to firms in Development Areas, Intermediate Areas and Special Development Zones. This policy is now concentrated on smaller regional 'assisted' areas and on Enterprise Zones. These are mainly designed to create jobs in areas where industry has been declining. The government also gives help to small firms and to industries in rural areas. The European Community also supports depressed regions through the European Regional Development Fund.

The problem of 'two nations'

One of the results of the government's policy to restrict its direct financial support for industry has been reduced funding for firms in areas of high regional unemployment. Because these regions are mainly in the traditional 'industrial 'North' of the country, we often hear reference made to a 'North-South' divide. There is no doubt that any economic recovery in the last five years has been concentrated in the more affluent South.

Solutions are not easy to find. With affluence in the South has come high house prices, restricting the ability of others to move into the more prosperous areas. With the sale of council houses, there is now less chance for families to be supported through local authority housing schemes – although the government is trying to make private rented housing more attractive to property owners.

POINTS TO REMEMBER

★ All governments take some responsibility for the control and support of industry but this varies according to their view. Socialist states control prices, investment policy and employment in a large section of the economy. Western capitalist countries tend to leave industry to private ownership.

★ Neither of these approaches is necessarily right or wrong. They are simply alternative strategies. Most countries, like Britain, have a mixture of the two systems. It is important to understand the arguments before you draw any conclusions.

Sid, Dave and Bert sell apples in a street market. They are all aware of the prices each of them charge.

Questions

1 Give two reasons why Sid charges 24p per kilo when Bert charges only 12p.

2 Give two reasons why they should all be forced by law to charge the same price.

3 What problems could this cause?

4 If Dave and Bert were struggling to stay in business do you think they should be able to get government help?

TASK 1

AN UPSURGE in the West Lancashire economy has been helped by the improving economy...and a former Basingstoke businessman!

Tony Woodley decided to leave the boom town so that his firm could expand—and he chose Skelmersdale.

Tony (30) who ran his leathercrafts business at Worting until last November, moved with his family to job-starved Skem.

And the father-of-four vows he would not come back to Basingstoke "even if you paid me £1,000"

The firm, called West Lancashire Equestrian, has proved so successful in Skem that Tony has now moved from his starter-unit to a shop in the town.

He said: "I left because the costs of industrial premises in Basingstoke does not encourage people to set up in business. It was too dear for us so we moved to a cheaper area."

"We wanted larger premises but were asked for anything from £8 a sq ft to £25 a sq ft in Basingstoke," he said.

"Down in Basingstoke they charge rent by the square foot because it is so much.

"But for what some businesses almost pay per square foot in Basingstoke, I am paying a week for the same sort of premises."

And he claimed that anyone who thought Skem was gloom and doom had been misinformed.

And our stories highlighting the north-south divide provoked a storm of protest.

Now the deep-rooted problems are still apparent but the mood seems to have changed for the better.

Unemployment is running at 19.5 per cent, but that's down on the figure of about 27 per cent 18 months ago.

THE NORTH-SOUTH DIVIDE

The article above is taken from the *Basingstoke Gazette* – the newspaper serving one of the South's fastest growing towns. It seems to suggest that all is not gloom and doom in Basingstoke's northern counterpart – Skelmersdale, Lancs.

What is the evidence for this optimism?

TASK 2

IT ▶ **DESKTOP**

SELLING SKELMERSDALE

Imagine that you are publicity officer for the town of Skelmersdale. Your task includes making the town attractive to business managers and their families – to encourage firms to come to the town.

Fold a sheet of A4 paper into three and use this format to design a publicity handout for the town. Suggest what makes it an attractive place in which to live and why it is a good location for industry.

You might like to do this for your town. Use the word processor to help with this task.

TASK 3

WHY JUNE 30 IS IMPORTANT TO A MAN IN YOUR POSITION.

If you're undecided about changing your company's source of energy, here's a timely reminder from British Coal.

The Government Grant Scheme, which could provide your company with up to 25% of the capital costs of converting to coal-firing, is due to close for new applications on June 30, 1987.

NO MORE GUESSING GAMES

British Coal has kept its steady competitive price profile through energy crisis after energy crisis. Meantime, oil costs have gone through the roof and back again with monotonous regularity. Oil prices are low now, but what happens next could make a nonsense of your company's forward planning.

RIGHT IN TOUCH WITH TECHNOLOGY

Today's coal-fired plant is a credit to British technology, bristling with new methods of coal handling and burning. And it comes in every shape and size – to suit every shape and size of company.

FOLLOW THE LEADERS

Leading British companies (like ICI, Reed, Tilcon, Bowaters and UML) have recently converted to British Coal. All with a little help from the Government Grant Scheme.

British COAL GET ALL FIRED UP BEFORE JUNE 30

BRITISH COAL

Look at the advertisement above. It represents a slightly different case from British Gas and British Telecom.

1 **Why should the government be prepared to subsidise a firm which is prepared to convert to coal fired power?**

2 **How does this fit into general government policy on the support for industry?**

TASK 4

	Incomes[1]	FE[2]	Owner Occupier[3]
North	170	N/A	55
North West	183	21.7	65
Yorkshire & Humberside	179	28.3	62
West Midlands	192	23.4	63
East Midlands	203	27.9	66
East Anglia	205	26.2	66
South West	209	29.4	69
South East	248	33.4	64
Scotland	198	30.6	41
Wales	187	25.5	67
Northern Ireland	172	31.1	61

1   Average weekly household incomes (£)
2   School leavers going into Further Education (%)
3   Households which own their own home (%)

Regional Unemployment (September 1987)

South East	7.2	Wales	12.9
East Anglia	7.2	North West	13.2
South West	8.2	Scotland	13.4
East Midlands	9.3	North	14.7
West Midlands	11.6	Northern Ireland	18.9
Yorkshire & Humberside	11.8	UK average	10.3

Vat registrations, 1980-85, % of 1979 stock.

Regions ranked by net registrations

	Net	Regist-rations	Deregist-rations
South East	14.9	94.3	79.4
N. Ireland	14.4	49.9	35.5
East Anglia	12.6	70.6	58.0
E. Midlands	11.9	75.0	63.1
South West	11.8	71.1	59.3
W. Midlands	11.4	78.9	67.5
Scotland	9.7	66.9	57.2
Wales	9.1	63.7	54.7
North	8.8	71.4	62.6
Yorks & Humb	8.7	74.5	65.8
North West	6.7	80.2	73.5

VAT REGISTRATION

The number of firms which newly register for VAT gives an idea of how many businesses are starting up. De-registrations show those which are closing down.

The net figure gives an idea of how many new businesses are being added in each of the regions.

Look at the indicators for regional inequality.

1   Do all the measures point to the same conclusion?

2   What is your view of the regional problem:
Should the government offer special support?
If so, what kind of support?
What are the dangers of this kind of economic policy?

TASK 5

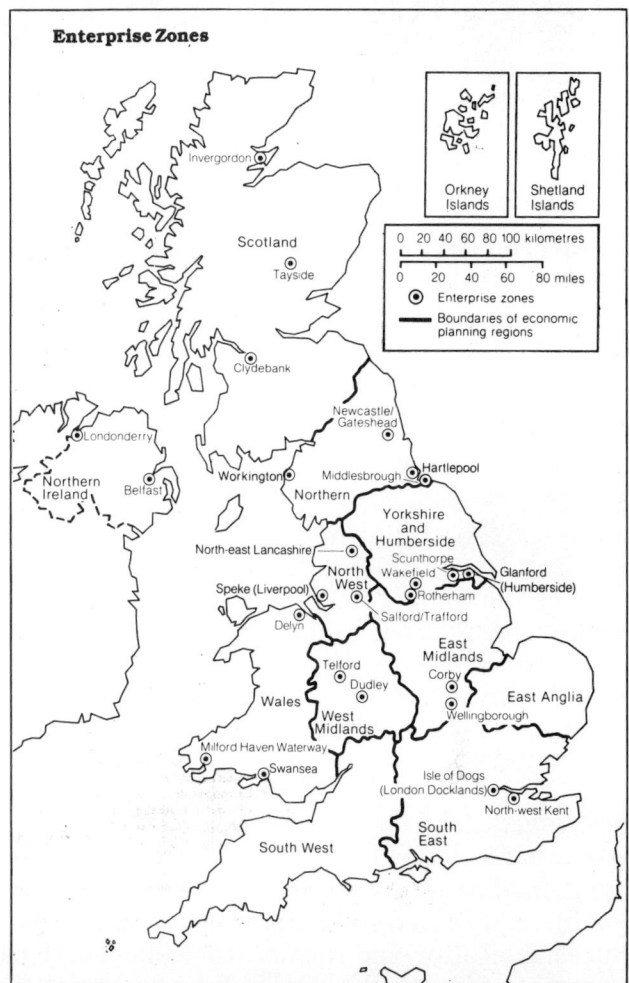

Enterprise Zones

ENTERPRISE ZONES

Since 1986, the government has set up 25 'Enterprise Zones'. These remove some of the taxes paid by firms within a small local area and make it easier for them to expand by removing planning regulations and all local rates.

1   What do you notice about the location of the 25 enterprise zones?

2   How would you measure whether or not they have been successful?

3   How do they fit in with government policy for supporting business enterprise in Britain?

Government and Welfare

The Government's social responsibility

In Britain, as in many other advanced industrial countries, the government takes on a major responsibility for people's well-being and pays for quite a lot of 'social welfare'. Some of this is run by local government – libraries, the police force, etc., and the rest by central government, which is responsible for the National Health Service and social security payments like pensions and child benefit payments.

Many of the arguments which have led to the 'privatisation' of firms in Britain have also led to a review of 'the welfare state'. However, we still have a government-financed health service, we still pay old-age pensions, give child benefits, unemployment pay and family incomes supplements. We can also include here other public spending on areas like education, defence and overseas aid.

Merit goods

These are 'goods' which the government chooses to provide free, or almost free, to all citizens. In Britain these include museums, support for the arts, health services, education and library provision. These can be supplied through the market by private firms as health care in the USA, but the UK government chooses to provide them free. This benefits people on low incomes, who get a service which they might not otherwise afford and it also ensures that the population as a whole gets a standard of health care, education etc., which is at least of a basic and guaranteed quality.

It might be argued that some of these provisions should be removed. Those who argue for a private insurance scheme for medical care, or for private schools and a 'voucher' scheme would take this view. On the other hand, others would argue for an extension of merit goods, basic housing and local transport could be treated as a basic right and provided free, or nearly free, by the state. There are many issues for you to consider.

National Health Service

86 per cent of health care is paid for through general taxation; the rest is met from National Insurance contributions from employers and employees and from charges for prescriptions and dental care. Hospital care and family doctor's services are free. Special attention is paid to the elderly (over 45 per cent of expenditure) and to the mentally ill. As medical knowledge has improved, so more treatment is available, but the system is not always able to keep pace with the growing demand which this creates. Attempts to keep costs down have resulted in arguments about the low pay and poor working conditions of nurses and hospital waiting lists.

Social security

This is designed to provide financial help for people

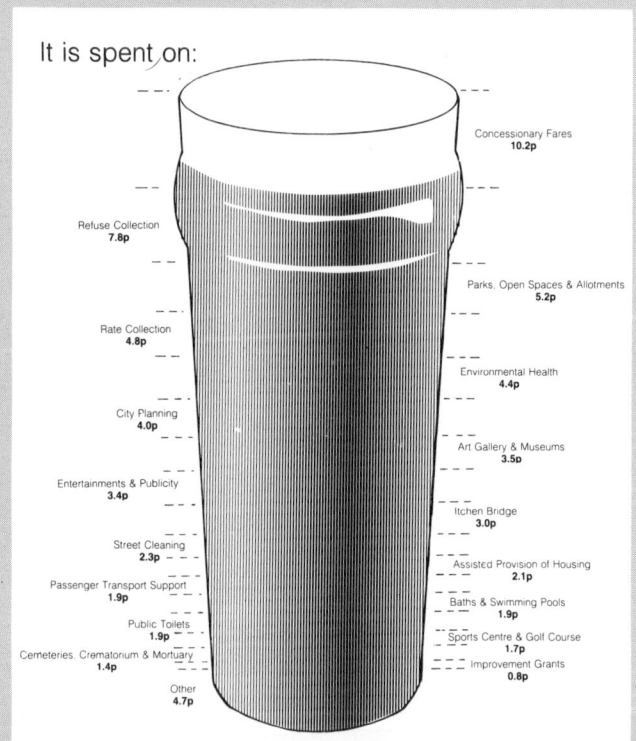

The Average domestic ratepayer pays just 65p per week for City Council Services – about the equivalent of a pint of beer.

It is spent on:

Concessionary Fares 10.2p
Refuse Collection 7.8p
Parks, Open Spaces & Allotments 5.2p
Rate Collection 4.8p
Environmental Health 4.4p
City Planning 4.0p
Art Gallery & Museums 3.5p
Entertainments & Publicity 3.4p
Itchen Bridge 3.0p
Street Cleaning 2.3p
Assisted Provision of Housing 2.1p
Passenger Transport Support 1.9p
Baths & Swimming Pools 1.9p
Public Toilets 1.9p
Sports Centre & Golf Course 1.7p
Cemeteries, Crematorium & Mortuary 1.4p
Improvement Grants 0.8p
Other 4.7p

Southampton City Council

Questions

1 Calculate expenditure on the following as a percentage of the total:
   a refuse collection.
   b art galleries and museums.
   c support for bus fares.

2 Prepare a brief report on city council expenditure in Southampton. You might like to comment on the reasons for its support of concessionary bus fares and housing. Where does the other revenue to provide these services come from?

who are elderly, sick, disabled, unemployed, widowed or bringing up children. Some of these are 'contributory' – paid from National Insurance – and others are available to all from general taxation. Even in real terms, expenditure on social security has doubled between 1970 and 1986. This is mainly because of the rising number of elderly people and because of the large rise in the number unemployed.

Social security accounts for one third of all public expenditure.

Education

Spending on education in 1986–7 was £17 500 million, about 10 per cent of public expenditure. 80 per cent of this is spent by local authorities on schools and colleges. On one hand, the fall in the number of children has allowed cuts in real spending to be made, many more young people stay on at school beyond 16.

Perhaps the greatest squeeze has been on university spending, although schools are now expected to control their own spending much more closely. Meals and cleaning services have been increasingly privatised.

Social security expenditure – The 1988 Social Security Act

The social security budget for 1988/9 was £48.5 billion, or 32p in the £ of all government spending. The Social Security Act, introduced in April 1988, introduced a new family credit scheme to help low-paid working families with children but the biggest losers were pensioners. Housing benefits were cut by £640 million and mainly affected pensioners with savings over £3000 – benefits were cut by £1 for every £250 saved towards retirement, affecting about 3 million old people.

Overseas aid

Britain is one of the largest private overseas investors. In 1985 £2550 million went into investment in developing countries. However, official government aid is much more often criticised. It amounted to £1181 million in 1985, which represents 0.34 per cent of GNP.

There is an internationally accepted guideline for aid by industrial nations to the third world – 0.7 per cent of GNP and 1 per cent including private flows. Britain accepts this in principle but has no timetable to achieve it. Total net flows are 0.81 per cent of GNP, short of the target. Sixty-five per cent of aid went to commonwealth countries.

The arguments about aid spending ask you to consider whether industrial nations have an obligation to help developing countries and to what extent aid should be in the form of emergency famine relief, or long-term investment. Should we provide support for education and medical care, for tractors and agricultural implements or should we lend foreign currency to governments to settle international debt?

BRITAIN'S PUBLIC SPENDING PLANS

Main public spending programmes (£bn)

	1986–87 est outturn	1987–88 plans
Social security	45.9	47.4
Education	19.3	20.1
Employment	3.9	4.0
Health	22.3	23.7
Agriculture	2.3	2.7
Defence	18.6	18.8
Law & Order	7.1	7.6
EEC and overseas aid	3.1	2.9
Other (net)	17.9	21.4
Planning total	**140.4**	**148.6**

GRAPHICS

Use your computer graphics package to produce this table in the form of two pie charts.

Compare the estimates for 1986/7 and 1987/8.

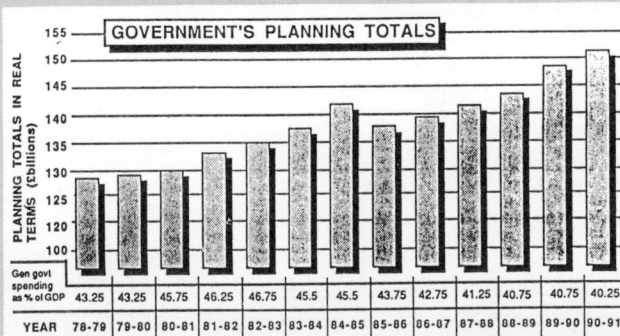

GOVERNMENT'S PLANNING TOTALS												
Gen govt spending as % of GDP	43.25	43.25	45.75	46.25	46.75	45.5	45.5	43.75	42.75	41.25	40.75	40.75	40.25
YEAR	78-79	79-80	80-81	81-82	82-83	83-84	84-85	85-86	86-87	87-88	88-89	89-90	90-91

Public expenditure plans

When we view statistics like those above, we have to remember that they are not always what they seem. Prices and costs go up each year with inflation so an apparent rise in public expenditure might not actually mean a rise in real terms.

Public expenditure has increased every year since 1979 (except 1985–6) but the real increase has been variable. Housing and local government spending have been cut and health care has risen by such small amounts that the service has struggled to meet the demands put on it.

Questions

1 What has happened to public expenditure as a percentage of GDP?

2 How might you account for this?

3 What are the three main categories of public expenditure and which have risen most in:
a money terms?
b percentage terms?

Defence

Whereas there have often been arguments for the privatisation of more and more areas of the economy, this has never been the case for defence. Everyone seems agreed that this should be provided from taxation on behalf of everyone. On the kind of defence policy adopted there is much less agreement. To some extent this is determined by UK membership of the North Atlantic Treaty Organisation (NATO) and the European Community.

The defence budget for 1986–7 was £18 000 million. It was 5.2 per cent of GDP, higher than just about every other country. Forty-five per cent of that budget goes on equipment, a higher percentage than any other NATO country.

POINTS TO REMEMBER

★ All governments need to consider how to provide a satisfactory standard of living for the population. This may be through private funding in the market system or through social welfare and related policies.

★ Merit goods are those which the government chooses to provide (more or less) free because it feels they are too important to leave to private provision.

★ We can categorise social welfare policy into
health care   defence
social security   overseas aid.
education

Defence expenditure

£ million

	1974/75	1975/76	1976/77	1977/78	1978/79	1979/80	1980/81	1981/82	1982/83	1983/84	1984/85
Total expenditure at outturn prices *of which:*	4 164	5 346	6 158	6 787	7 455	9 178	11 182	12 607	14 412	15 487	17 122
Expenditure on personnel	2 026	2 530	2 864	3 021	3 293	3 912	4 556	5 058	5 455	5 726	5 983
Expenditure on equipment	1 302	1 792	2 138	2 565	2 984	3 640	4 885	5 638	6 297	6 939	7 838
Other expenditure at	836	1 024	1 156	1 201	1 178	1 625	1 741	1 910	2 659	2 822	3 302
Total expenditure at constant (1984/85) prices	14 235	14 889	14 615	14 276	14 173	14 604	15 100	15 314	16 246	16 472	17 122

Questions

IT ▶ GRAPHICS

1 Use a suitable graphics package to draw a line graph which shows:
   a total expenditure at current (outturn) prices.
   b total expenditure at constant (1984/5) prices.

2 Compare these figures and explain how and why they are different.

3 Comment on the government's approach to defence expenditure in the period 1975–85.

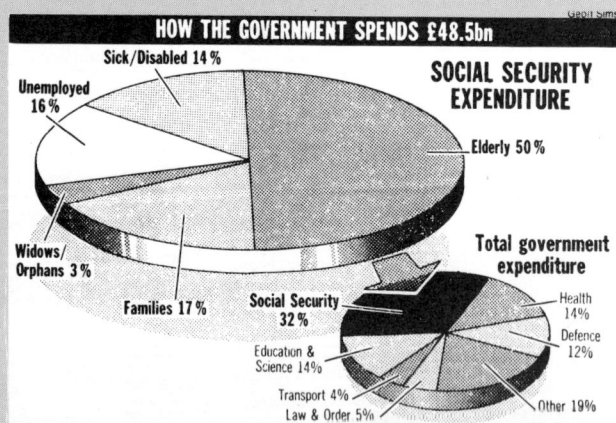

HOW THE GOVERNMENT SPENDS £48.5bn

SOCIAL SECURITY EXPENDITURE

Sick/Disabled 14 %
Unemployed 16 %
Elderly 50 %
Widows/Orphans 3 %
Families 17 %

Total government expenditure

Social Security 32 %
Education & Science 14%
Transport 4%
Law & Order 5%
Health 14%
Defence 12%
Other 19%

Education privatisation

It is proposed to privatise the ground maintenance provision at your school. This means that grass-cutting, pitch marking, etc. will be 'sub-contracted' to a private firm.

Use the word processor to design an advertisement for the local press inviting tenders for this service.

Question

What are the arguments for and against:
a reducing housing benefit payments to pensioners who have savings over £3000?
b reducing unemployment benefits for young people 18–25?
c reducing the support provided for free school meals for low-income families?

TASK 1

LOCAL AUTHORITY EXPENDITURE

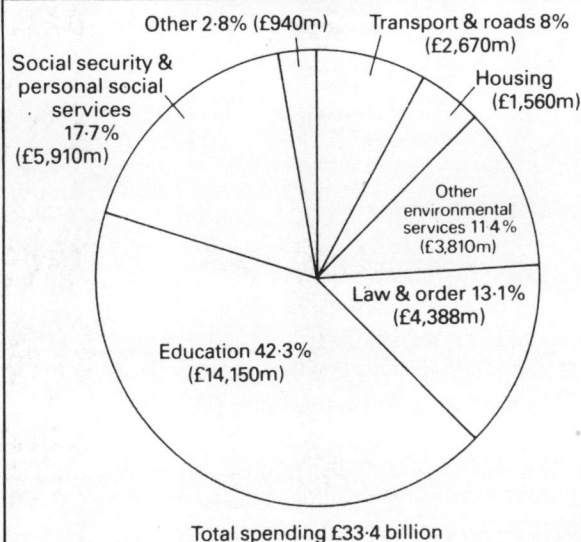

Local government expenditure is financed by a combination of central government funds – mainly the rate support grant – and local rates. Local authorities are free to decide on their spending within certain government constraints. Most capital spending is funded by borrowing and over 30 per cent goes on housing. Rates are levied on the value of a property and are fixed annually. It is likely that this system will be changed in favour of a 'poll' tax, levied on the number of people living in a property.

Local authority expenditure in 1986–7 was about £33.4 billion, about one quarter of total public expenditure. Education accounts for 40 per cent of the total. This is paid by the county councils in most cases, which are also responsible for major expenditure on roads, education and the police. District councils (the 'second tier' authorities) are responsible for environmental health, housing, etc.

Net, England and Wales 1986-87

Local authority expenditure

Other 2·8% (£940m)
Transport & roads 8% (£2,670m)
Social security & personal social services 17·7% (£5,910m)
Housing (£1,560m)
Other environmental services 11·4% (£3,810m)
Law & order 13·1% (£4,388m)
Education 42·3% (£14,150m)

Total spending £33·4 billion

Local authority expenditure in England and Wales

1 List the expenditure items in order of their size.

2 What is contained in each service provided? (Remember, these include the 'first tier' authorities – county councils or metropolitan authorities.)

3 Why do you think these areas of expenditure rest with local authorities in Britain and not with central government?

TASK 2

IT WORDPRO

THE NATIONAL HEALTH SERVICE

★ Spending on *private* health care has risen four times as fast as spending on the NHS over the past decade. In 1986 over £1 billion was spent on private treatment.

★ 300 NHS hospitals have closed and the number of beds available has fallen by 15%.

★ Waiting list for hospital treatment totalled 791,000 by the end of 1985, nearly 20% higher than in 1975.

★ Real expenditure on hospitals and community care has risen by only 0.5% a year, far short of the 2% growth rate needed to keep up with new demands.

The critical comments above are typical of those levelled at government spending on the NHS over the last few years.

1 Why has government expenditure on the NHS failed to keep up with public demands for an improved service in recent years?

2 What are the likely effects on the demand for health care of:
   a an increase in the average age of the population?
   b improved medical technology?
   c increased public awareness of new medical treatments?

TASK 3

NHS PRIVATISATION

The NHS has not been privatised as in the case of British Telecom, British Gas, etc, but there has been a growing involvement of the private sector in health care in recent years:

★ 5.2 million people now have private medical insurance, almost twice as many as in 1979 when Mrs Thatcher became Prime Minister.

★ Cleaning, catering and laundry services are subject to 'competitive tender'. If private firms can do these jobs more cheaply they are awarded the contracts. The government would also like to see more NHS patients treated in private hospitals and more cars for the mentally ill and mentally handicapped provided by the private sector.

★ Hospitals are to be encouraged to open shops, restaurants and fitness clubs.

★ Ultimately, plans are being considered to enable private companies to run NHS hospitals, or alternatively to give existing NHS managers much more control over the running of their own hospital units.

1 Why is the government supporting and encouraging the development of increased privatisation within the health service?

2 How is this view reflected in other areas of public expenditure?

Government Revenue

The need for taxation

In order to meet the costs of the government's expenditure programme, money has to be raised through taxes. Most people, from time to time, complain about having to pay income tax or VAT. However, if we want to live in the kind of country which looks after the elderly, the sick and those who suffer misfortune, we have to realise the need for taxation.

Most of us would agree that everyone who can afford to do so should pay into a common national 'kitty' from which the government can make payments for the services it provides. Many would also agree that the same kitty should sometimes be used to help industries which are in trouble, especially to create valuable jobs.

Different approaches to taxation

Some governments advocate a policy of 'low public expenditure and low taxation'. They would argue that people should keep most of what they earn but that they should be prepared to pay for the services they receive. In most cases this would mean low rates of taxation but charges for medical services, education, etc.

Others argue that this places a burden on the less well off who are then forced to pay for services which they cannot afford. In countries without free medical care, people sometimes die if they cannot afford to pay. If you want the kind of society which has a 'welfare state', then you have to be prepared to pay for it through higher taxes.

Policy alternatives

In Britain, what this generally means is that we are offered two alternative strategies:

1 Low income tax, say 20–25 per cent for most people.
Quite high taxes on spending, because we choose how we dispose of our money (VAT 15%).
More and more private health care through private insurance schemes, more independent schools with fees and less financial support for industry.

or

2 Higher income tax for most people, say 30–35 per cent.
Spending taxes such as VAT at 12–15 per cent.
Free health service, more state education, subsidies for industries like British Rail, British Coal, etc.

Chancellor's arithmetic (1988/9)

Where the money comes from
All figures in £ billion

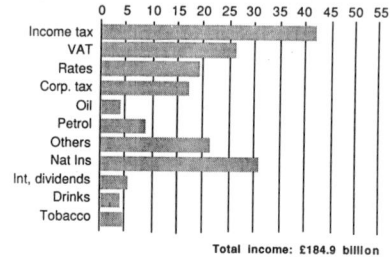

Income tax, VAT, Rates, Corp. tax, Oil, Petrol, Others, Nat Ins, Int, dividends, Drinks, Tobacco

Total income: £184.9 billion

How the money is spent

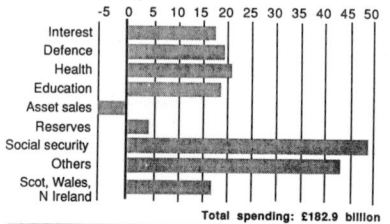

Interest, Defence, Health, Education, Asset sales, Reserves, Social security, Others, Scot, Wales, N Ireland

Total spending: £182.9 billion

Chancellor's income	£184.9 bn
Expenditure	£182.9 bn
Public and market borrowing	£1.2 bn
Budget surplus	£3.2 bn

A balanced budget

It has been traditional for the UK Chancellor to aim for a budget in which public expenditure just exceeds the amount taken in tax revenue. The difference is found by borrowing, the 'Public Sector Borrowing Requirement' (PSBR).

Not so in 1988. 'For the first time since the 1950s', says the Chancellor, public expenditure has been cut to levels where it can be financed from taxation. Indeed, more will be taken in taxes than is returned through government spending, a 'budget surplus'; and levels of 'direct' taxation are falling as well.

Questions

1 Where is most tax revenue coming from in 1988/89?

2 What is the difference between total anticipated spending and revenue?

3 How would these figures be affected by:
a a rise in the number unemployed?
b a fall in the level of smoking?
c an increase in the level of consumer spending on goods and services?

Direct taxes

Direct taxes are charged when money is earned. Income tax is the main direct tax, sometimes called PAYE, 'pay as you earn'. It is a 'progressive' tax which means that you pay not only more but at a higher rate as your income goes up, e.g. 25 per cent on the first £20 000, 40 per cent on the rest. This ensures that those who can afford to, pay most tax. It is often seen as a disincentive for well-paid managers to work harder because they pay more of their extra earnings in tax. The first part of everyone's income is tax free so that very low wage earners may pay no tax at all.

Company taxes

Companies also pay direct tax on their profits through corporation tax. Although this may seem high at 35 per cent, there are generous allowances against tax for re-invested funds. Football clubs, for example, sometimes use their profits to buy an expensive player because otherwise 35 per cent of that profit would be lost in tax.

Indirect taxes

'Indirect' taxes are mostly taxes on expenditure. Value added tax (VAT) is currently at 15 per cent and is paid on most goods and services we buy. There is no VAT levied on food, books, newspapers, heating fuel and bus and train fares. Almost everything else is taxed at the standard rate. It is argued that this kind of taxation is fair because it gives people a choice. If they don't buy taxable goods and services, they pay no tax.

Excise duties

We also pay extra indirect taxes on all alcoholic drinks, betting, tobacco, vehicle licences, new cars and on petrol.

This last group is often the most popular target for annual tax increases. The government can argue that many of these things are 'bad' for us and that taxation discourages bad habits. In truth, they are an excellent source of revenue and the government would find it hard to raise the same amount of money by other tax increases, at the same time persuading us that it was in our own best interests! In total they account for about 15 per cent of taxation each year.

POINTS TO REMEMBER

★ Economic policies vary on the matter of government spending and taxation. Some advocate low taxes and low spending, others higher rates of both.

★ High direct taxes are often considred fairer because they are 'progressive' but they do remove a large element of choice.

★ Indirect or 'expenditure' taxes give more choice but everyone pays at the same rate – rich and poor. They are sometimes called 'proportional' taxes.

Income tax

This is one of the most controversial areas of government economic policy. During the 1970s UK residents learned to live with quite high direct taxation. Once tax-free allowances had been considered, most people paid tax at 33 per cent of their income. This rose steeply to 85 per cent at the highest income levels.

The Conservative Government of the 1980s has been determined to reduce income tax greatly so that people keep a higher proportion of what they earn but may pay more when they spend it through VAT and other 'indirect taxes'. Overall, lower taxation has gone with lower government expenditure so that the level of support for health care, education, social welfare, etc., has been reduced, but people have more money in their pockets to start with.

The very high tax levels of the 1970s were reduced gradually and the government was able to meet its target of basic income tax at 25 per cent in 1988, with a top tax rate of only 40 per cent.

Questions

1 One central idea in taxation is that people should have the ability to pay their taxes. Think about a pensioner and a person earning £30 000 per year. Who benefits more from reducing higher rates of taxation?

2 If they both smoke 20 cigarettes per week who will pay a bigger percentage of their income in VAT on cigarettes?

3 Overall, what categories of people will benefit (a) most, and (b) least from shifting the burden of taxation from direct to indirect taxes?

IT ▶ **WORDPRO**

4 Compose a letter to your local MP expressing your personal views about government taxation policy. You should support your view with reasoned arguments and be prepared to think about the consequences of your stated policy ideas.

This letter should be composed on the word processor in formal style and addressed to the House of Commons. You may even wish to send it!

TASK 1

SOURCES OF REVENUE 1988-89

Total Consolidated Fund revenue £128.2 bn

Inland Revenue £68bn (53%)

Customs and Excise £47.9 bn (37%)

Other

Income tax £42,100m (32.7%)

Value added tax £26,200m (20.3%)

Petrol, derv etc. duties £8,400m (6.5%)

£5,000m (3.9%) Tobacco

£4,500m (3.5%) Alcohol

Betting and Gaming £890m (0.7%)

£1,260m (1.0%) Car tax

£1,670m (1.3%) EC own resources

(0.6%)£7,300m Other

£680m (0.5%) Interest and dividends

£1,140m (0.9%) Broadcasting receiving licences

£420m (0.3%) Gas levy

£2,770m (2.2%) Vehicle excise duties

Corporation tax £19,800m (15.4%)

Stamp duties £1,950m (1.5%)

Capital gains tax £1,950m (1.5%)

Inheritance tax £1,000m (0.5%)

Petroleum revenue tax £1,180m (0.9%)

Notes: Inheritance tax includes estate duty and capital transfer tax
National Insurance contributions are paid into a seperate fund; the budget forecasts a further £28.7bn from this source
EC own resources are taxes raised for the European Community

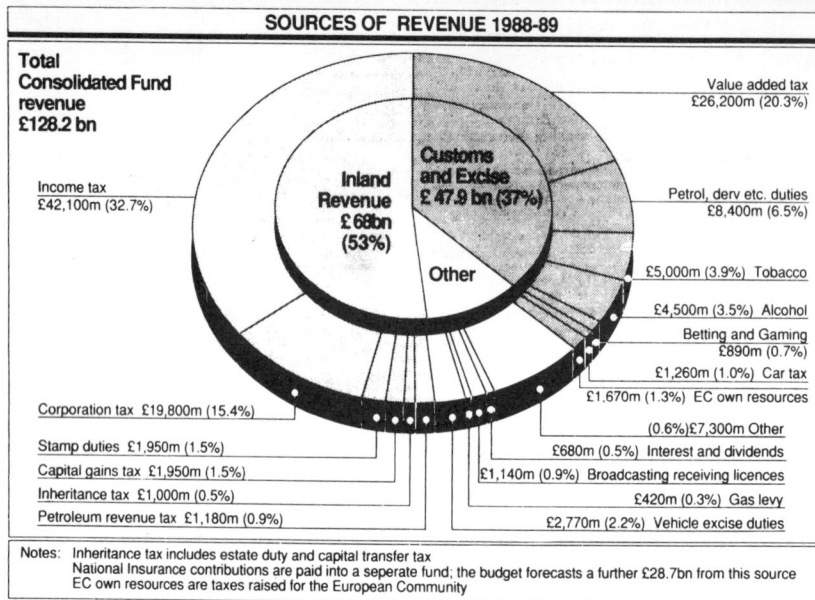

SOURCES OF GOVERNMENT REVENUE 1988–89

Examine the table, which shows the contribution to total revenue of each sector of direct and indirect taxation.

1 By how much does direct taxation (Inland Revenue) exceed indirect taxation (Excise)?

2 By how much is income tax revenue greater than VAT?

3 What is the revenue from:
   a vehicle excise duty?
   b tobacco duty?
   c corporation tax?

TASK 2

Consider the issues of taxation and public expenditure. Consider the benefits of different policy alternatives. Discuss with other members of your group their different views. What do your parents and other adult relations think?

Try to prepare a balanced list of arguments for and against different approaches. These could be displayed around the walls of your classroom so that everyone's views and different findings can be considered.

This might result in a classroom debate or discussion, hopefully based on informed and considered views of the issues involved.

TASK 3

How Britain compares

Taxes and social security contributions as percentage of GDP, 1985

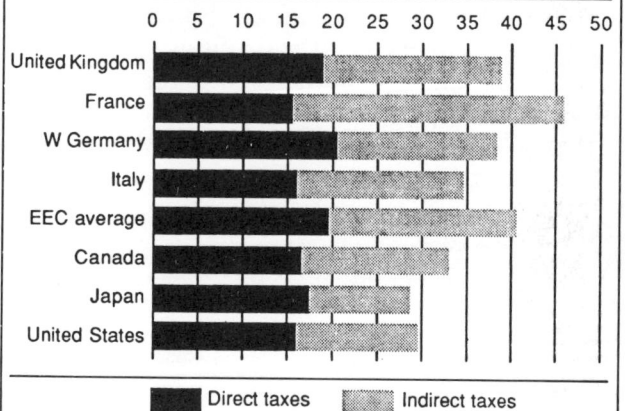

United Kingdom
France
W Germany
Italy
EEC average
Canada
Japan
United States

■ Direct taxes   ▨ Indirect taxes

INTERNATIONAL TAX COMPARISONS

Country	Starting rate	Starting rate threshold (£)	Top rate	Top rate threshold (£)
Canada	25.5%	5,003	43.5%	25,000
France	12.8%	6,698	56.8%	53,463
Germany	22.0%	3,439	56.0%	65,670
Italy	22.0%	3,358	62.0%	253,924
Japan	17.5%	4,286	78.0%	152,607
UK	25.0%	4,096	40.0%	19,301
US	15.0%	5,086	34.7%	22,086

Figures are for a married couple with no children and assume that the income of the couple is wholly employment income of husband. Figures relate to 1988 (1988-89 in case of UK)

Prior to the budgets of 1987 and 1988, British residents could claim to be fairly heavily taxed compared with their neighbours in the rest of the world.

Make a comparison between the UK and other nations based on:
a overall figures.
b direct taxes.
c indirect taxes.

TASK 4

THE EFFECTS OF TAXATION ON BUSINESS

The many different forms of tax not only affect individuals and governments but also businesses. They are very important for the creation of jobs and a prosperous economy is likely to be founded on business prosperity, and happy entrepreneurs and shareholders. How are business managers affected by the different types of tax?

The questions which follow are designed to make you think for yourself about the issues involved. It would be a good idea to discuss them in your group.

Income tax

This affects the 'take-home' pay of employees as well as the spending power of the whole population. If we have steeply 'progressive' income taxation, top income earners (£30 000+) may have to pay tax at 60 or 80 per cent. On the other hand, the system of tax allowances means that lower wage earners are able to keep most of what they earn. Employers may also be affected if company 'perks', like free company cars, are taxed heavily.

1 Do you think that high income tax may cause workers to press for high wage claims? What effects might this have on the economy?
2 Do you think that progressive tax rates are fair? Do you consider them a disincentive to top managers to work hard?
3 How do you feel about the taxation of company perks? What are the pros and cons?

Value Added Tax

It is argued that VAT is a fairer way of raising tax revenue than income tax because it gives people freedom to choose how they spend 'the pound in their pocket'. In fact, more or less everything but food is subject to VAT so we can only avoid it if we save our income. VAT puts prices up – at present by 15 per cent – so this must affect firms. A threat to put VAT on books or newspapers would have a great effect on producers.

1 What would be the effect on firms as a whole if VAT were raised to 20 per cent?
2 What would be the overall effects of a rate of 5 per cent on all foodstuffs?

Excise duties

The tobacco companies have been lobbying the Chancellor not to increase duties on cigarettes. Breweries suffer heavy tax penalties and it is said that taxes on spirits have escaped tax increases in recent years because of the effects on the economy of the Scottish Highlands if whisky sales were to fall.

1 What is the effect on the demand for differents types of motor vehicle if duties were to increase at different rates on leaded and unleaded petrol and diesel fuel?
2 What are the arguments in favour of replacing motor vehicle road fund licences with toll charges on bridges and motorways? Do you think this is a good idea?

Corporation tax

Companies pay corporation tax on their profits, after some allowance is made for the depreciation of their capital equipment. This is an incentive to firms to reinvest their profits rather than to pay them out to shareholders and be taxed. The main rate is 35 per cent and the rate for small companies 25 per cent. Company taxation in Britain is lower than most other industrialised countries.

1 Do you think that company profits should be heavily taxed? (The rate has fallen from 52 per cent in the last ten years).
2 What would be the effects on British industry if even greater company tax allowances were given for replacing and modernising machinery?

Local rates

Rates are often high in areas where the local council spends a lot of money to attract business. High rates, however, are a cost to firms and they are sometimes inclined to prefer low rate areas if they are to expand.

1 What are the arguments for and against high local authority rates?
2 How might local councils provide better local amenities without increasing the rates businesses have to pay?

IT▶ WORDPRO / DESKTOP

POLL TAX: DESIGN A LEAFLET

Imagine that you have been commissioned to design an explanatory leaflet about the poll tax system. This is intended for ordinary people to help them to understand what it involves. You will need to do some basic research.

Produce your outline document on a sheet of A4 folded in two, to create four pages. The front page should contain a suitable cover design. The text can be word processed.

The Budget

Government policy – The budget
The budget – usually in March or April – sets out the government's proposals for tax changes each year and the Chancellor of the Exchequer uses it as an occasion to review government economic policy. Plans for government spending are announced in a separate paper at the same time.

Three alternative budget strategies are: a balanced budget, a budget deficit and a budget surplus.

A balanced budget
Each year the government must state clearly how it is going to raise the money which it expects to spend in the coming year. For this reason the budget would have to 'balance', i.e. having decided to spend £100 000m on defence, education, health, industry, etc., the Chancellor would have to show how that £100 000m would be raised by taxes of different kinds.

A budget deficit
The chancellor can influence the economy very greatly if he decides not to make the budget balance, i.e. he might decide to spend £100 000m but to raise only £95 000m from taxes, leaving the exchequer £5000m short deliberately. This £5000m would have to come from somewhere, in fact it would have to be borrowed.

A budget surplus
On the other hand, the Chancellor may decide to raise more in taxes than he intends to spend, say £105 000m. In this case he has a spare £5000m to save or, more often, it will be used to repay loans from the past, sometimes referred to as 'the National Debt'.

We should also remember that sometimes the government gets its figures wrong and it sets out to balance a budget but falls short in revenue and has to 'borrow' anyway. This is quite normal, and usually expected. For example, higher than expected unemployment figures will mean more benefit payments than anticipated.

Budgetary policy
It may be surprising to think that a Chancellor might set out to overspend or underspend. The government may want to encourage economic growth by spending a lot on industry to create jobs and encourage firms to invest. It may not, though, at the same time, want to raise taxes. It will simply set out to overspend and borrow the difference.

The Chancellor may wish to stop economic ex-

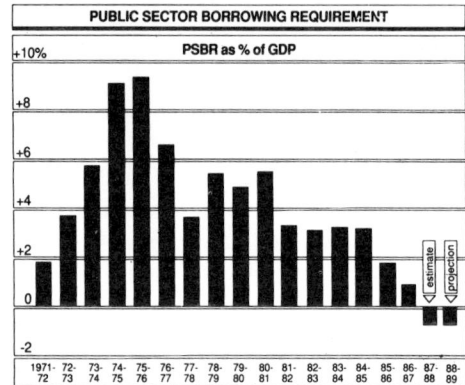

PUBLIC SECTOR BORROWING						
	£billion, cash					
	1986-87	1987-88	1988-89	1989-90	1990-91	1991-92
PSBR	3.4	-3	-3	0	0	0
Money GDP at market prices	386	424	456	486	516	545
PSBR as % of GDP	0.9	-¼	-¼	0	0	0

Public sector borrowing requirement (PSBR)

Questions

1 Explain what is meant by the term 'public sector borrowing requirement (PSBR)'.

2 Why has its level been falling since 1980?

3 What is significant about its level in 1988–1989?

4 Why are some politicians of the view that a higher PSBR would be healthier for the economy?

Public money 1988–89

Pence in every £1[1]

Receipts		Expenditure	
Income tax	23	DHSS: social security	27
National insurance contributions	17	DHSS: health and personal social services	11
Value added tax	14	Defence	11
Local authority rates	10	Education and science	10
Road fuel, alcohol and tobacco duties	10	Scotland, Wales and Northern Ireland	9
Corporation tax	9	Other departments	18
Capital taxes	3	Interest payments	10
Interest, dividends	3	Other	5
North Sea taxation	2		
Other	9		
Total	**100**		**100**

[1] Rounded to the nearest penny.
[2] Excluding North Sea.

Question

Public money 1988/89

IT ▶ GRAPHICS

Examine the figures above carefully. Imagine that they have to be presented to the public in clear diagrammatic form. You may wish to use a graphics package or to produce a suitably illustrated coloured diagram.

pansion for a while – perhaps if prices are rising too high as people and firms are overspending. Then he might choose to underspend by raising taxes but not raising real government spending. This is said to 'take money out of the economy'.

This kind of 'budgetary policy' has been used by governments not only in Britain, but all over the world to control a national economy.

Government borrowing: the 'PSBR'

If the government spends more money than it raises from taxation in any one year it is said to have a 'budget deficit'. This money has to be found somewhere; it has been, or is being, spent. In fact it must be borrowed and the amount needed is called the 'Public Sector Borrowing Requirement' (PSBR).

The government does not find it difficult to borrow this money but, of course, it has to be paid back with interest. In 1983 this figure was £11.6 billion and the government was determined to get the level down – by spending less and ensuring that taxes were high enough to cover most expenditure. They got the figure down to £7.5 billion in 1985 and, by 1987, it was £3.3 billion.

PSDR – Public sector debt repayment

This is a phrase which has been used to indicate a *negative* PSBR. In other words, it means that the government has raised more in taxes than it wishes to pay in expenditure. Not only does it not need to borrow, but it can use the surplus to repay some of its debt from the past.

The 'National Debt'

The government borrows this money from all sorts of sources. It sells government 'stocks' to the public (through the Stock Exchange), it borrows from banks and financial institutions and it raises money from National Savings certificates and bonds. Some of the borrowing is for quite long periods of time, 15 years or more. Because such stock is repaid by the government, it is considered very safe by savers, hence it is known 'gilt-edged'. By the end of March 1987 the total National Debt, i.e. money the government has borrowed over the years and which it repays bit by bit, was £186 000 million.

POINTS TO REMEMBER

★ The budget is the government's annual statement of income (taxation) and expenditure (public spending).

★ The Chancellor may present a budget which is intended to 'balance' (taxation = expenditure) or he may intend to inject money into the economy (budget deficit) or to take money out of the economy (budget surplus).

★ If public expenditure exceeds revenue, the difference must be borrowed – the public sector borrowing requirement. This is often an important indicator of government economic policy.

It's no evil to borrow for worthwhile projects
Roger Bootle says the idea of deficit need not be repellent

Public sector deficits are supposedly bad because they increase the competition for funds and hence drive up interest rates, which inhibits investment and restricts economic growth. But if private borrowers increased their deficits instead, surely the increased competition for funds would be the same, and with the same results.

But the real difference between these expenditures is not that one is public and the other private, it is that one is consumption and the other is investment. Compare instead public sector borrowing to increase investment in micro-chip plants with private sector borrowing to finance the mass purchase of video war games. In this instance, it is the public sector's expenditure which provides for the future and the private sector's which as good as goes up in a puff of smoke.

In making the reduction of public sector borrowing the cornerstone of its economic strategy the Government is dancing round a financial totem, bereft of real economic significance. Strip away the financial mumbo-jumbo and its lunacy is clear to the man on the Clapham omnibus. The message is extra-ordinarily simple. That is why it needs repeating again and again. It is this: increased spending on worthwhile capital projects is a different kettle of fish from spending on current consumption – whether public or private sector.

The case for a budget deficit

In the article above, Roger Bootle is arguing that the government should be prepared to borrow money to spend on 'public investment' programmes.

Questions

1 If the government borrows money to finance public expenditure which it cannot meet from taxation, why might this be thought to 'drive up interest rates'?

2 What is the difference between public expenditure on 'consumption' and 'investment'?

3 Why is 'the reduction of public sector borrowing the cornerstone of the Government's economic strategy'?

TASK 1

A BALANCED BUDGET

The UK government has been moving towards setting a 'balanced budget' since the Conservative administration began in 1979. Its case has been based very largely on three notions:

High taxation and high public spending do not make for a healthy and competitive economy. High government borrowing raises interest rates in the economy which inhibits business investment. All of these together cause high inflation and reduce our international competitiveness.

1   Write a report in the style of a newspaper of your choice which summarises the main features of the 1988 budget.

Include in it brief reference to the main measures but try to concentrate on the likely *effects* and on the intentions behind the main proposals – the 'balanced' budget, lower income tax, etc.

 WORDPRO

You can use the word processor to produce this in newspaper style – with columns of 75mm.

Use a suitable headline.

2   You might like to design an appropriate cartoon which captures the attitude of your chosen newspaper to the budget.

1988 budget

This was claimed as the first 'balanced' budget since the 1950s. In effect, it set out to reduce taxation and to reduce public expenditure. Since the two would be equal (at a lower level), there would not be any need for the government to borrow extra money in the year 1988/89.

The obvious result was that people would pay less in taxes but would receive less in public services of many kinds.

THE BUDGET

15 March 1988

The main features

The Chancellor announced:
- a balanced budget;
- substantial further tax reforms; and
- reductions in income tax at all levels.

The main tax changes include:
- double indexation of tax thresholds;
- a reduction in the basic rate of income tax to 25p;
- abolition of all higher rates of income tax above 40p;
- a new system of independent taxation for husbands and wives, to take effect in 1990;
- reform of capital gains tax;
- a major simplification of the tax treatment of covenants and maintenance payments; and
- a higher threshold and flat rate for inheritance tax.

"It's from my accountant, Friday. The tax situation in England has changed. I'm closing down the company here and returning home."

TASK 2

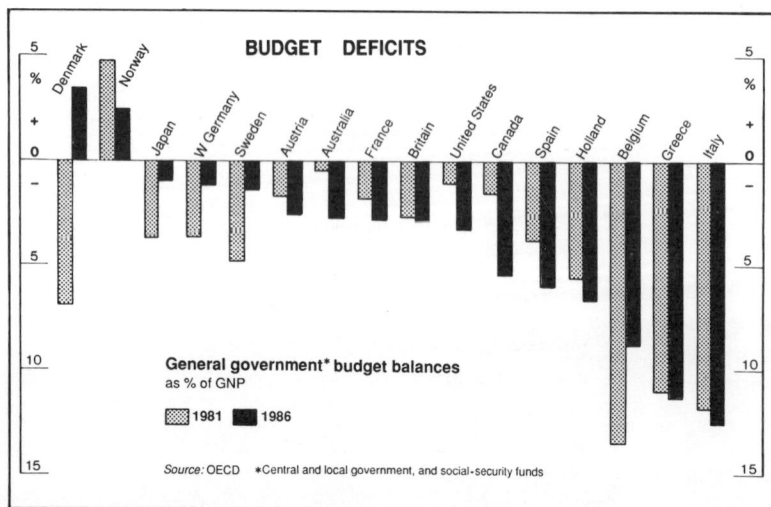

BUDGET DEFICITS

General government* budget balances
as % of GNP

1981   1986

Source: OECD   *Central and local government, and social-security funds

1   Which country in both years collected more in taxation than it spent?

2   Which country in 1986 came closest to having a balanced budget?

3   Which countries had reduced their budget deficits in the period from 1981 to 1986?

4   Is it 'good' for a government to have reduced its deficit?

TASK 3

In his April budget before the May 1955 election, Butler improperly cut 6d (2½p) off basic income tax, saying privately: "surely the most inflationary budget would be one that just let Labour in?" In an October emergency budget, he reimposed taxes with the same yield.

Before the 1959 election, Heathcoat Amory reduced income tax by 9d (4p), and cut purchase tax all round. But he was made to look almost responsible because Gaitskell promised that a peace-time Labour government would never increase income-tax rates again.

Maudling made huge tax cuts in 1963, but the opinion polls then stopped the Tories from running an election that year. By his April 1964 budget Maudling estimated his 6% annual rise in real demand was two points too high, but his higher booze and baccy taxes siphoned only half a point off.

Mr James Callaghan's 1966 pre-election non-budget was a classic. Before the March election, he said his budget would have to raise £8m through a new betting tax; a month later, he took £375m through a new selective employment tax, and three months later slashed another £500m from demand.

In April 1970, Mr Roy Jenkins did a Lawson. He introduced a responsible budget. But unlike Mr Lawson, Mr Jenkins had to raise taxes. His Labour party never forgave him: the Tories surged to power in the June election.

By the February 1974 election, the Tories' policy had turned wildly irresponsible, with money supply doubled in less than two years. Incoming Mr Denis Healey's bash-the-rich budget won the second 1974 election by making things slightly worse, but this soon propelled Britain into good government under the International Monetary Fund. Labour skipped a real budget before the May 1979 election.

In the March before the June 1983 election, Sir Geoffrey Howe fiddled the books to find £2¼ billion of income-tax reliefs. A month after the election, the new chancellor, Mr Lawson, cut £500m off government spending. Best honest guess: no measures this July.

CHANCELLORS' BUDGET POLICIES 1955–1983

1 Which taxes are mentioned in the article?

2 Name four people who have held the post of Chancellor of the Exchequer.

3 What evidence is there that budgets are mainly used to help governments get elected?

TASK 4

THE 1988 BUDGET

The cartoon shows the Chancellor of the Exchequer leading people down the path of lower rates of income tax and reduced government expenditure.

1 What is now the highest rate of income tax?

2 What has been the effect of the budget on spending on education and the unemployed?

3 What do you feel the government's future policy on income tax will be?

4 Who do you think will benefit most from the budget?

Investigating the INTERNATIONAL Background

'Why is my milk going down the drain?'

International trade

You have only to look at the labels on goods like televisions and stereo systems, or to listen to the accents and languages used by visitors to our major tourist attractions to realise how important international trade is to Britain.

Visibles and invisibles

Goods which we buy from other countries – like the Sony Walkman – are called 'visible imports', while goods which we sell abroad, like BL cars, are called 'visible exports'.

When a British company sells a service like insurance to somebody living in another country they pay us, just as if we had sold them a visible product. These sales are called 'invisible exports'.

However, if we buy the service of an overseas airline, we must pay out money to a foreign company and this is an 'invisible import'.

The rule is that if money comes into Britain from the transaction it is an export. If money leaves Britain it is an import.

Why is international trade needed?

The climates of some countries mean that they cannot grow enough food. Countries like Ethiopia therefore have to import from countries which can produce far more than they need for themselves.

There are many crops and fruits like bananas which can be grown in Britain only under special conditions like heated greenhouses. It is cheaper for us to buy them from countries like Jamaica rather than grow them ourselves.

Certain minerals like gold and silver are only found in particular parts of the world. If these countries did not export them to us we might not be able to have gold rings or silver teapots! This might not seem very important but some countries do not have coal or oil reserves with which they can power their factories and keep warm, so they rely on importing such commodities from other countries.

No country has the resources to provide everything that everybody wants. Therefore it makes sense to concentrate on making those things which the country is best at producing and import the goods that it cannot produce so well. If every country did this, we would all be making the best use of our resources and we could export the surplus goods we did not want. We would import the goods other countries were better at producing than us.

Should we have free trade?

For the last idea to work, each country should be free

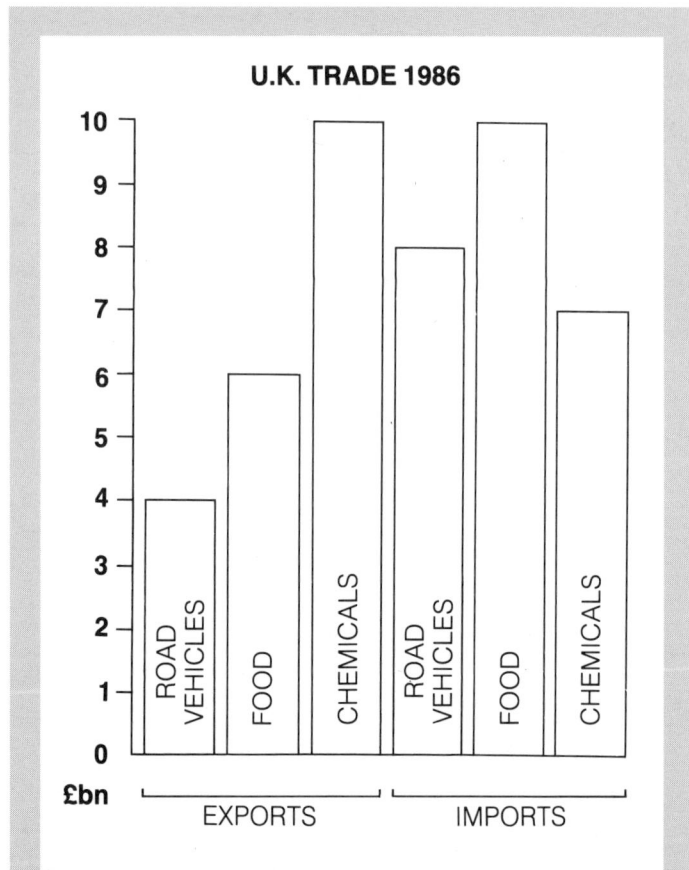

U.K. TRADE 1986

Questions

1 How much did the UK spend on importing
  a road vehicles?
  b chemicals?

2 How much more or less was this than was received from exporting road vehicles and chemicals?

3 Why does the UK both import and export food?

to sell its goods and services to other countries. This can lead to problems.

Britain makes a wide range of goods but they cannot always make them as cheaply as other countries. If we stopped making them many people would lose their jobs. Examples of this have been seen in the textile and car industries where better and cheaper imports have meant British jobs have been lost.

But if this happens on a wide scale, international trade would fall in volume and we would lose the benefits of being able to get goods from abroad because we would not be able to afford them.

Dumping

Another reason for stopping some imports is that the exporting country is 'dumping' goods. This means they are selling them very cheaply so that the firms who make them in the importing country may go out of business. The exporting firm then raises its prices because there is no competition.

Infant industries

Sometimes a country will restrict imports to help an industry which is just being set up. This is because 'infant' industries, as they are called, could not possibly compete with established ones overseas.

Ways of stopping imports

There are several ways in which a government can stop imports coming into a country.

It could put on 'quotas'. In this case it would only allow a limited number of goods, or goods of a limited value into its country. Another way is to put a 'tariff' on the goods. This is a tax and makes the goods cost more so people are less likely to want to buy.

Sometimes countries will make it very difficult to import goods by insisting on lengthy health and safety checks on goods or by asking for a great deal of documentation. Some countries also make it difficult for their importers to buy the foreign currencies with which to pay for the imports.

The problem of paying for your imports

Each country has reserves of gold and foreign currencies like dollars and yen. Every time we import goods and services we use up these reserves.

When we export goods and services we are perhaps paid for them in £ sterling, dollars and yen. This provides us with the reserves to buy more imports.

If imports are always greater than exports a country will gradually lose all its reserves and not be able to trade. For this reason it is very important that we export goods and services.

Exchange rates

An exchange rate is one country's currency expressed in terms of another country's currency. For example:

£1.00 = $1.75 = 225 Yen
UK   USA   Japan

The dumping problem

Japan's other disputes with the Community, particularly over its heavy taxes on imported liquor, got worse. In addition, the European Commission opened an investigation into claims by EEC competitors that Japan, Singapore and South Korea were dumping microwave ovens on the EEC market. At the other end of the household thermometer, penal anti-

dumping duties were imposed by the Community on cut-price deep freezes imported from Russia.

Questions

1 What benefits are there for those countries which 'dump' goods in other countries?

2 Why do 'dumped' goods benefit importing countries in the short term?

3 Why do some countries try to stop very cheap imports from entering their country?

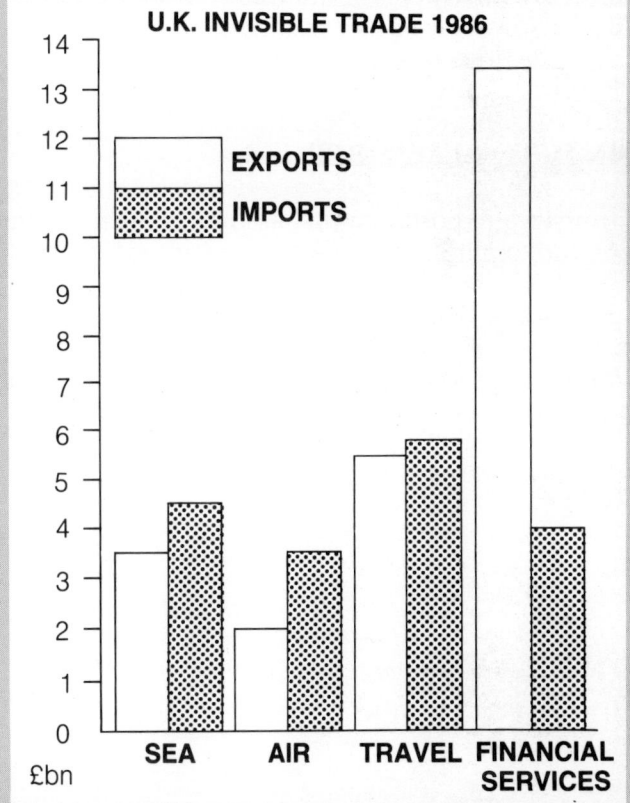

U.K. INVISIBLE TRADE 1986

Questions

1 Which of the above 'invisibles' created a surplus for the UK in 1986?

2 Can you suggest what is included in 'financial services'?

However, these rates do vary from day to day, according to the demand for and the supply of the currency.

If the UK imports a lot of goods from Japan, the UK will demand lots of Yen to pay for them. This extra demand for Yen pushes its price up so that £1 may be worth only 220 Yen. As this happens Japanese goods effectively become dearer for people in the UK to buy, so in theory less Japanese goods should be bought.

The outcome of this should be that any deficit in the balance of payments should be reduced because fewer Japanese goods are being imported. Also, UK goods become cheaper for the Japanese to buy, so we should be able to export more goods to them.

The recording of international trade

This is done in the balance of payments. It shows:

1. If visible imports are more or less than visible exports. (The Visible Balance of Trade)
2. If invisible imports are more or less than invisible exports. (The Invisible Balance of Trade)
3. How much investment there has been in foreign countries and how much foreigners have invested in Britain. This investment could be the buying of shares in companies.
4. How we have paid for our trade, either by using up our reserves or by borrowing from organisations like the International Monetary Fund.

POINTS TO REMEMBER

★ Invisible exports are just as important to Britain as visible exports.

★ Free trade benefits countries.

★ There may sometimes be good reason for restricting free trade.

★ Imports are paid for by exports.

Geographical Distribution of Trade 1986 of the UK

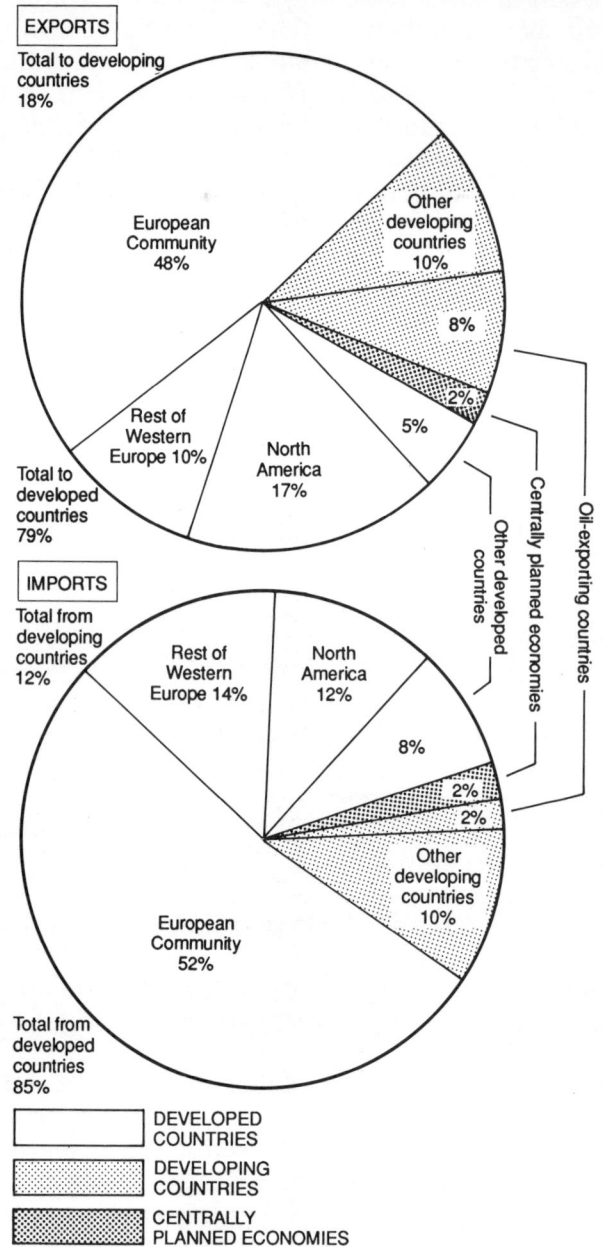

EXPORTS
Total to developing countries 18%
European Community 48%
Other developing countries 10%
8%
2%
5%
Rest of Western Europe 10%
North America 17%
Total to developed countries 79%
Centrally planned economies
Other developed countries
Oil-exporting countries

IMPORTS
Total from developing countries 12%
Rest of Western Europe 14%
North America 12%
8%
2%
2%
Other developing countries 10%
European Community 52%
Total from developed countries 85%

DEVELOPED COUNTRIES
DEVELOPING COUNTRIES
CENTRALLY PLANNED ECONOMIES

Differences between totals and the sums of their component parts are due to rounding.

Questions

1 Where are most of the UK's exports sold?

2 From where do most of the UK's imports come?

3 Why do you think we export and import so little from developing countries?

4 What sort of goods do you think we import from developing countries?

5 List three countries which have 'centrally planned economies'.

TASK 1

1 What does 'international' mean?

2 What is a tariff?

3 What is a quota?

4 Explain why it is important that we export goods and services.

TASK 2

Decide whether the following are invisible imports, invisible exports, visible imports or visible exports *for the UK.*

1 a British firm selling machinery to the USA.
2 a Fench tourist paying her hotel bill in the UK.
3 a UK firm buying TVs from Japan.
4 a British pop group paid to tour the USSR.
5 Lloyds of London receiving an insurance premium from Kuwait.
6 Lloyds having to pay insurance compensation for a Nigerian aeroplane which has crashed.

TASK 3

GROUP ACTIVITY – A JAPANESE PROBLEM

Imagine your group are the government ministers of Japan. For some years now your very efficient industries have been selling electronics goods all over the world. You have been able to export much more than you have imported. This has meant high levels of employment for your people and your reserves have been building up. Other countries have found it difficult to penetrate your markets because of problems with the language and their inferior goods.

However, several of these countries have got together and stated that they will put up tariff barriers and quotas against your goods unless:
(a) they can have access to your markets, and
(b) you agree to reduce your exports to them.

The world's press have gathered in Tokyo and you have to issue a press release explaining what you intend to do and your reasons for doing it.

TASK 4

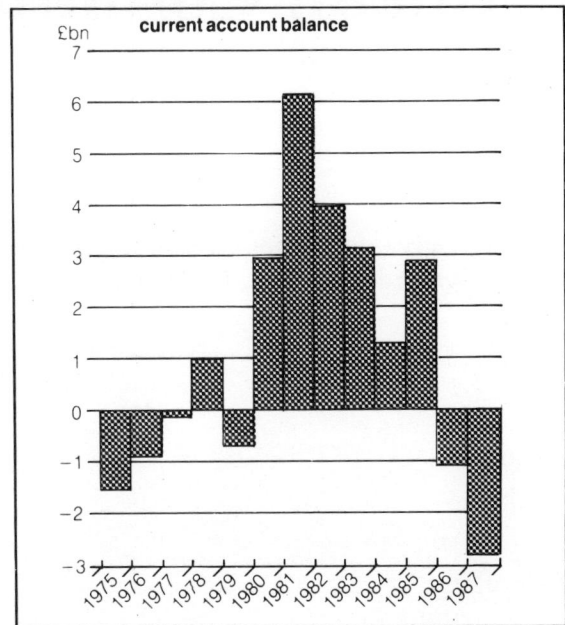

Balance of payments

The table above shows the current account of the balance of payments. It shows the difference between the value of all exports (visible and invisible) and all imports (visible and invisible).

If exports are greater than imports the current account is in surplus; if imports are greater than exports the current account is in deficit.

1 In 1986 were imports greater than exports?

2 In 1981 were imports greater than exports?

3 In 1980 was the current account in deficit or surplus?

4 In 1984 was the current account in deficit or surplus?

5 What was the greatest surplus achieved on the current account?

6 Can you suggest why the current account was in deficit in 1975 and why a surplus was achieved from 1980 to 1985?

7 Why can a country not run a deficit year after year?

European Community

There are twelve countries which belong to the 'European Community' (EC). These are

Belgium
Netherlands
France
Greece
Luxembourg
Denmark
Italy
Portugal
West Germany
United Kingdom
Eire
Spain

Whilst most of what you read about in the newspapers is concerned with the agricultural policy of the community, there is much more to it than that.

Of the many features of the EC, we need consider only those which most directly affect the business managers. These include:

European parliament

This sits in Strasbourg and Brussels and its members are elected from the twelve countries. They are known as MEPs (Members of the European Parliament). There are 518 seats in the parliament, 81 of which are allocated to the United Kingdom. One of the main jobs of the Parliament, along with the Council of Ministers, is to decide how much finance should be raised and how it should be spent. The EC gets its money from taxes on imports into the EC and countries also contribute a percentage of their value added tax (VAT). The Court of Justice is used to settle disputes relating to the treaties signed by member countries.

European currency unit (ECU)

All money dealings undertaken by the community are measured in ECUs. This is worth about 65p.

Economic and social policies

These operate in all member countries. Examples include:

Regional policy This provides funds to undertake projects like road building or offers incentives to firms to move to particular areas.

Social policy This tries to improve the living standards of people in the community. The European Social Fund has tried to reduce unemployment by providing money for investment projects and retraining schemes.

Industrial policy For example in the shipbuilding

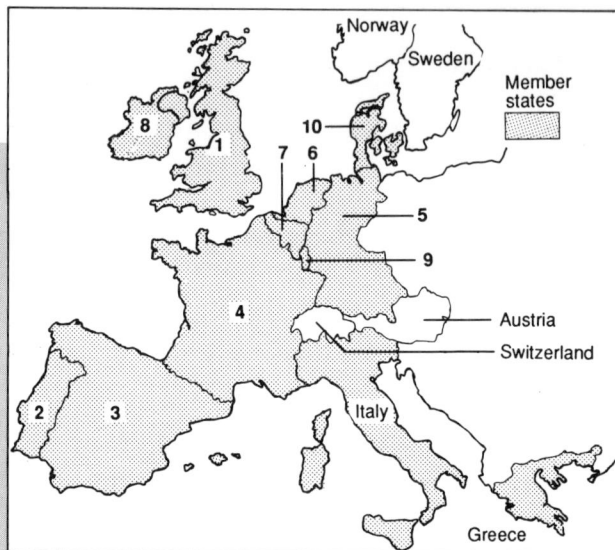

The European Community

Questions

1 Identify each of the EC countries.

2 Why are the countries between Italy and Greece unlikely to join the EC?

3 Can you find out which trading bloc Norway and Sweden are members of?

4 Which countries are members of Comecon?

IT ▶ DATABASE

5 Use your school or local library to create a database showing the following information about each of the European Community countries.

Control by which	Currency unit?
political party?	Main exports?
Population?	Main imports?
Area of country?	Birth rate?
Language spoken?	Death rate?

Interrogate your database and print out the answers to the following questions:

a Which countries speak French?

b Which countries have a currency called the franc?

c List the countries in descending order by area.

d Which countries are controlled by conservatives?

e Which country has the lowest birth rate?

f Which countries have agricultural products as their main exports?

g Give all the information in your database by countries in alphabetical order.

industry, the policy has been to organise a cutback in production in such a way that redundant workers can be retrained. In the aircraft industry, it promoted the 'European Airbus' project which is a joint design and building effort by several member countries.

The Common Agricultural Policy (CAP)

This policy is perhaps the most criticised of all the activities of the European Community. It accounts for most of the spending in the EC. The policy tries to:

Give farmers a reasonable standard of living.
Make sure we have enough domestic food production in the community.
Get farmers to become more efficient in their methods of farming.
Get food to consumers at a reasonable price.

The way these aims are achieved is by the CAP guaranteeing to buy what farmers produce at a set price. This then gives the farmers a guaranteed income and ensures we get enough food. Generally, it also causes overproduction in wine, olive oil, butter, meat and cereals because the farmers know that they can sell all they produce. If all these surpluses were put on to the European market the price of each product would fall and the CAP would get very little for each, although consumers would benefit greatly from low prices. So the CAP holds vast amounts of these products in storage (These are called the 'wine lakes' and 'butter mountains'.)

CAP – the over-production problem

Storage would be a good idea if there were poor crops in some years so the stocks could be put back onto the market to keep the price stable for the consumer. In Europe, however, crop yields are increasing, so stocks cannot be put back on the market. The CAP has then had either to sell off the stocks cheaply to non-EC countries or to give them away. This has led, in the past, to free butter and meat being given to the pensioners of Europe. At the start of 1987 the EC was holding stocks worth about £8 000 000 000. The first real action taken against such stocks was the setting of a milk production quota, which was a limit on milk output from dairy farms. This meant that farmers who produced more than their quota did not get paid for it.

You might think that one way round the problem would be for the UK to buy these goods again once they have been sold off outside the EC. The problem with this is that the EC is a customs union. This means that, whilst goods can pass between member countries without import taxes, if they come from a non-EC country they would be taxed to bring them up to the price which is ruling in the EC. As a result, there would be no benefit to the consumer.

The need for reform

Quite clearly the system is in need of reform. The UK government, in particular, has expressed its un-

Milk quotas

It has been common for farmers to obtain a guaranteed income from the Common Agricultural Policy fund, they often concentrated their efforts on one particular product, knowing they could sell it all to the European Community member states. Some farmers concentrated on the production of milk and built up large dairy herds of cows which gave high yields of milk. When limits (quotas) were introduced on the amount of milk the Community would buy from each farmer, problems began to arise.

'Why is my milk going down the drain?'

Questions

1 Can you answer the question asked by the cow?

2 Give two reasons why the European Community should feel the need to buy all the milk farmers could produce.

3 Why were quotas introduced on the quantity of milk each farmer could sell to the Community?

4 Why could the farmers not just change to another product?

5 If you were a farmer who had a quota imposed, can you suggest any other products you could create, at you own farm, with the surplus milk to save it having to go down the drain?

willingness to contribute funds to the EC which will be used to support such overproduction. The overproduction is, in itself, undesirable but the UK also receives little of the subsidy funding because fewer than 3 per cent of UK workers are farmers. In Greece, for example about 30 per cent of the workforce are in farming. Other EC countries, which have a lot of people employed in agriculture and benefit from this system, resist changes with equal fervour.

Competition policy

One of the areas in which the European Community is trying to have an effect is in encouraging competition between companies. For example, in 1988 the Commission finished a five year enquiry into price fixing by some multi-national companies.

Companies like BP, ICI and BASF were accused of secretly meeting to fix the price of PVC in order to keep its price high. This led the European Commission to impose multi-million pound fines on the companies.

The Commission is also keen to encourage competition amongst professionals like doctors and surveyors by letting them practise in any European country. This is part of the general policy of allowing free movement of labour across the countries of the Community.

POINTS TO REMEMBER

★ The EC comprises 12 countries.

★ It has a parliament and MEPs.

★ It has policies on social matters, economics, industry and agriculture.

★ Most of its funds are on spent on the CAP, which Britain feels is in need of reform.

HM Customs warning.

'Customers are reminded that all Duty Free goods must be exported intact from the UK and must not be consumed/disposed of until you have left the country'.

THERE'S 33% MORE IN OUR BIG BOTTLE

SAVE AT LEAST 20%* ON ALL PERFUME

* All savings are against UK Suggested Retail Prices.

Duty and Tax Free Shopping

Duty-free allowances

When people go on holiday to other European Community (EC) countries they often buy 'duty free' goods either at the ports or in an EC country. People save money because the UK taxes goods like wine and tobacco at much higher rates than most other EC countries. However, from 1992 all EC countries will be required to have the same taxes on such products so there will be no savings to be made. The British Airports Authority and the cross channel ferry operators like P&O are very angry about this because they make a great deal of revenue from selling these products.

Questions

1 Why are holidaymakers so keen to buy wine and tobacco on cross channel ferries?

2 Why do you think the government currently limits the quantity of goods you can buy 'duty free'?

3 How do you think the British Airports Authority and ferries might make up the revenue they will lose from 1992 on duty free sales?

TASK 1

NEWS
The Grocer February 20, 1988

EC plans to spend £5bn dumping surplus food

THE EC is planning to spend £5 billion on dumping surpluses of milk powder, cereals, sugar, wine, olive oil and beef on the world market over the next five years.

As part of last weekend's Brussels summit agreement on CAP reform, the EC governments have agreed to spend an average of approximately £800 million on subsidising the sale of surpluses at give-away prices. The money will be allocated at the rate of £864 million in 1988, and then at the rate of £1 billion a year for the following four years.

The EC currently has accumulated surpluses of 700,000 tonnes plus of beef, 600,000 tonnes of butter, up to 8 million tonnes of wheat, 600,000 tonnes of milk powder and hundreds of thousands of gallons of wine and olive oil. The EC leaders agreed to a scheme allowing the subsidised sale of these surpluses, with the cash coming from outside the new spending limit.

The new scheme is likely to mean that the EC Commission will be setting up new schemes to sell off the surplus involving subsidies financed by the EC taxpayer.

It is probable that the Commission will adopt the same sort of approach as it did after the December 1986 agreement on dairy sector reform. Some £2 billion was at that time allocated to selling off butter with subsidies sometimes greater than the price paid by the EC.

Major beneficiary of these sales was the Soviet Union. It is now likely that Russia will benefit from the cut-rate sale of milk powder, beef and wine.□

1 What is meant by 'dumping'?

2 Which products are being 'dumped' by the European Community?

3 What do the initials CAP stand for?

4 Who pays money into the European Community which finances the dumping?

5 Who will benefit from the products which are dumped?

6 Normally, countries do not like having products dumped on them. Why is this?

7 Why, in this case, do you think the country having products dumped on it is actually very grateful?

8 Why are the products not sold cheaply to the member countries of the European Community so that their own people can benefit?

9 Why is the surplus not shipped to third world countries where people are starving?

TASK 2

WINE LAKES

1 Where do you think the surplus wine is really stored?

2 Why does the wine lake keep on increasing in size?

3 Why do you think the EC does not just tell farmers to stop production until the surplus has been used up?

Third World Development

Whilst this section will look at the problems facing third world countries, it must be remembered that many of the countries we refer to as 'third world' do have millions of people employed in factories and offices who enjoy a good standard of living. In addition, direct comparisons with countries like Britain are often very difficult as what we value may not be the same as what is valued by people from other cultures. The problem of measuring living standards is considered in another unit.

What causes the problems?

The problems faced by third world countries were highlighted by the famines in Ethiopia. The difficulties faced by these countries, (often, and perhaps more fairly, referred to as developing countries) can include:

Relying heavily on agriculture.
Little investment in transport and manufacturing industry.
Extremes of climate varying between severe droughts and flooding.
Large numbers of people not able to read or write.
Poor levels of medical care.
Internal political problems.

At its simplest level, when harvests fail year after year and there is no food produced and no stockpiles of food from previous years, people will starve unless food comes from other countries. This can either be donated as food aid or the third world countries can buy it. The problem with having to buy food is that these countries do not have the means to pay for it. They export so little of their own production that they generate little or no foreign exchange.

Even if they do get the food, poor road and rail networks often mean it is very difficult to distribute it to those in need. In any case food aid alone, although it keeps people alive in the short term, does little to help improve the long term situation; this requires investment.

Investing for the future

In order to invest in capital goods like roads, railways, factories and schools, a country must use its resources to provide finance. This means that the current use of resources must be postponed, so if they are concentrating their efforts on producing food, they must divert some of this to making capital goods. The consequences of this are that, in the short term, food supplies will be cut and people will die. In the longer term, things should improve. This

Definitions

Birth rate – the number of births per 1000 of the population.
Death rate – the number of deaths per 1000 of the population.

Country	Birth rate	Death rate	Population
Britain	14	12	56m
Ethiopia	50	25	31m
China	19	7	1000m
India	33	12	685m

Questions

IT ▶ SPREADSHEET

This question can be attempted on a spreadsheet by using the table above.

1 Complete the following table:

Country	Births per year	Deaths per year
Britain		
Ethiopia		
China		
India		

2 By how many does the population of each country increase in a year?

3 By what percentage does each country's population increase in a year?

4 Which of the above countries would you describe as 'third world'? Explain the reasons for your choice.

5 Can you suggest three problems there might be for a country with a population which is rapidly increasing.

dilemma explains why the Band Aid charity and other charities like Oxfam and the Save The Children Fund, split their help between short-term food aid and long-term investment.

The climate

The problems of climate often dominate the life of a person in the third world. Crops can be ruined by either a lack of rain, or too much rain when monsoons wash the seeds away. These problems need investment help in terms of the building of dams or irrigation systems. Aid agencies report that it is often quite easy to get funds for prestigious investment projects through organisations like The World Bank. Such projects often mean jobs for people in developed countries who are involved in construction, design and engineering.

Education

The process of industrialisation needs an educated workforce as well as a lot of investment. Some third world countries find this very difficult to achieve, even if it is desired. Families often want the children to work and earn some income, no matter how little, rather than be educated. They also lack trained teachers.

Medical care

Poor levels of medical care lead to high death rates, short life spans with many children failing to survive infancy. Simple immunisation could save many lives.

Political problems

As with countries in the developed world, internal political problems can also dominate the development of a country. Firstly, there can be guerrillas or freedom fighters (depending on your point of view) waging civil war against the government. Either side can be supported, in terms of training or equipment, by pro-capitalist or pro-communist countries. In some countries this has led to food aid convoys being attacked and the food destroyed, or food being traded for arms by governments. Such acts of violence should not be viewed as peculiar to third world countries; people in the developed world are quite prepared to cause deaths in pursuit of political goals.

Just what is the picture?

Reports on TV and newspapers often show desperate levels of poverty in third world countries. In contrast it must be remembered these countries do have cities with jobs, food and housing but they do not yet have the capacity or sometimes the will to provide these for all the population.

International aid

In the meantime, as well as the aid agencies, many governments give a small percentage of their Gross National Product to helping third world countries. This is done partly for humanitarian reasons and

SQUARING OFF THE VICIOUS AID CIRCLE

CHARITIES supplying famine relief to countries such as Ethiopia actually worsen the situation in the long run it is often argued. Food aid, it is contended, prevents the development of an effective domestic agriculture because local farmers cannot compete against "freebies" from Europe and the US. Come the next drought, more food is needed, and all the time there is less and less incentive for self help.

This comment and picture appeared in a magazine called *Financial Weekly* in 1988. Write a letter to the editor giving reasons why you either support or disagree with the article.

IT ▶ WORDPRO

Try to write your letter straight onto a word processor.

partly because it helps stimulate these economies and, with it, world trade.

Gross National Product

Away from the visual portrayal of third world countries, there are more formal measures of how well a country is doing. Commonly used is Gross National Product (GNP) per head. This shows the average level of resources available to a person in a country. Third world countries usually have a low GNP but it is often not a good measure as much activity goes unrecorded and goods are rarely distributed evenly.

POINTS TO REMEMBER

★ Third world countries usually face combinations of problems.

★ Investment in capital goods and education is as important as providing food.

★ The developed world can give assistance in giving both food aid and capital aid.

★ We often get very negative ideas about third world countries, many do have lively economies and their people would not want our world.

Question

Write a paragraph about each of the above comments saying whether or not you think they are true.

TASK 1

Good shelter is necessary

Clean water prevents illness

Medical help prevents blindness

Food aid saves lives

GROUP WORK

There is a small village of 30 adults and 60 children in a third world country. There have been problems with the water supply and a new well would cost $1000. At present water is taken from a stream but increasingly many villagers and particularly children have been falling ill and the water supply is suspected as the cause.

Last year's harvest failed again and some parents have been going without food in order to feed their children. This has already led to five deaths. You estimate that $600 for food aid would stop this problem this year.

Part of the reason why the harvest failed was that the land was becoming more difficult to work and 3 new ploughs are needed. These will cost $100 each.

Twenty of the adults and 30 children are suffering from eye problems which need minor medical help. It costs $20 to stop each of these people becoming permanently blind.

The 15 huts used for shelter are in a very poor state and are unlikely to survive the next winter. It would cost $100 to make each hut weatherproof.

Your group has $1000 only to give in aid and it has to specify the purpose for which it is to be used. Discuss the issues raised and the way in which you would allocate the money between the various projects. Write a report for presentation to the rest of the class explaining what you decided to do and how you justified the decision. You should also mention why you think the other projects should be put off.

Ox-ploughing helps people to cultivate more land.

Investigating the FINANCIAL Background

Costs and Revenues

Selling ice cream – a case study

Gerry Baines is a young student who lives near the Lancashire seaside resort of Blackpool. He was looking for a summer job – the idea of making money during the holidays appealed to him.

He thought about selling ice cream, but how many would he have to sell to make a profit? He knew what his costs would be. They were quite simple: the bicycle, with a cold box on the front, was £300 to hire for the summer season and the cost of buying a cone with ice cream was 30p. He knew he could charge about 60p per cone because this was the price charged by other ice cream sellers in Blackpool.

Now he needed to work out how many ice cream cones he would have to sell to make a profit. Would it be tens, hundreds or thousands?

Fixed costs

He started to work out a break-even chart. This would tell him the minimum number of ice creams he would have to sell to cover his costs, without making any profits. First of all, the £300 for the bicycle was a fixed cost. No matter how many ice creams he sold he would have to pay this. This is shown on Graph A.

Variable costs

The ice cream he bought in bulk would be a variable cost, that is the more he sold the higher this cost would be. If he sold 1000 he would pay £300 but if he sold 2000 he would pay £600. This can be plotted on the graph as shown on Graph B. It is added to the fixed cost to give his total cost. This can now be plotted at different levels of sales.

Sales revenue

Gerry knows that if he sells no ice creams he will get no revenue; if he sells 1000 he will get £600 (1000 × 60p); and if he sells 2000 he will get £1200 (2000 × 60p). These points can be plotted as the sales revenue line. This is shown on Graph C.

The break-even point

Graph D puts all the information together. It shows the break even point where the total cost line crosses the sale revenue line. Here Gerry makes neither a profit nor a loss. If he sells more than this, the profit is the difference between the total cost line and the revenue line. If he sells less than this, then costs are greater than revenue and he makes a loss.

The important point to remember about fixed costs is that you have to pay them even if you produce nothing. They would include the cost of buying premises or machinery, but often they are not easy to identify. For example, wages are often put down as a variable cost because if you did not produce anything you would not employ anybody! But, in the real world, if you had no orders for goods, you would probably keep some of your workers in case you did need to start producing. You would not want to be delayed because you had to start finding employees.

Fixed or variable costs?

A similar problem arises with costs like electricity and gas. These are also often thought to be variable costs because if you produce nothing you would not use any power. This is not really correct. Even if a factory produced nothing it would still use some electricity, even if it was only to have a light on in an office, hoping that somebody would place an order! Also, if you look at an electricity or gas bill you will see that it contains a fixed charge that you must pay, even if you actually consume nothing. This part of the bill is likely to be a fixed cost whilst the rest of it could be considred as a variable cost. The reason why these bills are charged like this is because the electricity boards and British Gas have to maintain services to you even if you use no electricity or gas.

When costs are broken down like this, it can help a firm to decide whether it is worthwhile to take an order. Look at the following problem:

Cheap lunches

The Su Wong Chinese Restaurant has recently opened in Bridlington. It has fixed costs of about £2.00 per meal (this covers the rent, rates, wages and heating) and variable costs of £1.50 (mainly the food and the cost of cooking it).

Business is slack, especially at lunchtimes. The restaurant knows that it will stay in business in the long term as its reputation grows, but it needs to find ways of paying for its fixed costs in the early months. It has been asked by a local business if it would be prepared to provide 20 lunches per day for £2.00.

Mr Wong, the owner, at first thinks this order is not worth taking because the total cost of a meal is £2.00 + £1.50 = £3.50. Why should he provide meals for £2.00? However, after some thought, he realises that £2.00 per meal does cover the variable cost of the food and would leave him with £0.50 as a contribution towards his fixed costs. This would, of course be better than nobody eating in his restaurant at lunchtimes.

Contributing to fixed costs

The idea behind this contribution to fixed costs is

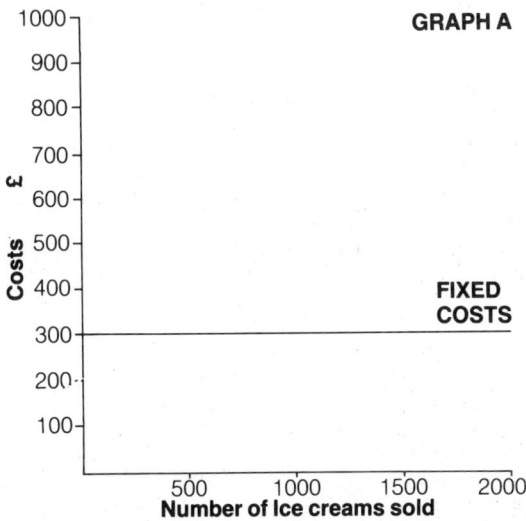

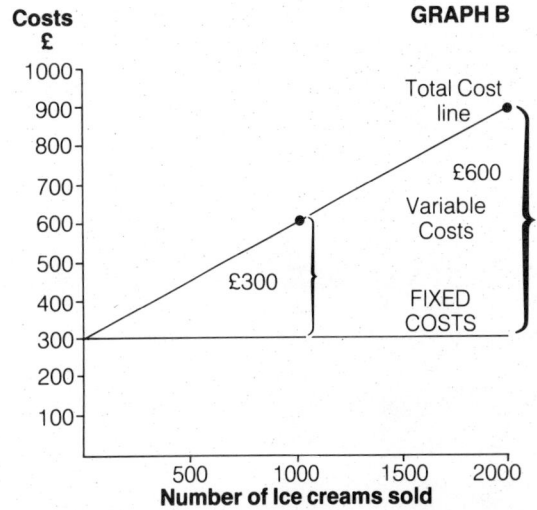

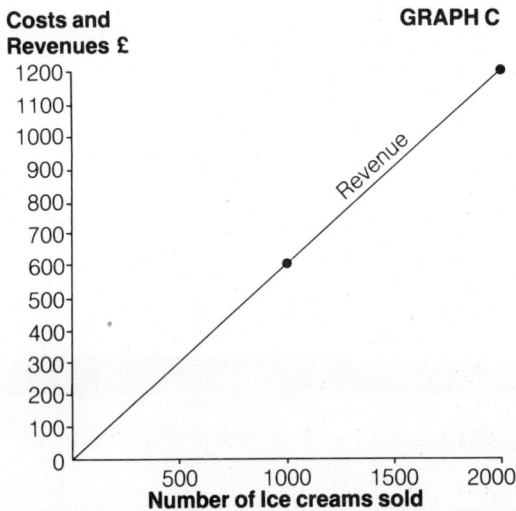

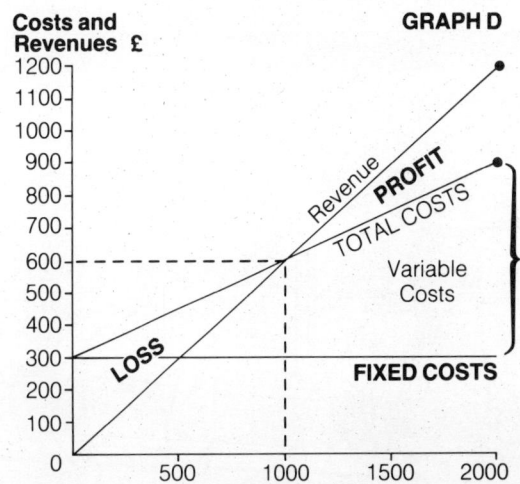

GRAPH A

Costs £

1000
900
800
700
600
500
400
300
200
100

500   1000   1500   2000
Number of Ice creams sold

FIXED COSTS

GRAPH B

Costs £

1000
900
800
700
600
500
400
300
200
100

500   1000   1500   2000
Number of Ice creams sold

Total Cost line

£600

Variable Costs

£300

FIXED COSTS

GRAPH C

Costs and Revenues £

1200
1100
1000
900
800
700
600
500
400
300
200
100
0

500   1000   1500   2000
Number of Ice creams sold

Revenue

GRAPH D

Costs and Revenues £

1200
1100
1000
900
800
700
600
500
400
300
200
100
0

500   1000   1500   2000
Number of Ice creams sold

Revenue   PROFIT
TOTAL COSTS
Variable Costs
LOSS
FIXED COSTS

Questions

1 What is the fixed cost of selling 1500 ice creams? (Graph A)

2 What is the variable cost of selling 1500 ice creams? (Graph B)

3 What is the total cost of selling 1500 ice creams? (Graph C or D)

Look at Graph D and use the information given about the selling of ice creams in the first paragraph of this section to answer the following questions:

4 How much profit does Gerry make if he sells:
   a 500 ice creams?
   b 1000?
   c 1500?
   d 2000?

5 What would happen to the break-even point if fixed costs rose to £500?

6 What would be the new break-even point if ice creams could be sold for 70p each?

7 What would be the new break-even point if the cost Gerry could buy ice creams for went down to 20p?

IT ▶ **SPREADSHEET**

This question is based on the information concerning Gerry Baines setting up as an ice cream salesman. Often it is difficult to read a graph accurately. Gerry wants to borrow £500 from the bank to get his small business started. He has decided to present the information in the form of a spreadsheet so he can clearly show his profit or loss at each level of sales. Complete the following spreadsheet for him.

FIXED COSTS	£300							
VARIABLE COSTS	£0.30							
UNITS SOLD	500	600	700	800	900	1000	1100	1200
SELLING PRICE	£0.60							
TOTAL COSTS								
TOTAL REVENUE								
PROFIT/LOSS								

seen in many businesses. If you think about train fares you can observe the same practice. At peak times, when trains are full, British Rail can base charges on total cost but, if it charges the full fare at off-peak times, people would use trains even less. Given that trains have to run to a timetable, it is better to have passengers on them paying something rather than to have them running empty.

POINTS TO REMEMBER

★ Costs are either fixed or variable.

★ Break-even charts show whether profits or losses are made at different levels of output.

★ Firms will accept orders if they cover their variable costs and therefore make a contribution to fixed costs.

TASK 1

THE PRICE OF HOTEL ROOMS

1 List three fixed costs which a hotel would incur.

2 List the variable costs of letting a room for one night.

3 What sources of revenue would a hotel have other than letting rooms?

4 Suggest why the offer of a reduced payment for one night might be accepted.

5 Would it be a good idea to accept such offers if they were made by customers early in the morning?

TASK 2

GOLDFISH BOWLS

A company making goldfish bowls has fixed costs of £50 000. The bowls sell to retailers for £2.50 each but have a variable cost of only £1.50.

Construct a break-even chart to show the level of output required to:
a break even.
b make a profit of £10 000.

TASK 3

BAROMETERS

A company making barometers has fixed costs of £10 000. It sells the barometers for £150 each. Variable costs amount to £75 per barometer.

Construct a break-even chart to show:
a the break-even level of output.
b the output required to make a profit of £10,000.

TASK 4

VALVES

Another way to calculate the break-even level of output is by the formula:

$$\text{Break-even level of output} = \frac{\text{fixed costs}}{\text{selling price per unit} - \text{variable cost per unit}}$$

An engineering company has received an order to make a special valve. They estimate the cost of a new machine, which will be used solely to make the valve, at £10 000. The variable cost of making the valve is £0.05. The order is for 20 000 units at £0.45.

1 Show the calculations necessary to suggest the order should be rejected.

2 What is the minimum order level that could be accepted if the firm wanted a profit of £2000?

TASK 5

SWIFT SANDWICHES

The increasing pressure on people to eat whilst working has created a gap in the fast food market. People want to be served fresh, tasty sandwiches and drinks without leaving their desks. Whilst you might think that this is a quick way to fall victim to the pressures of overwork, many people do this every day. George and Mildred thought that they might be able to meet the needs of this market by extending the service offered at present by their restaurant. In order to keep a careful check on whether or not they could make a profit out of supplying sandwiches they decided to operate it as a separate part of their business.

They decided to test the market over a three month period. The equipment needed would be hired to 'Swift Sandwiches' for three months from the main restaurant. One person would be employed on a fixed-term contract for the three months and bread and fillings would be provided at cost from the restaurant. As 'Swift Sandwiches' would be occupying valuable space in the restaurant it would have to pay a proportion of the rates and heating bills for the three-month trial period. It would also pay a charge for the use of the restaurant's van which would be used for deliveries.

Leaflets advertising the service would be sent to thirty companies operating in nearby offices.

These start up costs were estimated as follows:

Equipment	£50
Rent and rates	£100
Transport	£75
Cost of employee	£1500
Advertising	£20

The variable cost of making the sandwiches are given below:

Cheese and onion	20p
Prawn salad	25p
Ham	20p
Egg and cress	25p

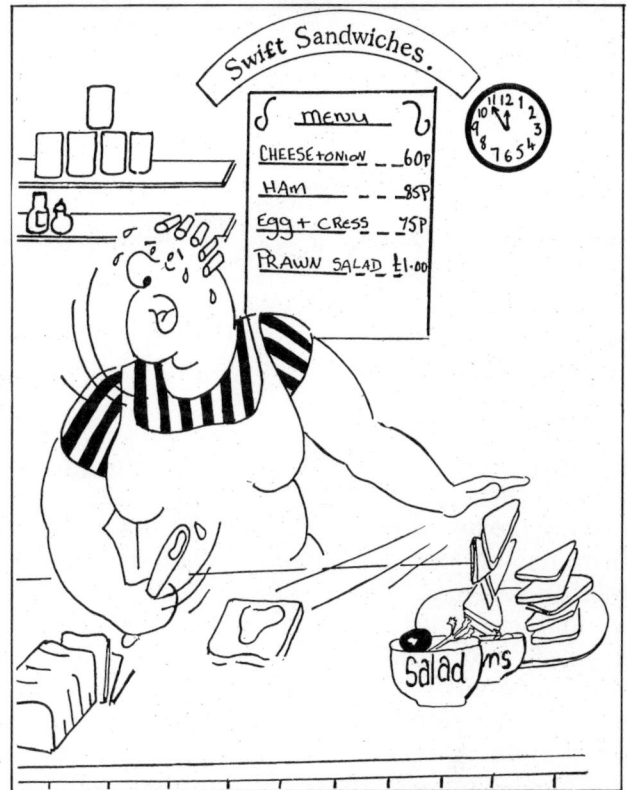

As demand is unpredictable 'Swift Sandwiches' will produce equal quantitites of each type of sandwich each day. Information on the selling price of the sandwiches is given on the menu board in the picture.

1 How many sandwiches would have to be sold to break even?

2 How many sandwiches would have to be sold to make a profit of £1000 over the three-month period.

3 If the sandwich maker could not cope and an extra person was employed at £1000 what would be the new break-even point?

4 If the cost of making the prawn salad sandwich increased to 30p how many sandwiches would have to be produced to keep the profit at £1000.

Cost Benefit Analysis

Cost benefit analysis is a way of looking at two problems. These are:

What price to charge for a product or service. Whether we should invest in a project like the new Channel Tunnel.

In order to answer these questions we need to look at four factors:

Private costs These cover all the items which a firm has to pay for directly when it produces goods or services. These will include rent, rates, raw materials, advertising, salaries, machinery, equipment and buildings.

Private benefits These are the advantages which a firm expects to gain from making a business decision. For example, a decision to launch a new product could mean they will make extra profit.

Social costs These fall on people who do not directly use the product. Examples of these costs include the costs of cleaning up water pollution from factories or the noise suffered by people living near airports.

Social benefits These again can be enjoyed by people who do not directly use a product or service. Examples of these are the benefits gained by those who do not become ill because others are given medical treatment for infectious diseases.

What price to charge?

Private costs and benefits are usually clearly identified by a firm when it produces a product. Problems do arise when trying to deal with social costs and benefits. These four factors all have influence on the price of a product.

For example, if a firm producing paper pollutes a river when it gets rid of waste products, should it include the cost of cleaning the river in the price it charges? This could put the firm out of business if nobody buys the product at the higher price. The alternative is to have non-users of the product pay through taxation to have the effluent removed.

On the other hand, if a firm improves the fishing in a river by depositing in it warm water from its cooling process, should the anglers who fish there pay the firm towards the improvement and help to reduce the costs of production?

Investment projects

The second main use of cost benefit analysis is in deciding whether to go ahead with a capital investment project. This may be judged in a local context, like a decision over the siting of a new pedestrian

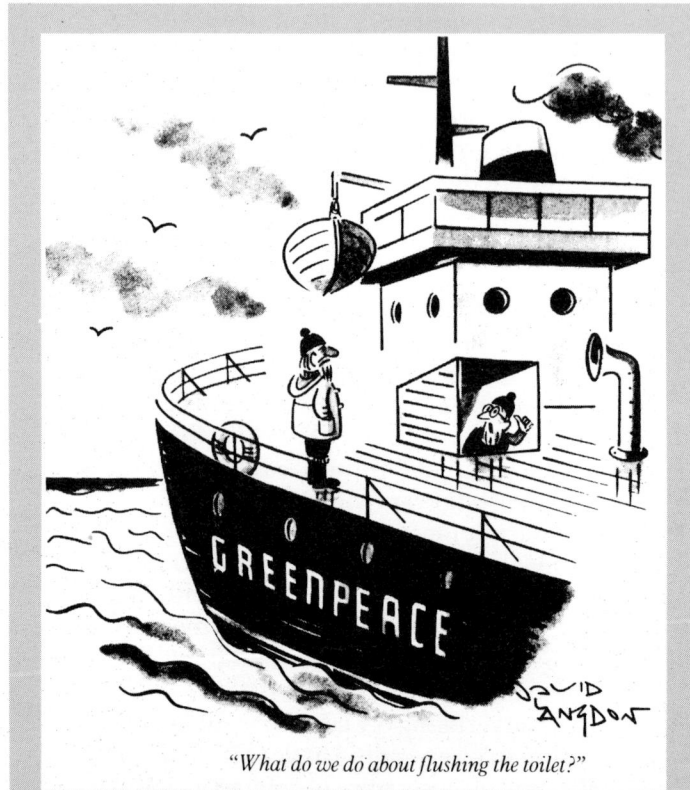

"What do we do about flushing the toilet?"

Questions

1 Why is the environmental group 'Greenpeace' concerned about dumping waste at sea?

2 Why is it so difficult to do anything about this problem?

3 Why do you think some companies are keen that there are no restrictions on sea dumping?

4 What are the social costs and benefits of dumping waste at sea?

crossing, or it may be a national or international decision like the construction of the new Channel Tunnel.

The Channel Tunnel

For a project like the Channel Tunnel, the private costs would be the construction costs, the development of the trains, track and administrative buildings. There would be obvious private benefits in terms of the profits which the company might make and to those people who would pay to cross the channel when the tunnel opened.

Problems do arise when looking at the social costs and benefits of such a project. The benefits could include the extra jobs that are created to run the tunnel, and the jobs in the building and construction industry. The social costs set against this are the spoiling of the countryside and the possible loss of jobs on the ferry routes. Given that it is possible to suggest what the social costs and benefits are, the real problem is how to measure them. In many projects, because of the uncertainty of the future, these are only rough estimates.

Pedestrian crossings

Whilst the Channel Tunnel represents a vast project, cost benefit analysis could also be applied to constructing a pedestrian crossing. The social costs are measured in terms of the lives lost and the social benefits in the lives saved; again monetary values are needed. The problem is that if you calculate a life to be worth millions of pounds, you would place crossings everywhere. In reality, if a life is worth £5000 and a crossing costs £15 000 then, when three people have died, the crossing would be built. This is a harsh and insensitive calculation but one which sometimes has to be made.

POINT TO REMEMBER

★ Decisions on what price to charge or whether to undertake a project should include a consideration of social costs and benefits as well as private costs and benefits.

"We'll have you on your feet in no time, Mr Perkins"

Question

What social costs and benefits are there in a decision to close a hospital?

OPEN ALL HOURS

NEW SHOPPING HOURS

MON	8.00 am	---	9.00 pm
TUES	8.00 am	---	8.30 pm
WED	8.30 am	---	9.00 pm
THUR	8.30 am	---	9.00 pm
FRI	8.30 am	---	9.00 pm
SAT	8.30 am	---	9.00 pm
SUN	9.30 am	---	5.00 pm

Given above are the typical opening hours of DIY stores. If a store decides to keep such long hours there will be both costs and benefits. Think of these from the point of view of the shop owners, the customers, shop staff and local residents.

Question

List all the costs and benefits that will follow from the introduction of longer shopping hours.

TASK 1

PROPOSAL FOR A BY-PASS TO THE TOWN OF WELLFIELD

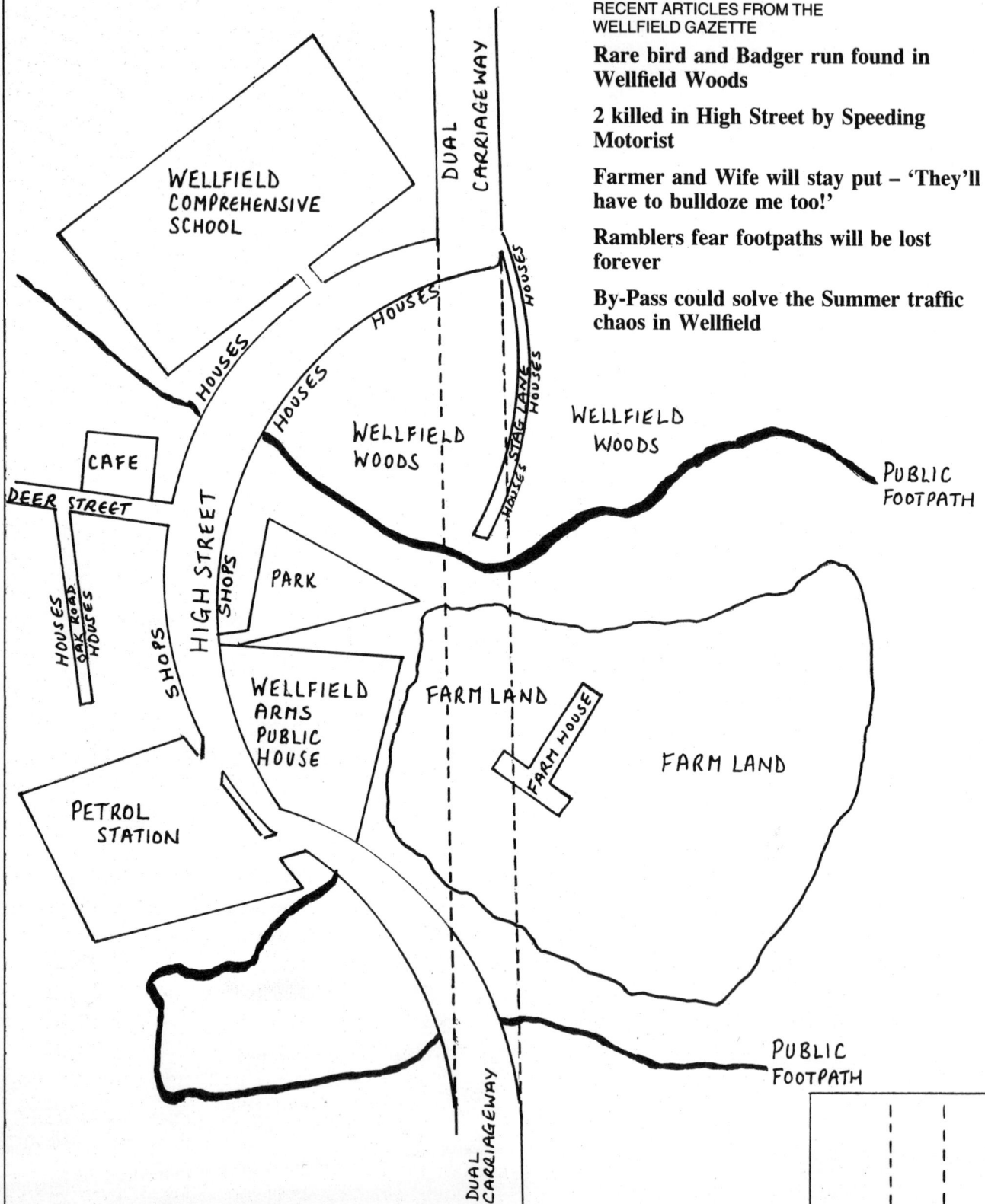

RECENT ARTICLES FROM THE
WELLFIELD GAZETTE

Rare bird and Badger run found in Wellfield Woods

2 killed in High Street by Speeding Motorist

Farmer and Wife will stay put – 'They'll have to bulldoze me too!'

Ramblers fear footpaths will be lost forever

By-Pass could solve the Summer traffic chaos in Wellfield

As planning officer you have been asked to prepare
a report for Wellfield Council stating clearly who
might benefit and who might lose if the by-pass was
built. You should reach a final decision stating
which arguments you found most important.

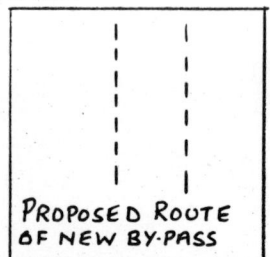

TASK 2

● The National Smokeless Fuel plant at Abercwmboi.

**By ROGER DOBSON,
Social Affairs Correspondent**

Valley leaders will get tough with the fuming factory

THEY CALL it Dante's Inferno.

The factory sends out fumes and flames around the clock as it takes the dirty smoke out of coal.

But while the newly-cleaned fuel goes away to heat homes in Britain's smokeless cities, Mountain Ash and the Cynon Valley retain the smoke and the pollution.

For years the Cynon Valley has put up with the Phurnacite plant at Abercwmboi because the need for jobs outweighed the pollution problems.

But now the Valley is planning tougher action against the plant. There are fears that the Phurnacite plant and its attendant pollution may be deterring industrialists.

The Valley has also lost hundreds of coal-industry jobs and may now be less dependent on the plant.

Cynon Valley Borough Council is now reconsidering its policy towards the plant after years of protests.

"It has been called Dante's Inferno and it has been a hideous site for years," said the council's chief executive, Mr Geoffrey Hosgood.

"The supreme irony is that many areas of the country have enjoyed the benefits of clean air while we, who have the plant, are denied the very benefits that the plant exists to give.

"We, as a council, have been cleaning up derelict land for years. It would be unacceptable if we clean up the environment, but the Valley is left with an industrial anachronism in the middle of it."

Mr Hosgood has told members of his environmental health committee the council is also anxious to attract new industry.

"The presence of this plant could well be counter-productive and discouraging to industrialists" he said.

Ideally, the council would like the plant cleaned up but the authority says that after years of protests and action by National Smokeless Fuels there is no evidence of any big improvment.

"We are reviewing our attitude to this plant," said Mr Hosgood. "We will be calling for facts and figures and making decisions. Our concern is the future of the valley."

A spokesman for National Smokeless Fuels was not available for comment.

IT ► DESKTOP

1 Read the newspaper article about the National Smokeless Fuels plant in South Wales. Prepare a report for the local council outlining the possible costs and benefits of closing the plant down.

2 Many issues raised in your locality give rise to costs and benefits. These might be new roads or a shopping centre, increased traffic or reduced bus services. Choose one such issue and prepare a newspaper report like the one above that sets out the issues on both sides. You may be able to take or find a photograph which you can use to illustrate the article. If possible interview local people to find out their views.

Business Accounting

Whether you are running a one person business or a large company you will need to keep accounts so that you can find out how well or how badly the business is doing.

Calculating the profit

In order to find out how well a business is doing it needs to calculate its profit. First of all, the 'gross profit' must be worked out. This is done as follows:

Stock of goods at start of year	+	Goods purchased for resale	−	Stock of goods at end of year
£10 000	+	£50 000	−	£20 000

= stock sold during the year (usually called 'cost
£40 000 of goods sold')

The firm should have kept a list of all its sales during the year. In this case, we will assume that sales were £100 000, which means that the firm sold goods costing £40 000 for £100 000. This results in a gross profit of £60 000. If the firm had got less than £40 000, it would have made a gross loss.

The usual layout for the above would be:

Trading Account for the period ending 31.12.88

		£
Sales		£100 000
Stock at start of year	£10 000	
+ Purchases	+ £50 000	
	= £60 000	
− Stock at end of year	£20 000	
Cost of goods sold	=	£40 000
GROSS PROFIT		£60 000

This does not give the final profit for the firm because all the other expenses of running the business have yet to be deducted, such as wages, salaries, rent, heating bills, advertising costs and rates. This is done in a profit and loss account as follows:

Profit and Loss Account for the period ending 31.12.88

Gross profit		£60 000
Rent	£5000	
Rates	£5000	
Advertising	£10 000	
		£20 000
NET PROFIT		£40 000

Questions

Work out the missing figures:

Opening stock	+ Purchases	− Closing stock	= Cost of goods sold
£8000	+ £20 000	− £2000	= ?
£2300	+ £16 780	− £3756	= ?
£200	+ £100	− ?	= £250
£3590	+ £5600	− ?	= £4530
?	+ £10 000	− £2000	= £9000
?	+ £9800	− £2350	= £10 670
£2m	+ ?	− £5 000 000	= £4m
£230	+ ?	− £23	= £600

Work out the missing figures:

Sales	− Cost of goods sold	= Gross profit or loss
£200	− £160	= ?
£3890	− £2900	= ?
£2312	− £3590	= ?
£120	− ?	= £32
£12 000	− ?	= £5000
£2300	− ?	= −£4500
?	− £1600	= −£600
?	− £389	= £452
?	− £372	= £4000

Calculate the gross profit percentage for each part of this question where a gross profit is made.

IT ▶ SPREADSHEET

These two sets of questions can be completed on a spreadsheet.

If you look at the Trading Account you will see that sales of £100 000 produced a gross profit of £60 000. In terms of buying stock and selling it, this means that every £1 worth of sales gave 60p of gross profit. This relationship can be expressed as the gross profit percentage.

$$\text{Gross Profit percentage} = \frac{\text{Gross profit}}{\text{Sales}} \times 100$$

$$= \frac{60\,000}{100\,000} \times 100 = 60\%$$

If this figure is worked out each year, reasons for changes would be looked for. If the percentage falls, it could be that the stock is now costing more to buy and the firm has not passed on the price rise to the customer. On the other hand, it could suggest that stock is being stolen or broken,

The next figure to calculate is the net profit percentage.

$$\text{Net profit percentage} = \frac{\text{Net profit}}{\text{Sales}} \times 100$$

$$= \frac{40\,000}{100\,000} \times 100 = 40\%$$

In this case the expenses, like rates and salaries, are being examined. If the net profit percentage falls, it means that expenses have increased but sales have not gone up as the firm would have hoped. For example, if the sales representatives were paid more, they would be expected to sell more. However, if electricity prices rise, the firm can do little more than increase its selling price to maintain the net profit percentage.

Final accounts

The trading account and the profit and loss account form part of the 'final accounts' of a firm. The last part of these final accounts is the 'Balance Sheet'. This lists all the assets of the firm (i.e. what it owns) and all its liabilities (i.e. what it owes). The balance sheet is always set out in such a way as to be in balance.

Picture above is the Smiths Crisps factory near Swansea, South Wales. Think about the process of making, packaging and selling crisps and then try to answer the questions below.

Questions

1 What are the two fixed assets shown in the picture?

2 Can you suggest three other fixed assets that the firm would have?

3 What sort of firms do you think are creditors of Smiths?

4 What sort of firms do you think Smiths has as debtors?

5 Most manufacturing firms buy in raw materials to make their products and unused stocks of these would appear in the final balance sheet as current assets. For example, at the end of the year, Smiths may have unused stocks of potatoes. Can you suggest two other items of raw materials they may have in stock?

Balance Sheet as at 31.12.88

Fixed Assets		(items kept in the
Buildings	£10 000	business on a long
Machinery	£5000	term basis)
Vehicles	£10 000	£25 000
TOTAL		

Current Assets		(items constantly
Stock	£20 000	changing on a
Debtors	£10 000	daily basis)
Bank	£5000	
Cash	£1000	
TOTAL	£36 000	

Current Liabilities		(items constantly
Creditors	£10 000	changing which
		are debts of the
		firm which may
		have to be paid off
		within a short
		time)

Working Capital	£26 000
(Current Assets	
minus current	
liabilities)	
	£51 000

Financed by		
Capital	£31 000	(Money put into the business at the start)
+ Net profit	£40 000	(Amount calculated in profit & loss a/c)
− Drawings	£20 000	(Money taken from the business by the owner for personal use)
	£51 000	

Having done the 'Final accounts' you now need to use this information to see how well (or badly!) the firm has done.

You can see that a net profit of £40 000 has been made, but that figure on its own does not mean a great deal. You need to look at how much was put into the firm to start with. This is the capital figure and was £31 000. So the firm invested £31 000 and made £40 000 in return.

What percentage has been made? This can be found as follows:

$$\frac{\text{Net profit}}{\text{Capital}} \times 100 = \frac{40\,000}{31\,000} \times 100 = 129\%$$

Investing an inheritance

You have just been left £30 000 by a distant relative who has died. Three of your friends have recently started their own business and each is trying to get you to invest £10 000. Having been poor for many years you are not inclined to throw your money away. Your local bank is offering interest on deposits of 6 per cent.

You have asked your friends to show you their accounts for last year. These show:

Name of business	Capital invested	Net profit
Supersox	£23 000	£3000
Cloud Ten	£90 000	£6000
Flashgun	£120 000	£10 000

Questions

1 Calculate the return on capital for each business.

2 Which one would you be most likely to invest in?

3 Why should investing in firms never be regarded as completely safe?

Net profit calculations

Gross profit	− Expenses	= Net profit
£6000	− £250	= ?
£7034	− £9800	= ?
£356	− £239	= ?
?	− £6300	= −£12
?	− £234	= £23
?	− £25	= £225
£2000	− ?	= £845
£9900	− ?	= £7900
£45	− ?	= £0

IT ▶ SPREADSHEET

These questions can be completed on a spreadsheet.

Questions

1 Work out the missing figures in the table above.

2 If sales were £10 000, calculate the net profit percentage in each case where a profit is made.

This represents an excellent 'return on capital', when you think that a bank or building society would give you only 5–10 per cent if you had invested the capital with them!

Another important factor to consider is whether a business can meet its immediate debts. These are shown as the current liabilities. Usually, if all the creditors required immediate payment, a firm would use its current assets to meet the debts. Current liabilities are £10 000, so creditors could be paid as follows: cash £1000; bank £5000 and £4000 from debtors. In this case the firm could probably manage. However, debtors are often slow to pay and the firm might have to sell stock cheaply to raise quick cash.

In order to be safe in this area, a firm usually needs £2 worth of Current Assets to cover every £1 worth of current liabilities. This is expressed by the 'current' ratio of:

Current assets : Current liabilities, i.e.
36 000 : 10 000
3.6 : 1

This should be adequate cover.

Often a business will want to check that it is liquid. The most liquid asset is cash. Other assets can be turned into cash but this can often take some time. The acid test ratio is:

debtors and cash : current liabilities
16 000 : 10 000
1.6 : 1

This shows whether a firm's most liquid assets could meet its current liabilities should the need arise. Generally, 1:1 is acceptable.

As well as being a useful guide to the changing performance of a firm over the years, these formulae can also be used to compare the performance of firms in the same line of business.

POINTS TO REMEMBER

★ Keeping accounts is required by law.

★ Accounts can be used to see how well a business is doing.

★ Keeping accounts helps to pinpoint the problems of firms.

TASK 1

British Airways Plc

BRITISH AIRWAYS
The world's favourite airline.

Extracts from published accounts

	1987	1986
	£m	£m
Sales	3263	3149
Cost of service sold	2993	2870
Total expenses	97	81
Fixed Assets	1300	1315
Current Assets	777	593
Current Liabilities	1140	988

1 What would constitute 'Sales' for British Airways?

2 What would the cost of sales comprise?

3 Work out the gross profit for each year.

4 Work out the net profit for each year.

5 Work out the gross profit percentage for each year.

6 Work out the net profit percentage for each year.

7 What is the working capital figure?

8 What problems could the answer found in question 7 bring about?

9 In which year did British Airways produce better results?

10 Think of the problems of operating an airline to a fixed schedule of routes and flights. Why is it difficult to reduce costs if you have fewer passengers?

11 During 1987 the chairman of British Airways pointed to the increase in terrorism and the Chernobyl disaster as major problems for the airline. Why should these events cause problems for an airline?

IT ▶ SPREADSHEET

This question can be completed on a spreadsheet.

Investigating
WATER
A Case Study

Business Case Study: Paying for Water

This case study looks at several business issues which relate to a common theme – water. Some of the text and tasks refer to domestic and industrial issues in the UK, others demonstrate that water supply is an even more sensitive issue in other parts of the world.

We drink it.
We wash with it.
We water plants with it.
We manufacture paper with it.
We cool electricity generators with it.

Water.

In business, we sometimes refer to 'a free economic good'. This is a good which is freely available to all of us, without the 'cost' of producing it. Sunshine is a free good to the farmer, so is the rainfall on his crops.

The water which we use in the home or the factory is not a free good because it has to be collected, stored, purified and distributed. In some parts of the world, water is a rare and expensive commodity. In Britain we often take the cost of water for granted. We turn on the tap and there it is. We pay a bill for our 'water rates' but, apart from that, most of us don't think about 'paying' for water at all.

How do we get our water supply?
Water is collected from rainfall either on the surface in reservoirs, or in underground rock layers where it can be pumped to the surface.

It is treated in a water treatment plant run by a local water 'authority', such as the 'Mid Southern Water Company' in Task 1. Sometimes a chemical called 'fluoride' is added because this is claimed to be good for healthy teeth and bones.

Your group may like to discuss the 'fluoride issue', finding out what is involved and whether or not it should be encouraged.

Purification is not the only costly process involved in getting water into the home. There is often a great deal of pumping needed if water is to be delivered under pressure to taps into domestic, commercial and industrial premises.

Local water companies
In the UK, private homes are charged for water according to the rates they pay. These charges have to reflect all the costs of providing a water supply to each home, regardless of where the home is situated. Like many domestic services, water is provided at the same rateable charge regardless of whether the site is on the side of a remote hill or on a densely packed housing estate.

TASK 1

DOMESTIC WATER SERVICES: MID SOUTHERN WATER COMPANY

The water charge for this domestic household is based on the rateable value of the property, in this case at 13.8p for each £1 of rateable value.

In addition there is a standing charge for providing the service and a fee to cover the extra use of water for garden hoses and swimming pools.

The water company also collects fees for the removal of sewerage through the main sewer system and for environmental water services like local river controls and local recreational amenities. In this case, these are paid to the Thames Water Authority.

MID SOUTHERN WATER COMPANY
P.O. Box 214, Frimley Green, Camberly, Surry GU16 6HZ : Tel Deepcut (0252) 835031

Office Hours Monday to Friday 9am to 5pm

WATER SERVICES ACCOUNT

FOR THE YEAR COMMENCING 1ST APRIL 1987

07/0147/067/07/0
PLEASE QUOTE THIS REFERENCE
ON ALL ENQUIRIES

SERVICE	CHARGEABLE VALUE	RATE	AMOUNT £	STANDING CHARGE £	AMOUNT PAYABLE £
WATER	£258	13.8P	35.60	13.70	49.30
SEW & ENV ✱	£258	14.5P	37.41	12.00	49.41
HOSE					9.50

✱ Sewerage and Environmental (if charged) are collected for Thames Water **TOTAL£** 108.21

00156630

Questions

1 What is the 'rateable value' of this property?

2 What is the 'standing charge' intended to cover?

3 Why should this family be expected to pay towards an 'environmental' water charge?

4 How else could this cost be met within the local community?

5 Is it reasonable, in your opinion, to charge for the use of a garden hose but not, for example, for the use of a bath or shower within a house? Give your arguments.

WATER SUPPLY

As soon as men began to settle into large communities they were faced with the problems of ensuring an adequate fresh water supply.

The ancient Greeks made considerable use of conduits, pipes and tunnels to supply water to their cities. Their techniques were refined and developed by the Romans.

Today water is supplied through an efficient purifying system, outlined on this page.

Reservoirs play an important part in the purification of water. While water is in the reservoir large solid impurities sink to the bottom and oxygen can attack other impurities. Such physical, chemical and biological conditions help to destroy harmful bacteria.

2

Pipelines which carry water from a reservoir to a treatment works are made from iron, lined with concrete

3

During the next stage the water is passed through a coarse screen, where leaves etc. are removed and often chlorine is added. This is followed by a much finer screen, done by a micro-strainer which is made up of holes 1 millionth of a metre wide.
This removes algae and small particles.

4

The water is then pumped into a service reservoir where it is stored and treated chemically to purify it almost completely. One process it goes through is called aerating where the water gets a higher level of oxygen which gives it a fresher taste.

5

After it is fully treated the water is pumped into the mains system, where pipes supply it to our houses etc.

A Roman aqueduct like this, at Segovia in Spain, is still used today. It carries water for 823 meters from Rio Frio to the old town. It forms the final stretch of a 60 mile system. The water flows in a channel along the top.

Surface water is collected in the higher rainfall areas of modern Britain and fed by pipeline to the areas of greatest population and highest use. Manchester and Birmingham collect water from North Wales and the Lake District. Elsewhere water is pumped from boreholes.

Charging an economic price for water

There are three stages in providing a domestic or industrial water supply – collection and treatment, transfer to urban locations, and provision of individual supplies.

Collection and treatment

This is currently undertaken by the local and regional water authorities. Rainfall is either collected and stored in reservoirs or is pumped from natural underground systems. The processes require investment – purchase of sites, collection, treatment, etc. In the past, government and local authority funding has subsidised these costs so that users do not pay for them directly.

Transfer to towns

This is a particularly sensitive issue at present because much of our water is brought in through very old lead and copper piping and this is now often in need of replacement. The same is true of rainwater and sewage removal – pipelines and sewers are often in a state of collapse and it is not always clear who should pay for their replacement.

Much of the water we use ends up in rivers. These are controlled by river authorities and funding for these is provided by government and local authorities. They are usually responsible for pollution control and clean-up processes.

Domestic and industrial supply

Large industrial users are metered so that they pay for the volume of water they use. They are also charged for effluent disposal and may be required to treat their waste for environmental reasons.

Domestic users pay for water according to their rates. We are going to look at other ways of charging for the actual volume of water we use.

TASK 2

STANDARD LETTER

IT ➤ WORDPRO

The Mid Southern Water Company is concerned that a number of customers are not paying their water services account on time. They are to send out a standard letter which you are asked to compose.

TASK 3

METERING WATER

Although most of us pay for water through a special charge based on the rates we pay, we are usually offered the chance to pay by the amount we consume. The disadvantage is that we have to pay for the installation of a meter to measure the consumption. If we are above average users, this would cost more than at present, when we pay an average charge. Low users would save on their annual water charge but this would be offset by the cost of the meter.

It is often argued that metering is a fairer system because it charges high users more for their consumption. It is also argued that charging for water in this way would reduce wastage and therefore cut consumption.

Some European cities already meter water, as the table shows:

Domestic consumption

	Litres per person per day	
Copenhagen	150	Recently metered
Helsinki	217	Metered
Oslo	185	Not metered
Stockholm	237	Metered
Amsterdam	120	Not metered
Rotterdam	138	Not metered
Vienna	133	Metered
Rome	290	Partially metered
Turin	270	Metered
Budapest	164	Metered
London	130	Unmetered

1 Is there a relationship between those cities which meter and the daily consumption of water per person?

2 Why can we *not* conclude from the table that the metering of water is one way of reducing water consumption?

3 What other factors, apart from metering, do you think might influence consumption?

4 If people reduce their consumption of water because they have to pay according to the amount they use, what problems might occur in terms of
a health?
b standard of living?

UK WATER USE

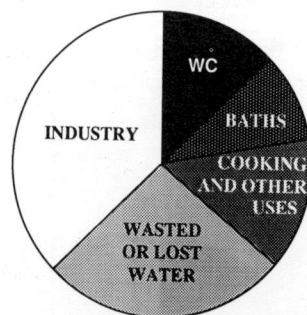

The environmental issues

Everything we have as consumers represents a cost to us in one way or another. In the case of water supply, a new reservoir will mean the loss of farmland and natural habitats for wildlife. People in towns and cities who suffer annual droughts from time to time may forget what the new reservoir they need will have a cost in terms of the quality of the rural environment.

Similarly, replacing old Victorian sewers and water pipes is expensive, quite apart from the chaos it causes in digging up roads. If we spend ratepayers' money on new sewage disposal facilities we either have to put up local rates or accept cuts in other areas of expenditure. If water is privatised, the consumer will pay for such improvements directly in higher charges.

TASK 4

DOMESTIC CONSUMPTION IN EUROPEAN CITIES

IT ▶ **DATABASE**

Transfer the information from the table in Task 3 into an appropriate database.

NAME OF FILE: water
NAME OF FIELDS: four
NO. OF RECORDS: eleven

NAME OF FIELD	FIELD WIDTH
City name	12
Litres per day	5
Metering (recent, metered, not metered, partially metered)	14
EC/Non EC (You will need to research this last entry)	10

Use the database to answer the following:

1 Select all those cities in EC countries where water is metered.

2 List those cities which have been recently metered in alphabetical order.

3 List those cities where consumption exceeds 200 litres per day, which are fully metered.

Take appropriate printouts.

TASK 5

WATER METERING

Use a spreadsheet to answer the questions below on supplying domestic water through a meter. The information and questions relate to a three month period.

FIXED COST of hiring a meter is £15
Water costs (i.e. the VARIABLE COSTS) 1.3p per 5 litres.

House name	Starting meter reading at 1 Jan litres	Meter reading at 31 March litres
Arcadia	6942	13 200
Blackwell	7295	16 222
Cumbria	6921	11 521
Downs	8397	10 111
Evesham	2911	17 694
Feltham	641	894
Gresham	2921	6655

1 Calculate the number of litres used by each house.

2 Calculate the variable cost of buying the water for each house.

3 Calculate the total cost of buying the water for each house.

4 Calculate the amount the seven houses would pay to the water board for supplying water.

5 Calculate the saving or extra payment that each house would have to make if a standard charge of £17.50 was paid by each of the houses and no other charges were payable.

TASK 6

WOULD A WATER METER SAVE MONEY?

Research indicates that, on average, one person uses about 7300 gallons of water each half year, about 40 gallons per day. It is on this basis that water rates are calculated, using the rateable value of the home as a guide. It is assumed that households with high rateable values use more water.

It is now possible to have a meter installed so that households can be charged for the amount of water thay actually use, rather than assuming the average figure.

Whether or not this would save money depends on:

the current charge for water supply.
how much water is used.
the cost of installing the meter.

Current charges (per half-year)

Rateable value	Amount payable for water
£200	£45.90
£250	£52.97
£300	£60.05

Metered charges
Typical Meter Bill - half yearly basis

Number in Household	If your water use is:- High £	Average £	Low £
1	36	33	30
2	51	46	41
3	64	58	52
4	78	71	64
5	91	83	75
6	105	95	85

Cost of meter
£178 including VAT
(Cost over ten years: £8.90 per half-year)

Calculation
Would it pay you to install a water meter, on the basis of the above figures, if you were:

a   a single person living alone, rateable value £200, low user?

b   family of three in a large house, rateable value £300, average user?

c   family of six, rateable value £250, high user?

Remember to include the cost of installing a meter.

MID SOUTHERN WATER COMPANY
Frimley Green, Camberley, Surrey

Domestic Water Metering
PLEASE READ THIS LEAFLET CAREFULLY

Commercial customers have already been given the option of metering under a separate scheme.

From 1 April 1984 you will be able to pay for water and sewerage services on a metered basis if you want to. This leaflet is designed to help you decide whether or not to have a meter fitted to the water supply to your home.

WHY ARE WE GIVING YOU THE CHOICE?

At present, your charges for water supply and sewerage services each consist generally of a standing charge plus a charge based on the rateable value (NAV) of your property.

This system keeps down administrative costs and is broadly fair: households with high rateable values pay more because, on average, they use more water. Charges based on rateable value will continue to be the better option for the great majority of our customers.

The choice is yours but, in fairness to customers who wish to go on paying on a rateable value basis, those who want a meter must pay a survey fee, bear the cost of installation and pay an extra annual charge to cover the costs of reading and maintaining the meter.

Meters at Customers' Option

You can choose to pay for your water supply and sewerage service by meter if you think that it would be to your advantage, provided that you pay the installation cost of the meter, currently £178 including V.A.T.

Most business people should find it financially worthwhile to have a meter, but there will be less benefit for household customers. As a rough guide, few three-person families in houses with rateable values of less than £500 are likely to be better off with a meter. For those who use a lot of water that figure could be much higher. For people living alone the corresponding rateable value is £250. Customers should note that it may take a number of years to recoup the installation costs of the meter from savings in the annual accounts.

Oi, that's enough! We're on a watermeter now!

Industrial water use

Many industries use a great deal of water. You will know that in the eighteenth century water was a major source of power. Factories were often sited in river valleys so that machinery could be driven by water wheels. The development of steam power from coal and, more recently, electricity from the national grid, reduced the reliance on locations near water.

However, water is still an important element in the requirements of many firms. Electricity power stations, for example, use millions of gallons of water in the cooling process and this is taken from nearby rivers and returned downstream. Purified domestic water is also important to many factories. In the food industry, for example, clean water is an important raw material.

TASK 7

CHARGING INDUSTRY FOR WATER

Nearly all paper is manufactured from wood pulp. This is made from the fibres of softwood timber and most of this is now imported into Britain. It comes in large, dry bales and needs to be soaked thoroughly at the start of the process which turns it into paper. Liquid pulp is 99 per cent water. China clay is added to give 'body' to the paper and make its surface suitable for printing. A ton of paper also needs an equal weight of coal to generate the electricity used in its production.

What else is needed?

MAKING PAPER

Pulp, china clay, coal: what else is needed? The answer is water, in large quantities. We have seen that the fluid entering the wet end of the machine is 99 per cent water. A power-station returns its cooling water for re-use; but a paper-mill uses up its process water: most of it is converted into vapour, and cannot be re-used. If the mill generates its own electricity it will need cooling water too.

Aylesford mills require about 20,000 gallons of water (for all purposes) to produce 1 ton of paper. Not all of this needs to be of high purity: the cooling water may be pumped from the river and returned to it after use; but the process water must satisfy strict specifications. It must be low in lime, magnesia, and iron. Lime would hinder the bleaching, and would form an insoluble residue on the pulp; either lime or magnesium oxide would counteract the effect of size, while compounds of iron would result in the yellowing of white paper, and in the dulling of coloured paper.

The purity of the water was one of the earliest localizing factors in the paper industry. The abundant soft water was undoubtedly significant in the concentration of paper-mills on the Lancashire slopes of the Pennines, and in the Aberdeen district. In Somerset, Hodgkinson, the owner of the Wookey Hole Mills, brought a successful action in 1861–3 against the lead-workers on the Mendips at Priddy, because the water from their operations was contaminating his supply down at Wookey Hole cave. Many large mills, however, find that the surface water is no longer sufficient for their needs, and draw on their own wells, keeping a careful check on its quality.

This is the wet end of Machine No. 5 at Bowater's Kemsley mill, near Sittingbourne, Kent. This is a newsprint mill, and No. 5 machine, with a wire width of 320 inches, is the largest in the world.

Courtesy, The Bowater Organisation

1 Why is water so important to the paper industry?

2 How should a paper-making firm be charged for the water it uses? State your reasons.

3 Electricity power supply is another industry in which water is an important cost. In this case, water is returned to local rivers after it has been used for cooling purposes. How should power stations be charged for water?

Privatisation of water

The Conservative government has made very clear its view that financial subsidies for industry should be removed wherever possible. This has been extended to include the water industry, although many experts do not agree that important services like water supply and sewage disposal should be put in the hands of private firms who set out to make as large a profit as possible. You need to think carefully about all the issues involved and then begin to make up your own mind. Remember, arguments are often very persuasive but they are not correct simply because they are put to you in a very forceful way.

TASK 8

Water goes private

If you can privatise the water industry, you can privatise anything. The government reckons it can (in England and Wales, at least). A year ago, it issued an unusually honest discussion paper examining how, and this week produced its answers. They are not convincing

Since 1974, ten water authorities—outside Scotland, where local government still does the job—supply 20.2m customers with 17 billion litres of water a day (a quarter of it through 29 "water companies", private-sector but closely regulated). They also collect and remove sewage. They manage rivers, handle land and road drainage, protect against flooding, control pollution, navigation, fishing and other watery recreation, and maintain sea defences.

Both by its nature and its particular structure in Britain, this is a hard industry to privatise while still protecting consumers:

● **Monopoly.** Piped fresh water is an essential, and (except, notably, for cooling-power stations) there is almost no substitute for it. Locally, "retail" supply is a natural monopoly, and wholesale supply is very nearly so. The same is true of sewage collection, though less so of its treatment and disposal. So how is the consumer in future to be guaranteed a proper service at a fair price?

● **Statutory powers.** Water authorities have regulatory powers over umpteen matters, notably control of pollution, in some of which they are also operators. They enforce the law, and indeed make bye-laws of their own. Who should in future exercise these powers?

● **Unprofitable duties.** Things like land drainage, flood protection and various conservation duties offer no prospect of charging customers. At present they are financed by raising a precept from local authorities or direct from the local ratepayer. Who would do them and how would they be paid for?

● **Commercial drawbacks.** Water supply might seem modestly attractive as a commercial proposition. It is no go-go business—demand rises about 1% a year—but a steady one and, albeit regulated, a monopoly. The water authorities have become much more businesslike, notably since the 1983 Water Act: manpower is down almost one fifth from its 1979 peak, to 51,800.

But the business has some unappealing oddities. First, charging. Over 99% of households, and half even of the 1.7m non-domestic customers, pay not for what they use but according to their property's rateable value. So the supplier cannot profit from better marketing. Meters would take time and £2 billion to install, although not much to read once that can be done electronically. But nobody knows how demand would respond for the 75% of water now unmetered; studies abroad suggest that it might fall by 15-30%.

Second, the water authorities' £27 billion (at replacement cost) of assets are largely underground: 160,000 miles of water mains, 120,000 of sewers. No investor can know what upkeep costs are likely to be, especially in places like Lancashire where pipes and sewers often date from the industrial revolution. A crude estimate is that the worst 20% of sewers need £1.5 billion spent on them—but nobody knows which they are.

TASK 8 CONTINUED

Thatcher emphasizes need to privatize water industry

By Robin Oakley, Political Editor

The Prime Minister used the Conservative Central Council meeting at the weekend to launch a new drive to sell the benefits of water privatization.

Setting out to restore the Government's image on the most unpopular item in its programme, Mrs Margaret Thatcher and Mr Nicholas Ridley, Secretary of State for the Environment, tackled head on the question of whether it was right to allow private profit from a natural resource.

Mr Ridley admitted: "There is a feeling that water is provided by the Almighty and should be free. He does in his munificence cause the rain to fall but he does not impound it, purify and pump it along pipes into our bathroom taps.

"Nor does he take it away, clean the water we pollute and return it pure to the rivers.

That is an activity requiring blue and white collar workers, scientists and engineers, and above all, managers. That sort of activity is done best in the private sector."

Mrs Thatcher echoed the call, agreeing: "Some people say water is different. It comes naturally from the heavens, ought we to be charged? What next — air?",adding that with the pipes and treatment works required costing huge sums "clean water does not come cheap".

A quarter of our water was already provided by the private sector "so there is nothing new about privatizing the rest."

The Prime Minister and Mr Ridley emphasized that the water industry would attract greater resources when freed from Treasury control.

They argued that consumers would be better protected by

price controls, policed by a new director of water services, and that the environment would be better protected by the new National Rivers Authority.

Mrs Thatcher signalled to the Conservative workers in Scarborough that there was no question of dropping the Bill. "Privatization of water was a manifesto commitment."

Mr Ridley insisted:"Our water companies have immense potential to offer their services abroad, to find new markets. Much of the water industry has long been private in France: their companies provide municipal services, housing, construction and communication and cable television as well as water.

"Why not our water companies too? Why should the French buy our companies and we stop ours from buying theirs?"

PRIVATISATION OF WATER

Read the article carefully.

1 Summarise the arguments offered against the privatisation of water supply.

2 What arguments can you find to support the government view that the industry should be privatised?

IT ▶ **WORDPRO**

Use your word processor to compose a letter to the local newspaper arguing for or against the privatisation of your local water authority.

Use your own name and address and use an appropriate style.

TASK 9

OTHER WAYS OF PAYING FOR WATER

A poll tax
This seems unworkable owing to the mobility of the population. It has been suggested that the voters' list would be suitable, but it would mean that some people would rather not vote than pay a water bill.

There is also increasing evidence, both in the United States and the United Kingdom, that water use is not very closely linked with the number of people in a household. This is because a bowl of water can be used to wash one cup or several.

An equipment and facility tax
This has its attractions. The consumer should be able to see a direct relationship between the quantity of his facilities and his water bill. This system would have to be rather arbitrary, with as few different elements allowed in it as possible, so that a bath is a bath whatever its size and likewise a dishwasher. The value of each would be measured in units. One benefit of this system is that a rising tariff could be integrated so that the first bath, lavatory or basin could be charged at lower units than subsequent ones. But if this is done then water charges are being used as another system of progressive taxation; and this might be difficult to justify.

1   Explain what is meant by a 'poll tax'.

2   How could it be used to charge for water?

3   What is meant by the term 'progressive taxation'?

4   Why is an equipment and facility tax described as 'progressive'?

A Rainmaker

TASK 10

THE EFFECT OF WATER CHARGES ON CONSUMER DEMAND

It can be argued that the amount we are currently charged for water is so little that it doesn't really influence the amount we use.

1   Why is it argued that an increase in water charges does not reduce consumer demand by very much?

2   Why are we having to reconsider this view every time there is a long, dry summer?

We do tend to take water for granted in Britain – until there is a period in the summer of unexpectedly low rainfall – then we panic!
In holiday areas especially, increased demand for water in the drier season causes acute problems from time to time. It is too expensive a solution to build new reservoirs for those few years when problems occur.

'Second grade' water

Water is purified to a very high standard – that at which it is safe to drink – and yet only a very small proportion is actually drunk. It is sensible to provide the same standard of water for all household uses, particularly washing, but equally to use water treated to a very high standard for industrial processes – for cooling, or for agriculture – is unnecessarily expensive. In certain areas, where second quality water is available, there could be a dual system. This is being considered seriously in several cities in the United States at the moment. Traditionally, water engineers have opposed such a policy owing to the risk of connecting the wrong supply to the pipes used for drinking water. However, modern engineering could overcome this problem, either by colouring the pipes, putting a reverse thread on the second supply or, as a last resort, adding a colourant to the second quality water.

In many drier countries, such as for example Israel, where water is much more scarce than in this country and conventional water resources tend to be fully exploited, the use of second class water is a necessity. There are occasions in this country when the same would be true. In last year's drought in some areas tanker loads of treated effluent were supplied to sports grounds in particular, when their normal supply of water was discontinued. Incidentally, the price paid for this second class water (the cost of transport) greatly exceeds the price of normal water supply.

3   If we did not bother to purify all water to drinking standard:
   a   How would we distribute 'second grade' water?
   b   How would we charge consumers for it?
   c   Why would it be more expensive?
   d   What extra costs would it involve?
   e   What dangers might it involve to public health?

TASK 11

THE OBSERVER. SUNDAY 29 JULY 1984

Reservoir delay worsens drought

ROBIN McKIE reveals a bureaucratic bungle

THE TAPS and water pipes of Plymouth will soon be turned off, bringing the first daily water rationing of the 1984 drought. Like many other people around the country, Devonians face a long, uncomfortable summer.

Yet their privations could easily have been avoided. In 1978 a public inquiry gave the South West Water Authority support for a 8,000 million gallon reservoir at Roadford, a scheme designed to eliminate all local supply problems.

For the next five years Local Government Minister Tom King and senior civil servants prevaricated over the project before finally giving approval last year. Construction is now due to begin in September.

'Devon and Cornwall would have all the water they need today if only we had been given that approval in 1978,' said a water authority spokesman.

The Roadford delay is a classic example of ministerial and bureaucratic indecision which has led Britain to the brink of the once unimaginable, the second major drought in less than a decade.

Already the drought has killed off grazing pastures in many counties in the West and

dairy production there has fallen; trout farms in South West Scotland report they have lost many thousands of fish; and 'non-essential' uses of water, from car washes to private swimming pools, have been banned in many areas.

In other regions, however, reservoirs remain full. It is the lack of a national water strategy which has meant there is no provision for moving excess supplies from areas with an abundance of water to those with none.

Kielder Water, Europe's largest man-made reservoir, is an outstanding example. It contains enough water to satisfy four million people's needs, and supplies are still being shipped to Gibraltar.

Infuriated

Only a few miles across the Pennines, the lakes and reservoirs of Cumbria are nearly empty.

The picture is even more depressing in Wales, where the south-western reservoirs contain healthy supplies while 1,500,000 people in Cardiff, Newport and the industrial South-East can expect rationing in September.

The area's plight, and that of other parts of Britain, has infuriated local people, and their MPs have backed growing

demands that a national water grid, similar to the electricity and gas grids, be set up.

The idea does not impress water authorities. 'A water grid would require control stations, pipe systems and a lot of very expensive equipment, a lot more than is used on our electricity grid,' said a Water Authorities Association spokesman.

Estimates put the total cost at around £6 billion and few engineers believe the scheme is necessary.

A far simpler solution would be simply to stop the leaks. Even in the middle of a drought a quarter of Britain's water supply disappears into the ground.

'With water costing an average 4.5 pence per 1,000 litres, that means £45 million worth of water leaks into the ground every year,' wrote water-system expert, Fred Pearce, in his book, 'Watershed, the Water Crisis of Britain.'

The source of the leaks is the cracked and corroded water mains and broken joints of our Victorian plumbing system, on which we still depend for our sewerage and water supplies.

Read the above article carefully.

1 The main reason for the delay in the construction of the Roadford reservoir was the level of local opposition from farmers, landowners and local people anxious to preserve wild habitats for animals and birds.
 Make a list of the points you think they would

use in opposing the drowning of a river valley for a reservoir scheme in Devon.

2 What are the arguments for and against a national water grid?

3 What are the arguments against repairing the many leaks in the water distribution system in the UK?

TASK 12

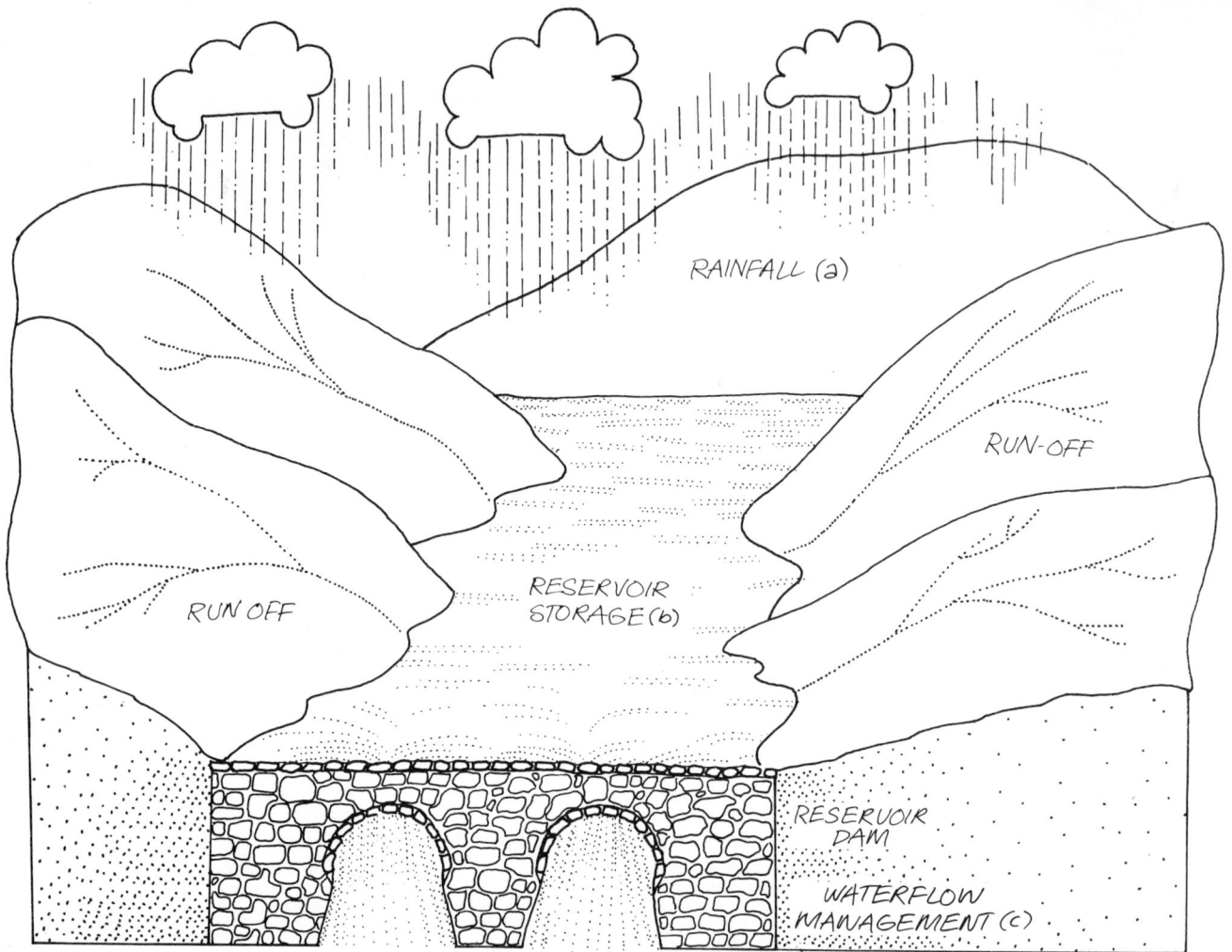

Labels in diagram: RAINFALL (a), RUN-OFF, RUN OFF, RESERVOIR STORAGE (b), RESERVOIR DAM, WATERFLOW MANAGEMENT (c)

FAIRNESS IN PAYMENT – FIXED AND VARIABLE COSTS

We often classify costs as 'fixed' and 'variable'.

Clarify what is meant by these terms and draw up a table on the word processor to list as many costs as you can think of involved in providing a water supply to your back door. Use the headings 'fixed costs' and 'variable costs'.

1 Which of the water-gathering processes are:
   a fixed costs?
   b variable costs?
   c free goods?

2 What does the article say about the variable cost of supplying water?

3 How does this compare with the fixed costs?

Metering would produce greater equity if charging on a volume basis covered all the benefits received from a mains water service, but it does not. The extra cost of putting water through the system is fairly slight, 3p to 5p per 1,000 gallons for chemicals and electricity in this country. It is really the availability of a water supply that is being paid for. The difference in the cost to the water authority, whether it is five gallons an hour or 100 gallons an hour, that goes through a particular system, is almost negligible.

4 What does the article say about the variable cost of supplying water?

5 How does this compare with the fixed costs?

The problem of water in other parts of the world

When an exciting cricket match ends in a disappointing draw because two days are washed out by torrential rain it is easy to forget that rainfall is a very precious and scarce commodity in some parts of the world. In many African countries expected rainfall often doesn't arrive and this can be repeated for several years at a time. Poor families may have invested all their spare money in seeds ready for the rainy season. If the rainfall is sudden and torrential, seeds and crops can be washed from the ground.

The unreliability of rainfall is a common factor in many developing countries. In many areas there has not been the capital available for water storage schemes, so rainfall, when it does come, is often wasted.

Sometimes the real problem is simply one of education. Local communities need to learn how to use water to its best advantage – how to store it, how to use it effectively to irrigate land, how to stop it eroding the soil when it comes in monsoon torrents. Farmers need to learn to plant the right crops and to manage water resources economically.

There is not much we can do if the expected rainfall does not come for several years. It is this problem which has led to extensive drought in eastern areas of Africa in the 1980s and which has resulted in the warm response of aid programmes like Live Aid and Band Aid. These responses to the crisis of drought are to be warmly welcomed but, for many people in the world, water shortage is a permanent problem.

TASK 13

THE PROBLEM OF WATER IN THE THIRD WORLD

'During a drought, people die of starvation, not thirst.'

'The first need of any village community is a clean water supply.'

'Water is a crop to be stored in the wet and harvested in the dry.'

'What third world countries need is not huge capital projects like dams and reservoirs but local schemes to bring water to village communities.'

These statements about the importance of water to developing nations show slightly differing views of the nature of the problem but, together, they reflect a key issue; unreliable rainfall and poor local organisation are a profound factor in restricting economic development. If the rains fail during the rainy season in equatorial regions, the land becomes parched, crops fail and local drinking water becomes stagnant and frequently contaminated.

This is not true in urban areas, and this is one of the problems of third world development, regional inequalities are so intense. People drift to the cities during times of crop failure and shanty towns grow up, often hotbeds for disease and famine.

1 Why do urban areas not suffer as badly as rural areas during a drought?

2 Why might people die of starvation rather than thirst during a drought?

3 Many countries solve the problem of having insufficient goods by putting their price up. This means that goods are allocated to people who can afford them. Do you think water should be allocated by this method?

4 What evidence can you find to support the view that the problem of third world countries is 'regional'?

TASK 14

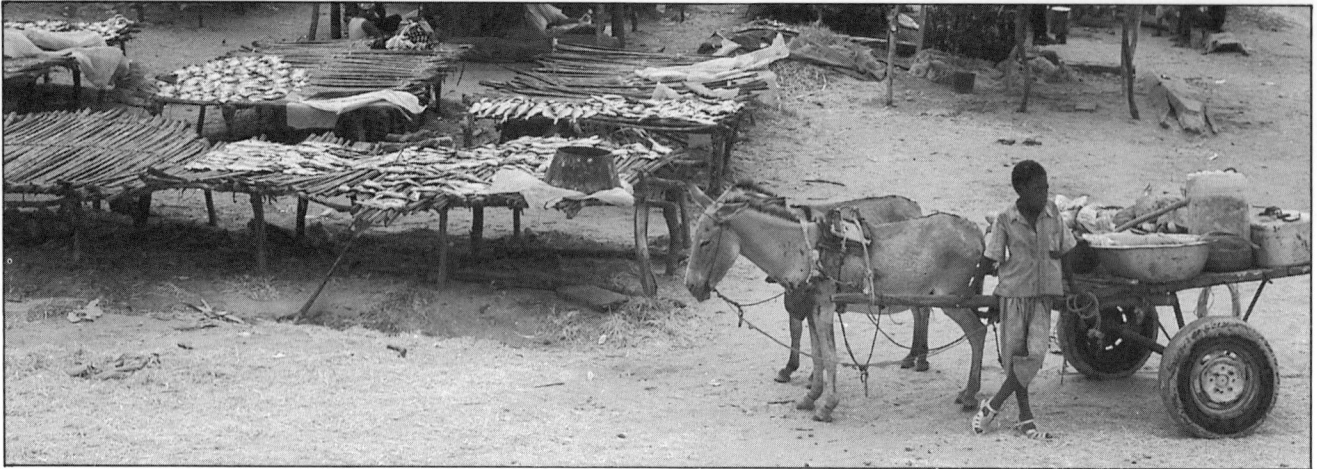

SELLING WATER

We have discussed alternative ways of paying for water in Britain. In many African countries, where water is scarce, it is sold commercially rather as we sell milk or lemonade.

1 Why is water a commodity which people will 'buy' at a given market price?

2 What do you think influences the price of water in an African village?

3 What are the likely effects of a rise in the price of a litre of water on a typical African village family?

TASK 15

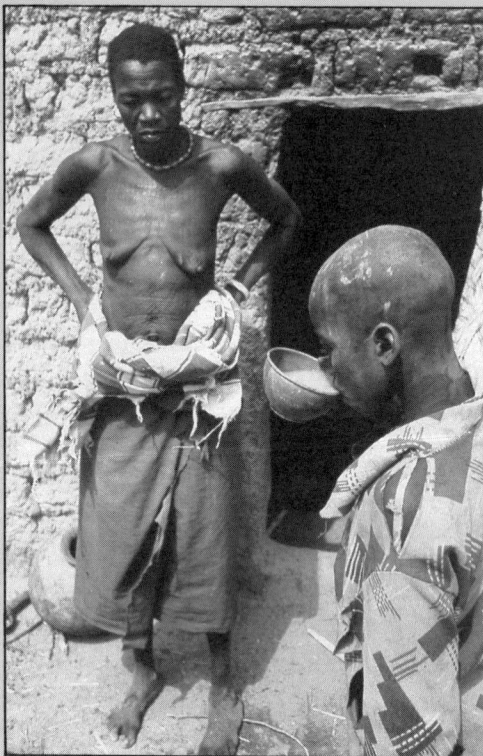

Drinking filthy water from the only available source

Making it last

At the hottest time of the year, from March, when the nearby pond dries up, to the first rains in mid May or June, a single earthenware potful of water has to last Kiemdé's family of four and their chickens and goats the whole day: about three gallons in all, less than six pints each, for all purposes. Every drop is carefully counted.

'No-one can drink enough to satisfy their thirst,' Kiemdé *(left)* explains. 'I give them one of these cups full [about half a pint], then they have to go away again until their thirst pains them. Only then will I give them another cup to calm their thirst.

'We eat only once a day in the hot months, when I get back from Kalsaka with the water. I use about 1 calabash full {about two pints} for the millet porridge, one cupful for the sauce.

'We wash our plates and hands before the meal. This takes about three cupfuls. But we don't throw this water away.'

'We keep it for one of us to wash in. We take turns. Today my husband will wash. Tomorrow I will wash, the day after my older son, then the younger.'

She laughs when I ask her what they do with the waste water from washing.

'There isn't any. It's hardly enough to wet every part of our body. If there is any left over in the jug, we put it out for the chickens and the little goats about to die of thirst.

'If you go to market, you can buy millet. But I have never seen water for sale in the market. Yet without water there is no life.'

1 Make a list of what Kiemdé uses water for during a day. Against each use put the amount of water used.

2 Keep a similar record of your own home's water usage during a day.

3 Prepare a wall display showing the comparison of your own usage and that of Kiemdé.

4 Can you suggest any reasons why water, if it is so valuable, is not available for sale in the market to which Kiemdé goes?

TASK 16

THE GAMBIA

Increasing populations inevitably need more food. This should mean increased food production. However, over the past 15 years the Gambia and the whole of the surrounding Sahelian zone has suffered from decreasing rainfall. In England, drought is declared if it doesn't rain for more than 15 days. Here, the climate is different. It is normal for there to be no rain from October to the beginning of June (the dry season) then in the remainder of the year (the wet season) up to 50 inches of rainfall are expected. At least, this was the case before the drought not only began to shorten the wet season, but to reduce the rainfall. 1983 saw the lowest for 97 years: only 17 inches.

Traditionally, the wet season is a lean time as far as food supply is concerned, with stocks from last year nearly finished and the new crops not yet harvested. In 1983, stocks of home grown rice ran out as early as December instead of the following June or July. The principle cash crop of ground nuts was greatly reduced too and so villagers were unable to buy rice to supplement their own poor yields.

From Brikama we are also running a well-digging programme which is available to help villages which, as a community, want to start and work vegetable gardens. Again we provide greatly subsidised input in the form of concrete lined wells for irrigating, as well as fencing and seeds. These vegetable gardens provide a valuable food supplement as well as cash to buy the rice which the drought has prevented them growing themselves.

SMALL SCALE SOLUTIONS TO WATER SUPPLY

1   What is the difference between 'drought' in Britain and 'drought' in the Gambia?

2   Why are there different definitions of 'drought'?

TASK – GROUP PRESENTATION

▶ GRAPHICS

Consider the passage above which describes the programe for digging local wells. Much international aid is concentrated on major prestige projects like dams and irrigation schemes.

This presents a problem. Often the best way of helping local village communities is to fund small scale, local projects.

Discuss this problem as a group. Try to find out what the problems really are, with examples. Use your graphics package to produce statistics in an attractive way and your word processor to present different views. Aim to put on a display in your classroom, hall or foyer which draws attention to the problem of water supply in the third world and to the problems of the food crisis in Africa. Some of the information in this case study will start you off and there are many newspaper articles which will help.

TASK 17

DROUGHT IN AFRICA

THE FACTS

The countries
31 countries are affected (see map) several economies near to total collapse

The food
production has dropped by about 10% since 1974

The people
3 Africans out of 5 are chronically malnourished
5 million children will die this year and 5 million suffer permanent physical and mental damage from malnutrition

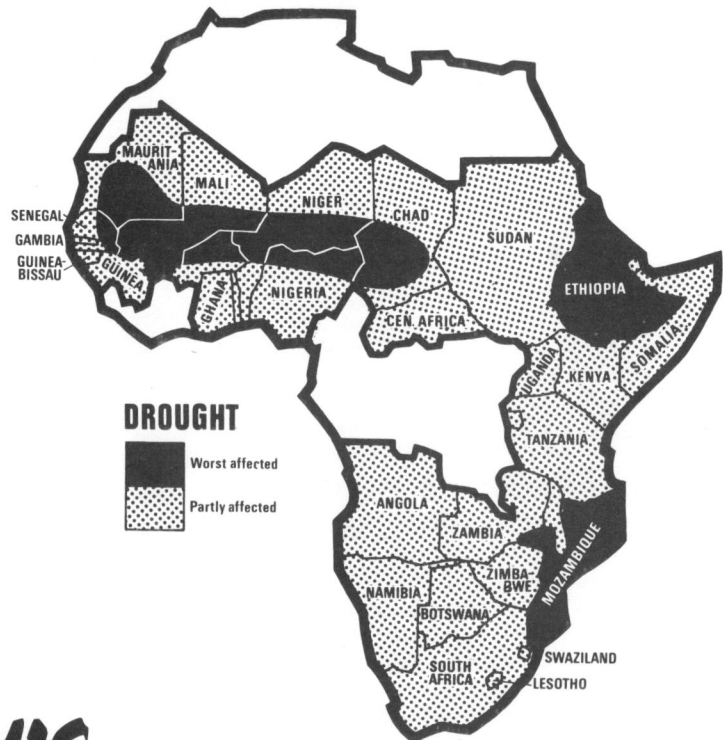

DROUGHT

■ Worst affected

▓ Partly affected

WHY HAS THIS HAPPENED ?

The short term lack of rain has triggered off the present crisis. But there are many other long term causes stretching back 15 years or more.

The environment – many parts of Africa have a semi-desert climate where droughts occur often. But some experts fear that the last few years indicate a long term change for the worse.

Government policies – have often discouraged farmers, encouraging town-dwelling military and government elites at the expense of others. The towns are growing; so there are more people to feed, while the number of farmers is declining.

The world recession – has meant increasing debts, compounded by falling demand for African goods and increased oil prices. This means cutbacks in imports essential for farming, and no money to buy from Western food mountains in times of crises.

The effects of wars – farmers cannot work, many are killed, many become refugees who them-selves have to be fed.

The wrong aid – badly thought-out or badly used, for instance, on big schemes needing much foreign money while village-level development is neglected. By 1975 for instance, the World Bank had invested over $200 million in Tanzania without supporting a single project designed to produce basic foodstuffs.

Vicious circles – for instance, people may be reduced to eating their seed corn one year because of drought. The next year they have no seed to plant.

– for instance, wells sunk after the drought of 1973 south of the Sahara provided plenty of water at first. So nomads were able to increase their flocks. They over-grazed the area. It is now desert.

*From DSR leaflet **Food Crisis in Africa***

TASK 17 CONTINUED

African rains are often either inadequate or torrential, intensifying problems of poor soil and desertification. In Mozambique the two years of drought which had crippled production in 1982–83 were swept away by rains when cyclone Domoina lashed the southern provinces in January this year. After drought rain robs the soil of vital nutrients, it becomes looser, more vulnerable to landslides and wind. If, in turn, the rain comes too fast, the soil cannot contain it. Silt-thick African rivers yearly sweep tons of topsoil into the sea.

The spreading of the Sahara and Kalahari deserts can be linked directly to overgrazing and overuse of land. Even shortages of rain, foresters speculate, are caused not by natural fluctuations in climate but by the rapid clearing of rain forests. Blaming the weather, moaning over acts of God and accusing poor farmers are superficial responses to a complex problem. It is more revealing to examine the policies which starve the poor, pressure the land and make entire countries vulnerable to drought.

'The hungry people of Africa cannot eat theories, slogans or empty ideologies. Africa needs to be invaded not with arms but with food, technology and substantial financial resources.'

Saihou Sabally, Agriculture Minister, the Gambia and UN World Food Council's Vice President

In Guinea Bissau, where children are often short of protein, local sales of ground nuts are banned in order to maximise exports.

The expansion of export crops is pushing peasant farmers to the margins of deserts and forests or into city slums . . . as a result, deserts are expanding and tropical forests being destroyed at an alarming rate.

*Report **Cultivating Hunger** by Nigel Twose*

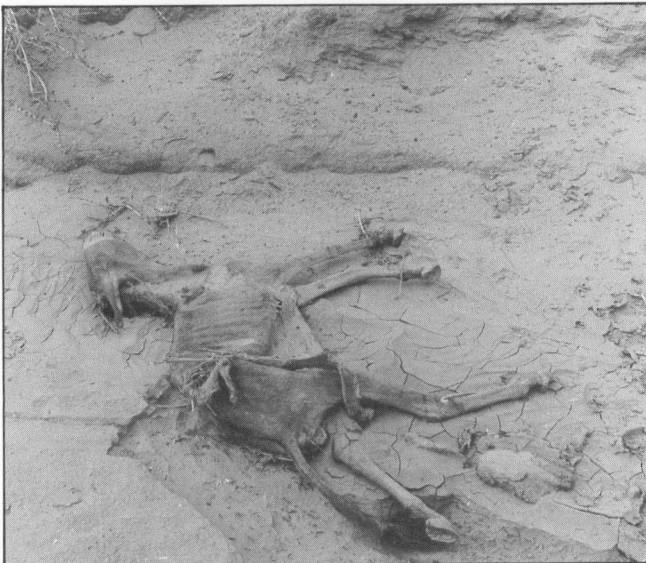

To what extent are the climate and 'poor' African soils responsible for food shortages in Africa?

In the mid-seventies a group of meteorologists and other academics organised a project to study the effect of climate on the great Sahel famine. After a few months an entirely different picture began to emerge. They found that the role of drought was much smaller than assumed and there was no simple cause-and-effect link between drought and famine. 'In 1976', their report argues, 'there was also a drought in Britain. We believe that nobody would have thought it "natural" for thousands of British children to die *because of the drought*. The loss of even a few dozen children would have been nothing less than a scandal.' Significantly, their report is titled *Nature Pleads Not Guilty*. People are to blame.

THE LINK BETWEEN DROUGHT AND FOOD SHORTAGE

1 **Is drought or heavy rainfall the greater cause of agricultural problems in Africa?**

2 **Is man a greater cause than nature of the problems of African famine?**

3 **Are poor management and ineffective government even greater causes?**

   Read the passages above and state your own views.

Index